holoca‹

hero

the untold story and vignettes of Soloman Schonfeld an extraodinary british orthodox rabbi who rescued 4000 Jews during the holocaust

Rabbi Solomon Schonfeld bringing the few existing relatives to meet the boatload of orphans he rescued from Poland.

holocaust hero

the untold story and vignettes of Soloman Schonfeld an extraodinary british orthodox rabbi who rescued 4000 Jews during the holocaust

david kranzler
with an appreciation
by the late chief rabbi
lord immanuel jakobovits

Ktav Publishers, Inc.
Jersey City, NJ
2004

Library of Congress Cataloging-in-Publication Data

Kranzler, David, 1930-
  Holocaust hero : the untold story and vignettes of Solomon Schonfeld,
an extraodinary British Orthodox rabbi who rescued four thousand during
the Holocaust / by David Kranzler ; appreciation by Lord Jacobovits ;
preface by Marcus Retter.
      p. cm.
  ISBN 0-88125-730-3 (pbk.) -- ISBN 0-88125-800-8 (hc.)
  1. Schonfeld, Solomon, 1912- 2. Rabbis--Great Britain--Biography. 3.
World War, 1939-1945--Jews--Rescue--Great Britain. 4. Holocaust, Jewish
(1939-1945) I. Title.
BM755.S297K73 2003
296.8'32'092--dc22

2003021135

Published by
KTAV Publishing House, Inc.
930 Newark Avenue
Jersey City, NJ 07306
Email: info@ktav.com
www.ktav.com
(201) 963-9524
Fax (201) 963-0102

This book is dedicated

in honor of

R' Mordechai (Marcus) Retter שליט"א

ng the Holocaust, one of the darkest periods in Jewish history, the legendary hero,

Rabbi Dr. Solomon Schonfeld ז"ל

single-handedly saved thousands of Jewish children and adults

by means of the now famous *kindertransports*

and other rescue schemes.

He also established the Chief Rabbi's Religious Emergency Council

Kedassia

and the network of Hasmonean Secondary Schools

which irrevocably altered the face of Jewish life in England.

As Rabbi Schonfeld's right-hand man during the war years and thereafter,

Mr. Retter was an important factor in Rabbi Schonfeld's spectacular success,

by implementing many

of Rabbi Schonfeld's projects and ideas

that reinvigorated English Jewry and planted the seeds

of revival and growth of Torah Judaism in England.

Upon emigrating to the United States,

e has continued his numerous efforts on behalf of many Torah institutions and individuals

in America and abroad.

In the merit of these efforts,

may Hashem grant him

אריכות ימים ושנים טובים ונעימים
and enable him to see much *nachas* from his children, grandchildren

and great grandchildren

until

ביאת גואל צדק במהרה בימינו אמן

shrei 5764   October 2003

The "Young Rabbi" Schonfeld (at the Adas Synagogue, London, England.)

Contents

ACKNOWLEDGEMENTS

One of the pleasures of completing a new book is being able to thank all those who have shared suggestions and constructive criticism with me. As always, I am grateful to the Al-mighty for having allowed me to spend many years, since my retirement from the City University of New York, doing research and writing about rescue and rescue attempts during the Holocaust.

This work, like all my others, has its own history. During the first of many trips to London, beginning in the 1970s, I had the privilege of meeting two outstanding Jewish personalities who left their mark on history.

One was Dr. (Rebbetzin) Judith Grunfeld z"l, a pioneer and contributor to Jewish life who made a significant difference in the quality of Jewish life in Poland and England. As one of the three primary builders of the Bais Yaakov movement in Poland during the twenties, she was sent from Frankfurt to Cracow by Jacob Rosenheim, the president of World Agudath Israel. She arrived in Cracow in 1923, when the Bais Yaakov Seminary created by Sarah Schenirer was officially "adopted" by the Agudah during the First Knessia Gedolah (in Vienna). The other person who was influential in that movement was Dr. Leo Deutschlander who helped Sarah Schenirer develop the seminary on a solid pedagogical foundation. Dr. Deutschlander also helped Dr. Grunfeld smooth the transition from the Frankfurt of Rabbi Samson Raphael Hirsch to the Orthodoxy of Sarah Schenirer and prewar Polish Jewry. In the seminary, she was the teacher and guide to most of the students who later became teachers and principals in the Bais Yaakov movement.

She married Rabbi Isidore Grunfeld in the early 1930s and became the headmistress of the Hasmonean Girls' School, founded by Dr. Solomon Schonfeld in England. During World War II, she headed the Shefford evacuation center for five hundred and fifty youngsters, under Rabbi Dr. Schonfeld's direction.

Dr. Grunfeld's pioneering efforts in Cracow with Bais Yaakov and her Shefford experience during the Second World War fascinated me, and when I interviewed her, we needed six sessions and filled many tapes. In the following decade, I encouraged her to work on her auto-biography. She asked me to remember her efforts in my work, and as a result, I included one of her charming vignettes of the Shefford story in this work.

Dr. Grunfeld also introduced me to the second great personality of the period, a true hero—Rabbi Solomon Schonfeld. By that time, he was suffering from an illness that left him, once a formidable, handsome man, partially paralyzed. Although I specialized in rescue and rescue attempts during the Holocaust, I had never heard of him or his efforts to save Jews.

When Dr. Grunfeld arranged for our interview, he dismissed me with a typical Schonfeld gesture, "I have no time for the past, I'm too busy working on the future." I did manage to convince him to grant me a fifteen-minute taped interview. Even more important was his permission to microfilm his enormous collection of papers (lying in scores of dusty packages in the attic of one of his schools) that related to rescue efforts of his organization, the Chief Rabbi's Religious Emergency Council (CRREC).

After much effort, and with Dr. Grunfeld's help, I had succeeded in microfilming most of the papers, when they were suddenly transferred to the Southampton University Archives. My deepest gratitude goes to both of these great personalities, who gave so much to the Jewish community in the Diaspora, but have yet to receive their due. I hope this volume will help them earn recognition for their efforts, and that they will become role models for the future, although it will be posthumously.

I have done what I can to convey the enormity of their work, but this book does not do justice to Rabbi Schonfeld's manifold activities, and he deserves his own detailed biographical work devoted to his enormous rescue, educational and communal efforts.

I have made the CRREC Papers (plus some papers photocopied courtesy of the Southampton University Archives) available to Dr. Pam Shatzkes, whom I inspired to write her (soon to be published) dissertation on rescue efforts in the Holocaust by Anglo-Jewry, including Rabbi Schonfeld's. Dr. Shatzkes, in turn, provided me with other relevant documents. My thanks go to her.

In later years, Rabbi Schonfeld became very ill and required full-time nursing care. Since he never took a penny for any of his rescue efforts, though he raised millions of dollars for this cause, he lived on his meager salary as rabbi of the Adas Synagogue and as presiding rabbi of the Union of Orthodox Hebrew Congregations.

Again, it was loyal Dr. Grunfeld, long retired—and not any of the four thousand Jews he rescued during the decade of 1938–1948—who made it her business to help out this unsung benefactor. She personally typed and sent hundreds of letters to those saved by her mentor, requesting financial help and arranging for a public tribute to him in the Hendon Adas in honor of his seventieth birthday.

This late show of appreciation by hundreds of former Schonfeld charges gave the forgotten hero some pleasure, as did my small contribution of the original book, edited by Gertrude Hirschler z"l, which consisted of forty vignettes by people he rescued.

It is, therefore, Dr. Grunfeld who is responsible for any recognition he received during his lifetime. I am grateful to Rebbetzin Lady Emily Jakobovits for permission to reproduce her late husband's "Appreciation" upon the occasion of that celebration.

It was also Dr. Grunfeld who convinced me to use part of my sabbatical from CUNY to produce the original book. She asked me to include a selection about her Shefford experience in my work on Rabbi Schonfeld; a request I willingly granted. I also appreciate the permission to use Daniela Grunfeld's charming drawing of Sheffield and her very apt suggestions for my sketch on the book jacket. I especially appreciate her careful proofreading of the manuscript. I also appreciate Ms. Barbara Barnett's permission to use her unfinished manuscript on Schonfeld's last transport from Czechoslovakia.

Mr. Marcus Retter is the worthy subject of the dedication of this book by his highly accomplished and loving children. Mr. Retter was one of the many youths rescued by Schonfeld, who became his closest assistant and confidant during those crucial years of rescue—he even represented Schonfeld in a number of important rescue missions. It is also his very informative "Setting" that lays the stage for the Schonfeld story and it is his "Preface" that places Schonfeld and his rescue efforts in historical perspective.

My appreciation goes to Rabbi Yisroel Lefkowitz, communal activist par excellence, for his mission to disseminate my works to inspire our youth in the Yeshivos and Day Schools.

I am also grateful to Dean Geoffrey Alderman, the foremost historian of Modern British Jewry, for assigning me to write the piece on Schonfeld for the New Dictionary of National Biography (which inspired me to write this new work) and for critically reviewing the first draft of this manuscript.

My profound gratitude to the Schonfeld family, especially to Jonathan, for the photographs, and to Dr. Jeremy Schonfeld, who carefully reviewed the manuscript. I thank both academics for preventing the inclusion of some egregious historical errors, though any errors still in this work are strictly my own. I am also grateful to Ms. Henya Mintz for many of the photos.

I was most fortunate to have Ms. Jeanette Friedman, an editor par excellence, working with me to polish this work and reminding me to keep the reader in mind. Her superb sense of style and appreciation of the subject matter transformed this story from a routine historical work into a book I hope the reader finds engaging and educational.

Last, I am grateful to be a recipient of the greatest blessing of all—a wonderful, inspiring family who encouraged and helped me during some difficult moments.

TO THE PAST:

To my dear parents, Reb Yerachmiel and Chana Kranzler z"l, the paradigm for erlichkeit and hachnossas orchim (honesty and hospitality), whose home was always open to countless strangers, refugees and yeshiva students in Wurzburg, Germany, and later, after the war, in Williamsburg and Boro Park, Brooklyn;

To my dear in-laws, Rav Yaakov and Dinah Bein z"l, who were directly involved in rescue efforts in Budapest and who also opened their homes in Williamsburg and Boro Park;

To those of my siblings who passed away prematurely—my sister Mali and brother-in-law Gershon Loebenberg z"l, who were pioneers at Kibbutz Chofetz Chaim in Israel, and who took care of our home and me, after the untimely demise of my mother;

To my sister, Rose Halberg z'l, whose constant concern for me always made me feel very special, and my brother-in-law, Rabbi Eli Halberg z'l, one of the first talmidim of Reb Aaron Kotler z"l in Lakewood.

To my brother, Dr. Gershon z'l, who was a pioneer in America, writing books for Orthodox Jewish youth, initiating the first serious sociological studies of Orthodox Jewish communities, creating several important secular high school departments in various Bais Yaakovs and yeshivos, inspiring thousands of students to utilize their talents on behalf of Yiddishkeit and especially for his work in rescue (with Mike Tress of the Zeirei Agudah), which served as an inspiration to me;

To my artistic and talented brother, Henry o"h, whose lifelong challenges to me inspired me to dig deeply into Yiddishkeit and our Jewish heritage and to specialize in modern Jewish history.

TO THE PRESENT:

To my sister, Dr. Bella Weisfogel, my greatest supporter and severest critic, and my brother-in-law, Rabbi Alex Weisfogel, who, like Gershon, was directly involved in rescue as assistant to Rav Kalmanowitz during the Holocaust years, and who also inspired me in my research in this area;

To my dear brother, Rabbi Dr. Moish, and my sister-in-law, Eveline, whose close relationship has greatly enriched me;

To my dearest children, Moish, whose incredible administrative and deep empathy has contributed much to higher Jewish education,

and my talented daughter-in-law, Faigi, my Shani and son-in-law
Rabbi Shaye Greenwald (who spread Torah in Eretz Yisroel), and my
dear Yaakov Meir, who spent many years absorbing Torah at Mir
(Jerusalem) and Lakewood before embarking on his legal career.

I applaud all their efforts on behalf of Yiddishkeit in their various
capacities.

To my dear nephews, Dr. Gerald Weisfogel and Dan Kranzler
without their steady encouragement during some very difficult times,
I should not have been able to produce this book and the last few that
preceded it.

TO THE FUTURE:

My dear grandchildren, Aliza, Yonatan Boruch and Elisheva
Kranzler; and my dear Dena Brocho, Rivka Tehillah and Tova Gittel
Greenwald (in Telstone, Israel). They are the sources of my greatest
nachas (pleasure). May they gain inspiration to work on behalf of the
Jewish people from the many heroes and heroines of rescue who were
responsible for rescuing tens of thousands of Jews during the
Holocaust era;

Finally, to my life's partner. I am especially grateful to my dearest
wife, Judy, the exquisite link between the rich legacy of the past and
the hopeful future.

PROLOGUE

The young Rabbi Schonfeld with colleagues at the Slobadka Yeshiva in Poland.

PREFACE

BY MARCUS RETTER

I come to bear witness!

I consider it a rare privilege and honor to have the opportunity to share with you my most cherished memories of Rabbi Dr. Solomon Schonfeld, OBM. His legendary feats on behalf of his fellow Jews that took place more than fifty years ago and spanned a decade are recorded in this volume.

Despite his *"Oberlandisch"** (strict Hungarian Orthodox-Jewish) upbringing and his years of study in the Nitra Yeshiva, Rabbi Schonfeld was able to bridge the strictly Haredi/Orthodox world and the secular and "foreign" world of Her Majesty's Government. He did this with his heroic and successful efforts to save more than four thousand children and adults from Hitler's inferno. He thereby contributed to the preservation of tens of thousands of Jewish lives, including the descendants of those he rescued.

Rabbi Schonfeld was the right man in the right place at the right time. By virtue of Divine Providence, the rabbi was able to see that European Jewry was in mortal danger.

He carried himself regally, was approximately six feet tall, was able to speak the King's English perfectly, and was respected by most who met him. After the war, he did not rest on the laurels he earned with his rescue efforts. He devoted himself to the establishment of Jewish secondary schools in London. These Anglo-Jewish schools taught thousands of boys and girls to study Torah and secular subjects. His objective was to turn them into proud Torah-observant Jews, and in this, he succeeded admirably.

Sadly, Rabbi Schonfeld died in 1984 at seventy-two, almost forgotten by Jewry in general and British Jewry in particular. Two years before his demise, Dr. Judith Grunfeld, a devoted headmistress at one

xix

of his girls' schools, drew attention to his heroism when she organized a testimonial dinner in his honor. She also inspired the historian Dr. David Kranzler to write and publish a book of vignettes, edited by Gertrude Hirschler, about the people Schonfeld saved.

This new work about Rabbi Schonfeld by Dr. Kranzler is the rabbi's biography with an emphasis on his rescue efforts. Many of the original vignettes are reprinted in the second and third parts of this work. Dr. Kranzler's extensive research into these areas is greatly appreciated. The stories make it possible for Rabbi Solomon Schonfeld to posthumously become a role model for the youth of today.

I pray that by perpetuating his memory I have somewhat repaid my debt to him for saving me from Hitler's ovens.

Marcus Retter's arrival in London from
Vienna, 1938.

THE BIOGRAPHY
PART ONE

THE SETTING

BY MARCUS RETTER

I was born in Vienna and lived in the Twentieth District with my parents. In April or May 1938, after the Nazi annexation of Austria, I found out that Rabbi Dr. Solomon Schonfeld in London, England was engaged in organizing a *kindertransport* (children's transport) from Vienna to London to bring children to study at a yeshiva there. I first heard about this at the *Jugendgruppe* (youth group) of Agudath Israel (the Agudah) in Vienna. I was not an active member of the group, but I belonged to it and was told that my application to go to England could be made through the Agudah. In Vienna, the man with the decisive voice in the arrangements was Julius Steinfeld, who is remembered by hundreds of Viennese Jews as the man to whom they owe their lives.

After Hitler's *Anschluss* (the annexation of Austria) in March 1938, my parents—like the other Jews in the country—wanted to leave. They were Polish citizens and hoped their Polish citizenship would protect them until they could emigrate. My father lived in Vienna practically all his life, served in the Austrian army during World War I and married my mother there, but he never became an Austrian citizen. He was completely non-political and not associated with any Jewish party. He was a strictly Orthodox Jew, but not an Agudist.

As a youth I studied English for six years and always dreamed of going to England. I had a working knowledge of the language, and my admiration of English culture and the English people increased my desire to go to London and study at a yeshiva there. I also hoped I could attend an English college and earn a degree.

By the time I found out about Rabbi Schonfeld in London, I was seventeen, too old to apply for the *kindertransport* because the cut-off age was 16. I contacted the rabbi directly and asked to be included in a special transport he was arranging for yeshiva *bachurim* (male students). I had a younger brother and younger sister, but I felt that if I—

as the eldest—succeeded reaching England first, I would be able to obtain visas for my family. I wrote letters to Schonfeld in Hebrew, telling him about my background. I promised that if he could get me to London, I would do whatever he asked. Perhaps he needed a secretary to do his Hebrew correspondence?

I wrote at least twenty-four letters before there was an answer from London. Shortly after the *Kristallnacht* pogrom of November 9–10, 1938, I received a carbon copy of a letter Dr. Schonfeld wrote to a Rabbi Hoffman in Mandate Palestine, telling him that he, Schonfeld, had an interest in the case of a young boy named Marcus Retter and would Hoffman do whatever he possibly could on my behalf. It was important to me to learn that I had not been abandoned.

In February 1939, I received a letter from the British consulate in Vienna advising me that an entry visa to England was available and that I should report to the consulate in person to pick it up. The letter was stamped *"Nur durch die Agudas Jisroel in Wien"* (issued only through Agudath Israel in Vienna). It seemed that the Agudah, under whose auspices Julius Steinfeld was working, had sixty British visas for students headed to London to enroll in Yeshiva Ohr Yisroel at 109-11 Stamford Hill. Dr. Schonfeld had organized Ohr Yisroel expressly as a tool for bringing out young refugees. Schonfeld enrolled sixty young men from Vienna, including me, in Ohr Yisroel, and it turned out that I knew all of them. Most studied in the yeshivos of Pressburg or Nitra and were my age; some were a little older and had already finished their yeshiva studies in Vienna.

Schonfeld did these things at the request of his mentor in the Nitra Yeshiva in Slovakia, Rabbi Michoel Ber Weissmandl, his teacher and the assistant Rosh Yeshiva (head of the school), the son-in-law of Rabbi Shmuel Dovid Ungar, the Rosh Yeshiva. This same Rabbi Weissmandl eventually earned the title "Genius of Rescue" for his activities before, during and after the Holocaust years.

Ninety-five percent of the students in the transport were from the *Schiffschul*, the famous separatist synagogue, mostly descendants of Hungarian and Moravian Orthodox Jews. They lived in Vienna's Second District, citadel of the *Schiffschul* community, as distinct from the Twentieth District, where most of the Polish Jews lived, as did a great many Zionists.

I picked up my British visa early in February 1939, and in May, I left Vienna without my family, by train, traveling through Germany and Belgium. The Nazis gave me no trouble, probably because I had a so-called "stateless" passport (a Nansen pass issued by the League of Nations). Most of us in the transport from Vienna did not travel as a unit; we traveled in groups of three or four, as individuals who happened to be accepted as students at the same school in London. Our student visas meant that British authorities expected us to return to our countries of origin when we completed our studies.

In addition to, and separate from the yeshiva students, there was a *kindertransport* that took 250–300 children to London. These children left Austria as a group in March 1939. An earlier transport of about three hundred children left in December 1938. When I left Vienna for England, I estimated that Schonfeld was responsible for bringing about 750 children and young people out of Europe.

I arrived in London's Victoria Station, and went directly to the yeshiva, where I introduced myself and announced that I was ready to begin my studies the next morning. They said, "We are very happy to have you, but there is no dormitory in this yeshiva," and directed me to the youth hostel set up for us at 65 Lordship Road. We were supposed to be taken into homes in the Orthodox Jewish community, but we had to wait. At 65 Lordship Road, I found many of my friends from the *Jugendgruppe* in Vienna. I was duly assigned a bed, and stayed there from May 1939 until the end of September.

Approximately 10 percent of the students in the hostel came from Germany and arrived in England because their relatives—who settled in England years before World War I—brought them to London and took them into their homes, making it easier to get a student's visa for German Jews living in Germany than for young Jews in Austria. These families included the Weils, the Lunzers and a man named Meyer—of whom all of them are members of Schonfeld's Adas Yisroel Congregation, who asked him to get visas for their relatives. He managed to obtain, I would guess, 20–25 such visas for German students in much the same way he secured them for the rest of us. By then Schonfeld was bringing in rabbis and teachers from Germany and Austria, mostly from Berlin or Frankfurt, and asked the Home Office to grant permits to certain rabbis, teachers and Jewish scholars to fill the shortage of Jewish clergy in England.

Dayan Grunfeld (Judith's husband and a religious judge for the Court of the Chief Rabbinate) had two brothers, Moritz (Mor'le) and Frank, who were two of these teachers. When Dr. Schonfeld asked the authorities to issue visas for the clergymen, he explained that they were "ecclesiastical officers" singled out by the Germans for special persecution.

In other cases, he obtained permits for his teachers through the Ministry of Labor and secured positions for them as functionaries in synagogues or as teachers at day schools and *yeshivos*. He could do that only after he went through various legal formalities to prove that the Jewish functionaries would not jeopardize British jobs. Schonfeld submitted guarantees from the Union of Orthodox Hebrew Congregations, which were considered "ironclad" by the British Home Office. Later, Schonfeld used endorsements from the Chief Rabbi's Religious Emergency Council (CRREC). In other words, Schonfeld had the Chief Rabbi tell the authorities, as it were, that he would "personally guarantee that the refugees issued entry permits will never become a burden to the British Government or the Public Assistance Board."

Two or three weeks after my arrival in England, I visited Dr. Schonfeld to thank him for what he had done. When I finally met him, he said, "You really have no idea what problems I had with you." There was trouble with Steinfeld, who demanded priority for the young people he personally chose for the transport. Steinfeld told Schonfeld that those children had no other way to leave Vienna, while others—presumably, young people like me—would be rescued by others.

Rabbi Schonfeld told me, "As you know by now, I am not one to take no for an answer. I told Steinfeld, 'Look here, I also have something to say in this matter.' Steinfeld suspected you must be a relative of mine. He just could not believe me when I said that I did not even know you. I explained to him that you were a boy who continually wrote to me, and that I became interested in you because I believe in people who are persistent! I believe in people who bet on the wrong horse."

Schonfeld was the busiest man under the sun and I had some trouble finding him. He spent at least twenty hours a day on rescue work, arranging the transports to England and trying to arrange transports to

Canada and the United States that required transit visas for refugees to travel via England. These transatlantic transports never sailed, but Dr. Schonfeld, a born optimist, firmly believed that the students, loosely organized as the Yeshiva Ohr Yisroel, would evolve into an established yeshiva in the mode of the Etz Chaim Yeshiva, one of the older *yeshivos* in London.

Most of the Ohr Yisroel boys were eighteen years old or older— officially we were sixteen to eighteen—and we were finished with our yeshiva studies. We were concentrating our time and energy on the business of getting our families out of Europe. After a while, Ohr Yisroel (which existed until late 1944–early 1945) moved from 109-111 Stamford Hill to 65 Lordship Road, and the house in Stamford Hill was turned into a hostel for pre-teens. At the time, Dr. Schonfeld appointed Rabbi Yosef Babad as the yeshiva principal. Babad later left to become the communal rabbi in Sunderland.

When World War II began on September 1, 1939, Schonfeld was desperate. Providing for the children at the hostel and yeshiva required a great deal of money and Schonfeld did not have it. There were major Jewish relief organizations like the Central British Fund and the German-Jewish Aid Committee specifically geared to meet the needs of German and Austrian refugees, but these "establishment" agencies would have nothing to do with Schonfeld, the independent operator.

In fact, the German-Jewish Aid Committee did everything possible to undermine the rabbi's rescue activities because they considered him a religious "separatist" and an interloper. To them, he was a threat and nuisance, and therefore, if Schonfeld felt like rescuing children on his own, they argued, that was *his* problem.

In general, even strictly Orthodox Jews in Austria were challenged because they insisted on being independent. Many belonged to the *Adas Yisroel Schiffschul*, a separatist community and Agudah stronghold, which stood apart from the Vienna Jewish *Kultusgemeinde*, Austria's official all-inclusive Jewish religious community. Since the *Kultusgemeinde* arranged for the emigration of Jews from Austria after Hitler came to power, they made it difficult for Orthodox Jews to escape.

Julius Steinfeld, the Agudah leader who conducted rescue work in Vienna after the *Anschluss*, was a *shtadlan* (a traditional term—one

who intercedes with authorities on behalf of his fellow Jews). Since
World War I, he maintained excellent connections with the Viennese
police. At the conclusion of that war, many Jewish refugees from
Galicia and other parts of Eastern Europe illegally crossed into Austria
and were arrested. Steinfeld, though then still young, bailed them out
and turned them into legal immigrants. Steinfeld had a good reputation
among the Jews and at police headquarters. He was a man of principle,
who was never "money-mad" and never asked for or received any
financial remuneration for his efforts.

Steinfeld considered *hatzalah* (rescue) and *pidyon shivuim*
(redeeming captives) vital *mitzvos*, divine commandments that every
Jew is obligated to fulfill. In the course of his rescue activities,
Steinfeld met Adolf Eichmann in Vienna sometime after March 1938.
At the time, Eichmann was in charge of the German immigration
bureau set up in a palace the Nazis had confiscated from the Rothschild
family.

There were striking similarities between Steinfeld and Schonfeld—
excluding their physical characteristics. Each was a one-man organization and neither of them could tolerate bureaucrats, red tape and the
rigamarole generated by committees and sub-committees. After the
Anschluss, Steinfeld, at least officially, no longer operated on his own
and made it known that he was doing rescue work as a representative
of the so-called *Auswanderungsamt* (emigration office) of the Agudath
Israel of Vienna.[1]

Steinfeld was a businessman who never became wealthy. He was
partner to Kalman Pappenheim, an active member of the Agudah who
played a prominent role in rescue work. Unfortunately, Pappenheim
and his wife did not survive the war—they were eventually deported to
the ghetto in Riga and it is assumed they were murdered.

Despite his lack of wealth, Steinfeld set an example with his own
generous donations to the cause and urged others to donate funds for
rescue. After the *Anschluss,* he traveled back and forth between Vienna
and London, with no entourage or secretariat. In London, he spent a
day or two with the daughter of Rabbi Yosef Yonah Horowitz, former
rabbi of the "separatist Orthodox" community of Frankfurt. She volunteered her time to be his amenuensis, and he would dictate his letters, in German, at a fast clip. (I saw some of them before they were

mailed.) Most were addressed to individuals in the United States. The main thrust of each was that something, no matter what, had to be done to save Jewish lives.

I remember one letter Steinfeld wrote to Rabbi Abraham Yehoshua Heschel, the Kopitzinitzer Rebbe, who left Vienna and settled in New York City in the 1930s. The letter explained that visas for the Dominican Republic could be gotten for Jewish refugees, provided they had enough money to bribe Dominican officials. He did not suggest that these matters be handled by or through him; he merely noted that this was something that needed to be done and that American Jews should be willing and able to do it.

Meanwhile, in London, Schonfeld wrestled with his own particular problem—the desperate shortage of funds for further rescue work. By that time, he was already personally responsible for almost a thousand refugees of all ages who had made it to England. He was twenty-eight years old, unmarried and rabbi of the Adas Yisroel Congregation, then a very small community with probably no more than a hundred member families. Most of his congregants were of German origin, and among them were quite a few native Englishmen. Schonfeld was also the presiding rabbi of the Union of Orthodox Hebrew Congregations, founded by his late father, Rabbi Dr. Avigdor Schonfeld.

This Union consisted of no more than twelve or fifteen *shtiblech* (one-room synagogues) in London's East End—which joined the Adas Yisroel for cemetery privileges for their members; other than paying their dues, they did not support the Union. The relationship between Schonfeld's Union, the Anglo-Jewish establishment and the Chief Rabbinate was then the same as that between the independent Orthodox communities in Austria and the official *Kultusgemeinde*.

The Union of Orthodox Hebrew Congregations, under Schonfeld, considered itself independent of the Chief Rabbinate, and, as a consequence, the Anglo-Jewish establishment and its affiliated institutions refused to recognize Schonfeld. They regarded him as the rabbi of a small ultra-Orthodox group of troublemakers and would have nothing to do with him. They did so despite the fact that the Union of Orthodox Hebrew Congregations had two representatives on the Board of Jewish Deputies of British Jews—Harry Goodman, the leader of the Agudah in Great Britain, and Dr. Isaac Levy, a British-born grandson of the great German exponent of neo-Orthodoxy, Rabbi Samson Raphael Hirsch, and author of the first English translation of his grandfather's commentary on the *Chumash* (Pentateuch). Later, I became one of the Union's two representatives on the Board.

Although Schonfeld was ideologically an Agudist, there were several reasons he chose not to be officially identified with them. One was because he was principal of the Jewish Secondary Schools and did not want to create a situation where Orthodox Jews or others would refuse to give him financial support for the schools by telling him to go to the Agudah. At the time, most of the Orthodox synagogues were Mizrachi-oriented (they were Zionistic and observant). If Schonfeld were to be labeled an Agudist, they would be closed to him when he needed to make appeals for funding.

People sometimes ask how it happened that Schonfeld became involved in the rescue activities carried on by Julius Steinfeld and the Agudath Israel in Vienna. Schonfeld, like Steinfeld and most of the *Schiffschul*-type of Viennese Agudists, was of Hungarian descent. His father was born in a small village in Hungary, his mother in Budapest. Although he studied in Slobodka for almost two years, Schonfeld knew little about Lithuanian Jewry. He was British-born, but like his father he considered himself an "*Ungarisher Yid*," a Hungarian Jew. Steinfeld, for his part, knew about Schonfeld's family because they had many relatives—mostly his mother's cousins—living in Vienna, all of them Orthodox and some of them affiliated with Agudath Israel.

Solomon Schonfeld was also a former student of Rabbi Shmuel Dovid Ungar's yeshiva in Tyrnau (Trnava), a bastion of "Oberland" Hungarian-style Orthodoxy. There he met Rabbi Michoel Ber Weissmandl. It was Weissmandl who suggested to Steinfeld that he organize *kindertransports* and most likely also asked Steinfeld to get in touch with Schonfeld (his former student) in London.

On one of his trips to London in the 1930s, Weissmandl developed a friendly relationship with the then-Archbishop of Canterbury, Dr. Cosmo Lang; Schonfeld also drew on the goodwill of his successor, Dr. William Temple, for a heroic rescue effort during the war years. While the effort did not yield results, it was a testament to Schonfeld's originality of thought and vision.

I have always associated a number of main character traits with Rabbi Schonfeld. First, he really enjoyed doing good deeds. Then, he was very human and wanted to know that people appreciated what he had done for them, yet he never sought tangible rewards and he never accepted financial compensation (as a consequence, he never had any money).

Schonfeld never hesitated to speak candidly on behalf of what he called "undiluted" Judaism. He wanted to show the Anglo-Jewish establishment that Orthodoxy counted, not as a "political" force, but as an entity of like-minded people. In his view, every *ehrliche Yid*, every truly religious, earnest Jew, regardless of his/her Jewish political affiliation, was important. And there was his love for his own "independent" Orthodox congregation, his network of schools, and his delight in watching them grow.

Even as an independent operator, Schonfeld was ready and willing to work with others on equal terms when conditions, in his view, demanded it. For instance, after the war, he found that an ever-growing number of refugees from Vienna's *Schiffschul* had joined his congregation, so he asked the membership to take on Rabbi Shlomo Baumgarten as associate rabbi. Baumgarten's father, Rabbi Joseph Baumgarten, was the *dayan* (judge) in the *Schiffschul* in Vienna and represented a type of Hungarian-style Orthodoxy that was considered extreme even in Orthodox circles. Yet Schonfeld was so secure, he was able to put someone more stringently Orthodox than he into his congregation in order to meet their needs.

At the same time, Schonfeld concluded that his rescue work would be more successful if he had the official approval of the Anglo-Jewish establishment. To this end, some time in 1938, he approached Chief Rabbi Joseph H. Hertz, who, as distinct from the lay leadership and congregations of the United Synagogue in those days, was personally Orthodox in his religious observance and orientation.

Schonfeld asked Hertz to join him in creating what he originally called the Chief Rabbi's Religious Emergency Council for German and Austrian Jews. Schonfeld, the independent operator, was willing to let the Chief Rabbi be presiding officer of this new body, while he, Schonfeld, would be the behind-the-scenes activist. The Chief Rabbi agreed. Eventually the name of the new organization was shortened to "The Chief Rabbi's Religious Emergency Council," (CRREC) or more simply, "the Council." When Schonfeld approached the British authorities for official permits or went to Jewish communal leaders for financial or moral support, he was able to say, "I come before you as a representative of the Chief Rabbi's Religious Emergency Council."

My official job title was Secretary to the Union of Orthodox Hebrew Congregations, and my unofficial title, the one I appreciated more, was Assistant to Rabbi Solomon Schonfeld, Rescue Activist. With their permission and approval, I would frequently write and sign letters for Rabbi Schonfeld and the Chief Rabbi, with accurate facsimiles of their own handwritings. Chief Rabbi Hertz was happy working with Schonfeld, who would go on to marry his oldest daughter, Judith.

Despite the blessings of the Chief Rabbinate, the Board of Jewish Deputies of British Jews and the Anglo-Jewish establishment did not accept Schonfeld and did not approve of his rescue operations. These organizations complained to Chief Rabbi Hertz: "This is not an activity in which the Chief Rabbi should engage," and he responded,

As Chief Rabbi, I am supposed to care for the needs of Jewish religious teachers, scholars and clergy. Schonfeld's activities come under this heading. This is not a communal matter, but a religious matter. When it comes to religious matters, no communal organization has the right to dictate to the Chief Rabbi. Remember, Chief Rabbis seldom die and they never retire!

Schonfeld, in his turn, was a pragmatist. He realized that while the idea of a "separatist" Orthodox community might have been good for Jewish communities on the Continent, it was not entirely relevant in England, where the Chief Rabbinate and the United Synagogue were at least officially Orthodox. He explained to his congregants that the time was not yet ripe to form an "independent," "secessionist" Orthodox community (*Austritt*).

He modeled his own educational and communal activities, in a manner of speaking, on the pattern of the British Commonwealth and its constituent states—independent entities under the umbrella of an overall community. True, he set up an independent *schechita* facility (slaughterhouse) in Letchworth, but did it only after the arrival of large numbers of *Schiffschul*-type refugees, made it necessary. He still permitted the "Shechita Board" of the Chief Rabbi to supervise his own *shechitah* and to place its seal upon his food products—as long as his own organization, which he named Kedassia, could exercise its own special supervision of these products.

In October 1939, about a month after the war broke out, Schonfeld called me into his study. He said, "Retter, do you remember the letters you wrote to me from Vienna saying that you would be willing to help me if ever I needed your services? Well, now is the time for you to make good on that promise. I have a job for you."

I must confess I was not particularly anxious to take him on because I was eager to complete my studies. I think I was the only refugee yeshiva student who had passed the *matura* examinations in Vienna, marking the completion of my academic high school studies and qualifying me for admission to an institution of higher learning. I was given no chance to protest. "I don't want to waste time," he declared. "Meet me here next Sunday at 12 o'clock!"

I did as instructed. The rabbi took me to London's East End to attend a meeting of the Executive of the Union of Orthodox Hebrew Congregations. The president at the time was Joseph S. Stern, an immigrant who had lived in England since well before World War I.

I remember two vice-presidents present were Harry Goodman and Dr. Isaac Levy, along with several others. Stern said to me, "Young man, Dr. Schonfeld told us you are a refugee. He said you have not been in the country very long but that you do speak a little English. We are appointing you secretary of the Union of Orthodox Hebrew Congregations. Your salary will be ten shillings a week." Even then, this was not a decent living wage. A more appropriate salary would have been a minimum of £5 a week. But Stern said to me, "We, the Union, do not have any money. If you find money for us, there will be more money for you, too."

The Union, at the time, was approximately twelve years old. I threw myself into the work and learned that twenty *shtiblech* [small congregations, usually located in an apartment or one room in a house] were affiliated with the Union. I saw an opportunity, and under Schonfeld's guidance, set out to recruit at least another twenty to twenty-six unaffiliated synagogues. There were new *shtiblech* emerging as a result of the influx of refugees from Germany and Austria. They weren't *shtiblech* in the East End sense of the term, but German-type Orthodox groups based on the Hirschian principle of *Torah im derekh eretz.* By the time I left England in 1950, I am proud to say that the Union had almost seventy constituent congregations.

My sole employment was as secretary of the Union. The CRREC never officially employed me, and I never did receive any money from it. In theory, Schonfeld kept the activities of the Union and those of the CRREC strictly apart because he did not want anyone to say that the Union was being financed by funds belonging to—or collected by— the Council. Still, in practice, Schonfeld's activities were interrelated.

The rabbi became my mentor and I became his friend and closest confidant. As such, I took an interest in the work of the CRREC. Eventually, Schonfeld, with the Chief Rabbi's full approval, entrusted me with several important missions on behalf of the Council. He did so at my initiative and, in each case, I volunteered.

In October of 1939, which was about the month after the war broke out, there was a rumor that young men from the ages of between seventeen and nineteen who had been given permission to stay in England as refugees, would become conscripted to the services. I then wrote a letter to the Home Office offering my services as a volunteer in the Censorship Department, stating in the letter, that I had a fair knowledge of the English language and of course German was my "mother" tongue. I figured, that this would be my contribution to the war effort. It took four weeks, and I was requested by the Foreign Office (although I had written to the Home Office), to appear for an interview. I was interviewed by a young man, Lord Linlithgo of the Foreign Office, and after an interview that lasted about three hours, Lord Linlithgo told me that there would be a position for me, and that I would hear very soon from him. Instead, I received a telephone call from Lord Wedgewood of Barlaston, the former Col. Josh Wedgewood, requesting me to appear before him. He lived in an apartment house in the Whitehall area. When I arrived at his apartment, I looked out of his sitting room window, and I could see the Thames River. Lord Wedgewood at first asked me whether I had heard of him, and what I knew about him. I told him we all knew that he was Col. Josh Wedgewood, and that he was a member of the House of Commons, and that he was considered a friend of the Jews. Lord Wedgewood then told me that he was both the head of the Censorship Department and also the chairman of the History of Parliament Committee.

At first, he showed me letters in German and asked me to translate these into English, and also to tell him if I could discover anything in the contents that would smell of illegal activity. After this interview, he appointed me as his adviser on German Jewish Affairs. I worked for Lord Wedgewood for a year and a half or more, and was given access to documents, which really were considered of vital importance. I then told him that I was associated with Dr. Solomon Schonfeld of whom he had heard, and that I was bound to continue working for Dr. Schonfeld's organizations, because I had written to him from Vienna, and I told him that if he were to obtain a visa for me to come to England, I would work for him and be of assistance to him. Lord Wedgewood was impressed by this, and he said: "Oh!, You are a very good letter writer; with your letters you came from Vienna. and with your letter you came to me here". The work was very interesting and I made use of this position (it was only a part time, half a day) to try and help Jewish refugees who lived in Belgium and Holland, who were trying to come to England, with the help and under the aegis of the Chief Rabbi's Emergency Council, which had been established by that time, by Dr. Schonfeld.

I then introduced Dr. Schonfeld to Lord Wedgewood and a friendship evolved, and Lord Wedgewood was always willing to help, especially when it concerned the possibility of obtaining certificates or immigration visas to what was then Palestine. Palestine, as we all knew, was a British Mandate and immigration to Palestine was controlled by the Colonial Office in London.

As a result of my working for Lord Wedgewood, and being very close to him, I was exempt from internment on the Isle of Man. All Austrian and German refugees came before a tribunal, and the tribunal ruled and classified a person either as a friendly enemy alien, or one that should be interned. I was one of very few persons of my age, who were exempt from interment to the Isle of Man. I used this relationship and connection to help in the provision of Kosher food to the Orthodox Jewish refugees who were interned in the Isle of Man. This was done with the help and boundless energy of Dr. Solomon Schonfeld.

On one mission, in 1940, I visited four internment camps on the Isle of Man, where German and Austrian refugees, were housed with German and Austrian enemy aliens. I went as a representative of the CRREC, not as representative of the Union. I spent ten days there and my arrival caused quite a stir. I was a refugee myself, one of their own, but I escaped internment and I was free, because somehow Schonfeld proved to the British authorities that I was indispensable.

My next mission involved Chief Rabbi Hertz's appeal to the Jewish community of England to donate kosher canned and non-perishable foods to the religious Jewish survivors. This upset the British authorities because the man in charge of the Division of Kosher Food at the Ministry of Food, Sir Robert Waley-Cohen (Lord Woolton), a Jew himself, loudly protested to the Chief Rabbi. He declared that the CRREC was creating the impression that Jews hoarded food in Great Britain while the rest of the country went hungry on rations. Waley-Cohen did not like being criticized by non-Jews, but the Chief Rabbi had more pressing concerns and was annoyed. He called me and asked me to prepare a draft response to Waley-Cohen and send it to the Ministry. In my draft, the Chief Rabbi wrote as ecclesiastical head of the Jewish Community of Great Britain.

Of course, we had no right to state officially that the canned food we sent to Germany was solely to be given to Orthodox Jews, though it was true that they needed it more than others. All we could do was to make sure they would receive at least the share of food to which they were entitled. Getting it done required our constant tact and vigilance. Though refugee organizations in the Anglo-Jewish establishment were in existence, they functioned as fundraisers, and were not intended to engage in any practical rescue activities. Their role was solely to allocate money to groups actively engaged in rescue work—they were not interested in bringing displaced and orphaned Jewish children to England. They would have preferred that Schonfeld, or, for that matter, anyone, take the children to Mandate Palestine or to the United States.

Another mission occurred immediately after the war. I visited the DP camps in Germany on behalf of the Council. My job was to organize the Orthodox population and see to it that the money and kosher food sent by the CRREC would be duly allocated to the people for whom it was intended. I spent about ten days in Bergen-Belsen; two days with what was left of the Jewish community of Berlin, and several days in Frankfurt and Hannover. Since I had not yet become a British citizen, I traveled on special "stateless" papers issued by the British Home Office, which guaranteed my readmission to England when I was ready to return. I also represented Schonfeld on several other postwar trips to the Netherlands and Poland.

Among the high British officials particularly helpful to Schonfeld were Lord Linlithgow and Baron James Chuter Ede, who later became Home Secretary. Another official who was most helpful was the First Secretary of the British Embassy in Warsaw. These were relationships that only Schonfeld was able to develop, and they were very personal. The rest of them, the Waley-Cohens and other leaders of the Anglo-Jewish establishment, were too stiff for him. In those days, in the 1930s and 1940s, British government officials never addressed communications to individuals. The salutations simply read: Dear Sir or Dear Madam or Dear Sir or Madam. At the CRREC, we were perhaps among the first to receive letters addressed to us as individuals: "Dear Dr. Schonfeld" and "Dear Mr. Retter" were the salutations we often found in our correspondence.

There are some who claim Schonfeld paid too little attention to *Eretz Yisroel* (the land of Israel) in his rescue schemes because he was opposed to the concept of *Eretz Yisroel* as a Jewish homeland. Nothing could be farther from the truth. Unfortunately, during the Holocaust years, Britain adamantly refused to open the doors of Mandate Palestine to Jewish refugees.

Schonfeld realized that this negative attitude could hardly be expected to change until after the war, when Britain would no longer need the Arab world in her struggle against Nazism.

This was why Schonfeld, the pragmatist, devoted the thrust of his rescue activities to possibilities that to him seemed within reach. To him there was only the Torah's dictum; immediate rescue of Jews transcended any long-range political aims. Schonfeld did not regard his sympathy for the religious objectives of Agudath Israel as anti-Zionist. He loved *Eretz Yisroel* as much as the most ardent Zionist, and desired the restoration of the Jewish homeland in the spirit of the Torah. Unlike the secular Socialist-Zionist establishment that actively worked for the creation of a postwar Jewish political state—even if it contravened the more urgent call to find immediate refuge for European Jewry—Schonfeld, the pragmatic idealist, was guided by only one goal: obedience to the Divine commandment which placed *pikuach nefesh*, the saving of lives, above all else.

Marcus Retter
New York, NY

INTRODUCTION

Poland 1946. The survivors of the Holocaust were confronted with the implacable hatred of their former Christian neighbors—who believed they should finish the job Hitler began. Hitler was dead, but Jews in Poland still were afraid to go into the streets or speak Yiddish in public. Their fears were justified when fifty Jews were killed and hundreds were wounded in a pogrom in Kielce.

A young rabbi in London, Solomon Schonfeld, heard reports from Poland, and wearing an officer's uniform of his own design, suddenly turned up in Warsaw. Word quickly spread among the surviving remnant of Jews that a British rabbi had come to Poland to take Jewish war orphans to England. Schonfeld had no time to lose, because the Communists, especially Jewish Communists in power, wanted the Jews to remain in Poland to help create a "new Poland," built on the ideal of a socialist utopia. That ideal, they believed, would solve all problems, including that age-old "Jewish problem"— antisemitism.

Schonfeld, who never believed in a Communist utopia, knew better. He rushed to bring out the orphans as quickly as possible. Armed with several hundred cartons of cigarettes—the most valuable post-war currency available—the rabbi chartered a boat in Gdansk and escorted 150 Jewish boys and girls aboard.

The crossing from Gdansk to England took four days. Aside from the ship's crew, the rabbi was the only adult on board. He spoke no Polish and the orphans spoke no English. Many of the orphans, hidden in non-Jewish homes for years, spoke no Yiddish either, but somehow they managed to communicate. Schonfeld talked to the children, in a mixture of English and Germanized Yiddish, about the beautiful country he was taking them to and how wonderful it is to be Jewish.

Many of the children were bewildered and seasick, and the young rabbi assumed the role of rescuer, father, mother, English teacher and nurse. Young and handsome, he exuded an infectious air of self-confidence and warmth. The boys and girls didn't understand everything the rabbi told them, but he did answer their unspoken questions enthusiastically: "Yes, life is still worthwhile, you *are* human beings worthy of love and affection, and yes, it is great to be a Jew!"

* * *

Who was this rabbi—this one-man, large-scale rescue operation—who had gone into action when the Nazis overran Austria? What impelled him to risk his peace of mind, his family contentment, his health—and, at times, his life—in order to ceaselessly pursue the divine commandment of *hatzalahs nefoshos,* the physical and spiritual rescue of his fellow Jews?

Rabbi Solomon Schonfeld, at the tender age of twenty-two, succeeded his father as rabbi of a small Orthodox congregation of approximately one hundred families and as principal of England's first Jewish Day School. Just six years later, in 1938, when Jewish cries for help came from Nazi-dominated Germany and Austria, he jumped into the fray as an outstanding rescuer—and fought the good fight for a decade. He remained at his calling, despite the opposition of virtually the entire Anglo-Jewish establishment, the Zionists, and, at times, his own Orthodox camp.

As a charismatic, formidable, handsome young man, with a quick mind, limitless energy and great memory, Schonfeld was given entrée to the offices, homes and hearts of all sorts of people. His sympathetic and pragmatic approach allowed him to work with government officials who might easily have rejected him as a Jewish "loner" in favor of the Jewish establishment. Though the British often liked to play both Jewish sides against the middle, Schonfeld preferred not to play the game at all and was thus able to accomplish more by sheer dint of his personality. He had total spiritual and physical passion devoted to his mission—rescuing the Jews of Europe. An inspired idealist, Schonfeld had enough common sense to wield the practical tools of his personality to fulfill the needs of those he served—and he preferred to do so as a one-man committee. He was outspoken and sometimes unpopular because of his single-minded views on rescue and Judaism, but his personal charm and diplomacy enabled him to set them forth with impressive effectiveness.

As the spiritual leader of his community in London, founder of a network of Orthodox day schools, as a welfare activist *par excellence,* teacher and preacher by his words—written and spoken—he was a most original phenomenon in modern Anglo-Jewry. Totally committed to Torah Judaism, he felt secure within the religious Jewish world as well as in the British secular world. Still, he did not work within the framework of any single political or religious party in Jewish life. Though he considered himself independent, he was ready and able to enlist proponents of views different from his own in order to carry out his rescue missions. *Chacham* Dr. Solomon Gaon described him as a "savior of the bodies and souls of thousands of Jewish people."

Schonfeld's style was unique. In the midst of large-scale planning and myriad administrative details, he found time for little personal touches that "his" children—now parents and grandparents living in many parts of the world—remember with admiring gratitude. By word and deed, he convinced his charges, young and old, that they were not impersonal case histories in a bulging refugee file. He convinced them they were individual human beings worthy of love and concern, and that no matter what they suffered at the hands of the Nazis, it was worth their while to persevere physically and spiritually as proud Jews.

Schonfeld's creative streak was manifest in all his endeavors and frequently allowed him to fulfill his objectives, regardless of the circumstances. His offbeat approach as a strictly observant Jew often brought him into conflict with the assimilationist Anglo-Jewish establishment, which hated making waves—especially on religious issues—fearing they would create antisemitism. They preferred, for example, to place the Jewish refugee children in non-Jewish homes, regardless of the consequences on the children's religious lives.

These conflicts had ramifications that crippled the ability to rescue and care for Jewish refugees in Britain before, during and after
the war, and had an impact on the Orthodox Jews in particular,
because the greater Jewish community generally ignored their needs.
Schonfeld's objective was to keep Orthodox youngsters together in
Orthodox homes or kosher hostels. He brought older youth to
England to study in existing yeshivos and Secondary Schools and to
participate in Orthodox youth groups like Chevra Ben Zakkai and
Zeirei (Agudah).

Schonfeld's methods would preserve the children's Jewishness,
and eventually many of them later became teachers and leaders in the
Jewish community. He established Yeshiva Ohr Yisroel for youths
between ages sixteen to eighteen who were ineligible for the *kindertransports,* and reestablished Rabbi Moshe Szneider's Frankfurt
Yeshiva in London, providing additional space for refugee students.

Just before the Blitz, during the mass evacuation from London,
tens of thousands of British children had to be moved to the countryside. Schonfeld met the challenge by creating a Jewish enclave for
more than 550 youngsters in non-Jewish villages on the outskirts of
London. The town of Shefford was the central hub for five villages
that took in his children. Schonfeld, in his congenial way, was able to
deal with villagers who had never seen Jews before, persuading them
to host Orthodox youngsters and make them feel at home.

To foster a Jewish atmosphere, Schonfeld set up an organization
called the National Council for Religious Education (NCRE),
responsible for establishing and elevating Jewish life in evacuation
centers and other communities. He raised funds and supplied those
communities with teachers—rabbis and functionaries he had rescued
from the hell of Europe. He supplied his charges with prayer books,
matzohs, *esrogirn* (citrons) and other religious articles. During the
war, HMG appointed him the sole importer of religious articles from
Eretz Yisroel, which he distributed to Jews throughout the British
Empire and later, in post-war Europe.

Schonfeld took care of the Jews in the internment camps. The
British, fearing a fifth column, established them in 1940, but

Schonfeld helped even when the refugees were interned in Canada and Australia. He solved the shortage of Orthodox leadership in those places by sending in his religious functionaries,[1] strengthening Jewish life in his communities.

Because Schonfeld was as concerned with the souls of Jews as he was with their physical well being, soon after the war he created synagogue-ambulances, also known as mobile synagogues. The appearance of these large trucks provided a much-needed psychological lift to the Jewish DPs. Schonfeld and his assistant, Marcus Retter, served the refugees a friendly welcome and the first kosher food many of them had eaten in years. At the same time, they urged the survivors to create their own Orthodox communities.

On Schonfeld's seventieth birthday in 1982, Chaim Bermant, an astute British-Jewish journalist, wrote an article in the *Jewish Chronicle of London*. Bermant appreciated Schonfeld's talents and the ten years he devoted to rescue, ten years that had a profound and lasting impact on British Jewry.[2]

CHAPTER 1

BACKGROUND

Solomon Schonfeld was born in London on February 21, 1912, the second son of seven siblings. His father, Rabbi Dr. Victor (Avigdor) Schonfeld, had come from Vienna three years earlier to assume the spiritual leadership of a small Orthodox congregation in North London. The elder Rabbi Schonfeld received a traditional yeshiva education in his native Hungary, and then went to Vienna for graduate studies. He served his London community for two decades—with one brief interruption—and distinguished himself as a pioneer in Britain's Orthodox Jewish life.[1]

Avigdor, who was the *force majeur* in Solomon's life, was born in 1880, in Süttö, Hungary, to Jakob and Betty Schonfeld. He was named for his grandfather, a rabbi in Vac, Hungary.[2] Avigdor's father was a shopkeeper and a learned man, and when Avigdor showed early promise, he sent him to *yeshivos* in Gross-Tapoicany and the Shevet Sofer's (Rabbi Simcha Bunim Schreiber's) yeshiva in Pressburg/Bratislava for his *smicha* (rabbinical ordination). The latter location, then part of the Austro-Hungarian Empire, later became part of Czechoslovakia. Unlike others, Avigdor completed his secular studies at a non-Jewish *gymnasium* and attended the University of Vienna, eventually earning a doctorate in education in 1914 from the University of Giessen with a dissertation, *Die Ethik Shafstbury*, written in English—a language he taught himself. Because he did this while he remained true to his Torah heritage, he stood out among his peers.[3]

In 1909, Avigdor married Rochel Leah (Ella) Sternberg (1890–1971), a descendant of the nineteenth-century scholar, Rabbi Akivah Eger. She bore him six sons and a daughter. Her strong personality and ambitions for their children—and her husband's ability to deal with the secular world while remaining committed to his Orthodoxy—were pivotal factors in shaping Solomon's personality.[4]

Avigdor espoused the *weltanshauung* of Rabbi Samson Raphael Hirsch—*Torah im Derekh Eretz*—that allowed Orthodox Jews to accept the secular world and secular knowledge as viewed through the prism of the Torah, while acknowledging the Torah's sovereignty. He also believed in Hirsch's concept of *Austritt* (separatism), a philosophy which posited that Orthodox Jews should develop their own totally separate, independent, recognized communities (*kehillos*) where they set themselves apart from the *Einheits* or *Grossgemeinde* (general Jewish community)—that included all factions of Jewish belief: Orthodox, Liberal and Reform. Rabbi Hirsch founded an *Austritt kehillah* in Frankfurt-am-Main in the latter part of the nineteenth-century, although many Orthodox Jews there preferred to remain part of the overall Jewish community.[5]

In time, six other congregations in different German cities followed Hirsch's example and set up their own *Austritt* communities. Still, most Jewish communities followed his ideological opponent, the great Talmudic scholar, Rabbi Seligman Ber Bamberger (1807–1878), the "Wurzburger Rav," who felt that it was incumbent on the Orthodox community to remain within the *Grossgemeinde*, as long as the Orthodox controlled the religious institutions (*shechitah* [kosher slaughter of meat], education, cemeteries, etc.).[6]

The concept of *Austritt* had a parallel development in nineteenth-century Hungary. (The separatists here were called the Orthodox *kehillah*, while the purely Reform *kehillos* were known as "Neolog." The remaining overall *Grossgemeinde* were known as the *Status Quo.*) Rabbi Moshe Sofer (1762–1839), the Chassam Sofer, inspired the struggle for independent Orthodox *kehillos* in Hungary. He was a leader and scholar who founded a famous yeshiva in Pressburg. He sought to retain Orthodox control over Jewish institutions that were challenged by the rising secular and Reform movements. While fully consonant with Hirsch's concept of *Austritt*, Hungarian Orthodoxy vehemently rejected Hirsch's second ideology of *Torah im Derekh Eretz.*[7]

While the battle between Hirsch and Bamberger raged in Germany during the 19th century and quieted down during the early part of the twentieth, history has shown that the separatists retained their loyalty to "Torah-true" Orthodox Judaism to a far greater degree than did those Orthodox who remained within the *Grossgemeinde* or *Status Quo*. Moreover, the mere existence of the separatist *kehillos* prompted the Reform elements in other cities to permit the Orthodox control over certain key institutions, such as education and *shechitah*.

The impact of these philosophical and religious splits in the Jewish community cannot be underestimated. They had an impact on the rescue and relief efforts involving the Continental Orthodox Jewish refugees and, after the war, the survivors.

* * *

In 1904, Avigdor Schonfeld was appointed to a position in the Montefiore Synagogue in Vienna. When he received his *smicha* from Pressburg in 1908, he went to London and became the rabbi of the London *Beth HaMidrash*, whose president, Julius Lunzer, also believed in Hirschian ideals. The congregation saw the young rabbi as a kindred spirit who inspired their hopes for a revitalized Orthodox community in Britain.

Soon after his arrival, Rav Avigdor realized that the British Jewish community was disorganized and weak, so he followed Hirsch's *Austritt* blueprint for rebuilding the *kehillah*, with *Torah im Derekh Eretz* as the principle on which it was based.[8]

In 1910, because he viewed youth as the future of Orthodoxy, he established the Chevra Ben Zakkai to encourage Torah study in young people (*Chevras Limud Hatorah*). It was the first such institution in England and was named for Rabbi Yochanan Ben Zakkai, the Talmudic scholar, who had witnessed the destruction of the Second Temple and reinvigorated Diaspora Judaism—that needed to survive in a world without the Holy Temple—by studying Torah.[9]

The Chevra Ben Zakkai was more than just a learning group. In addition to *shiurim* (lectures), Rav Avigdor offered boys and girls social activities like hiking and concerts, following the examples set by Zeirei Agudah and Esra, the German Orthodox youth groups. Young women were offered special lectures on the importance of women in Jewish history and their crucial role as homemakers.

As a result of his programs, Rabbi Schonfeld was able to make Orthodox Jewish youth feel proud of who they were and what they believed in. In 1911, the *Beis HaMedrash*, under his leadership, spun off the Adath Yisroel Synagogue (the Adas), whose name was symbolic of the Hirschean ideal. Later that same year, Rabbi Schonfeld organized the first English Conference of Orthodox Rabbis in Leeds.[10]

The First World War (1914–1918) had an enormous impact on the European Jewish community and on Avigdor Schonfeld. More than 1.5 million Jews served in the armed forces of all the belligerents, out of proportion to their numbers in the general population. The heaviest fighting on the Eastern Front took place in the heartland of the East European Jewish community, which ran from the Baltic Sea in the north to the Black Sea in the south. Hundreds of thousands of Jews were uprooted and turned into refugees. (For example, Galicia, part of the Austro-Hungarian Empire, was taken and retaken six times between the Austrian and Russian armies. Each time they caused more destruction and created more refugees. Over 200,000 Galician Jews fled to Vienna, while a smaller number fled to Germany.) With their way of life torn asunder, and their religious institutions destroyed, many Jewish communities simply disappeared.[11]

Thousands of Jewish soldiers were captured and became prisoners of war in various countries, including Britain. At the same time, the British implemented the precedent-setting policy of interning "enemy-aliens"—people who were born in Germany or any other country fighting with Britain. These "enemy-aliens" included Jewish refugees from Belgium, Austria-Hungary and Eastern Europe. Although himself an "enemy-alien," Avigdor Schonfeld was exempt as a rabbi and was able to work with Dr. Joseph H. Hertz, Chief Rabbi of the British Empire, risking everything to help those in need. He even intervened with the military authorities to provide kosher food and other services for Orthodox and other Jewish internees.[12]

In 1917, buoyed by the Balfour Declaration that promised a future Jewish homeland in Palestine, Rabbi Schonfeld, who loved *Eretz Yisroel*, founded the British branch of Mizrachi, the religious Zionists who helped establish a Jewish homeland in British Mandate Palestine (the *Yishuv*). In 1920, he attended the Mizrachi World Conference in Amsterdam, was elected to its Central Bureau and given the assignment to lead the Mizrachi school system in the *Yishuv*.[13]

That same year, he met Harry Goodman, an active Mizrachist who later became secretary of World Agudah when Jacob Rosenheim, a refugee from Germany, was its president. Both Rosenheim and Goodman would later be members of Adas Yisroel when it was under Solomon Schonfeld's leadership.[14]

In 1921, leaving behind his unfinished work at Adas Yisroel, Rav Avigdor moved to Eretz Yisroel and confronted the challenge of building a Mizrachi Talmud Torah system following the principle of *Torah im Derekh Eretz*. He tried, without success, to get the Mizrachi and the Agudah to cooperate on educational efforts, advocating that the Mizrachi follow Hirsch's principle of *Austritt*—to remain separate and independent from the Jewish Agency (the *Sochnut*). [15]

The Mizrachi, however, preferred to benefit from the largesse of the *Sochnut* and accepted funding so as not to have to raise funds from other sources. In his letter of resignation, written in 1923, Rav Avigdor complained about the politics of it all:

> The battle of the Mizrachi still rages more fiercely to the right [Agudah] than . . . to the left [the dominating labor Zionist organization]. And so long as this prevails, the enthusiasm of traditional Jewry cannot be awakened in the cause of Mizrachi. The Mizrachi has been making concessions to the Zionist organization for the last 25 years. It must now do the same toward the Aguda [*sic*] for the sake of a unified Orthodoxy.[16]

The disillusioned rabbi returned to London and the Adas, where he was welcomed with open arms and rebuilt the synagogue according to its original founding principles. He revitalized the Chevra Ben Zakkai youth groups and spent the next seven years working to assure that the fruits of his labor would blossom. At the same time, he hammered away at the British establishment Jews (United Synagogue) who called themselves Orthodox but were lax in their observance. He interested himself in the plight of Ethiopian Jewry, whose identification had been a subject of dispute since the late 19th century, and took a personal interest in one young man from Africa. Then, in 1925, the Adas purchased a cemetery in Enfield to meet its congregants' needs.[17]

The following year, Rav Avigdor created the Union of Orthodox Hebrew Congregations as an "amalgamation of synagogues which profess and practice Traditional Judaism," with its own *beis din* (court of Jewish law), *kashrus* authority, cemetery and other services. The creation of this independent Orthodox community (following his adherence to the *Austritt* philosophy) put him at odds with the United Synagogue, the established British Jewish community, whose leader, Rabbi Dr. Joseph H. Hertz (1872–1946) was recognized, by most, as the Chief Rabbi of the British Empire.[18]

There was a third Orthodox synagogue group, The Federation of Synagogues, under the leadership of Rabbi Meir Tzvi Jung (1858–1921) that was not part of the heated conflict. According to Retter, Jung and Schonfeld were very different personalities. Rav Avigdor was an activist, a public figure who built a "competing" Jewish community to face off against the British establishment Jews in United Synagogue. Rabbi Jung was passive and not seen as a threat by either Hertz or Schonfeld.[19]

In 1927, Rav Avigdor organized the Yavneh Union to "unite all the Orthodox youth societies of the [London] metropolis," anticipating by decades the Yavneh societies that would flourish in America among Orthodox college students in the 1950s and 1960s.

In 1929, he attended the World Conference of Shomrei Shabbos (Sabbath observers) in Berlin, and later that same year established a Jewish Secondary School in London, a dream that took a long time to realize and was not without controversy.[20]

Many of Rav Avigdor's congregants and fellow Orthodox Jews felt that the British school system was the place for their children. In order to become an accepted part of British society, they were not willing to create self-imposed ghettos or train their children for the rabbinate. An analogous situation existed in the United States, where it was assumed that between the traditions their children learned at home and in the Talmud Torah afternoon schools, the Jewish future was assured.

Rav Avigdor spent enormous effort to convince parents that their children could live as Orthodox Jews and still be accepted within English society. He told them that such a school would be:

> . . . a centre [which] would be saturated with Judaism, where the boys and girls may be brought up in an up-to-date, but thoroughly Jewish atmosphere, where they will acquire the knowledge of Judaism along with other subjects, where the study of Judaism is not going to be a burden, as at the present, robbing them of their hours of leisure, and where they will take pride in exercising their best faculties as Jews.[21]

The first Jewish Secondary School opened at Finsbury Park on September 17, 1929 with a non-Jewish headmaster and with Rav Avigdor doing double-duty as principal and Judaism teacher. He was a role model for his students and saw his success in this endeavor as the beginning of a secondary school movement in the Orthodox world. Unfortunately, he did not live long enough to see his prophecy fulfilled. On January 1, 1930, when he was just forty-nine, Rabbi Avigdor Schonfeld died of blood poisoning from an infected cut that today could have been simply cured with penicillin.[22]

Thousands of mourners accompanied the rabbi's casket to the Enfield Cemetery. Among the numerous eulogies delivered that day was one from his second son, Solomon, who quoted from his father's last Rosh Hashanah sermon: "We do not just want life, but a purpose in life." That phrase was to set the standard for the young law student, who was chosen by his mother, the Rebbetzin, to take his father's place.[23]

Solomon immediately left the law school at the University of London to return to the yeshiva in Nitra, Czechoslovakia, still under the leadership of Rabbis Ungar and Weissmandl. His mother arranged for the temporary appointment of Rabbi Eliyahu Munk—recently arrived from Germany—to her late husband's pulpit. A year later, as Retter noted, she approved the first memorial address by Rabbi Zvi Hirsch Farber, a learned and well-known preacher. He delivered it dramatically, pulling away the curtains of the Holy Ark while intoning the verse from Psalms: "No stranger shall sit upon his throne." (A pointed hint to Rabbi Munk to understand his temporary position in the congregation.)[24]

While her son was preparing for his future on the Continent, Rochel Leah and several devoted friends managed to keep the day school and secondary school afloat in the face of fierce opposition from the Anglo-Jewish establishment and some members of the Adas congregation—who remained unconvinced of Rav Avigdor's ideology.[25]

In the meantime, Solomon had switched from the yeshiva in Nitra to the more advanced yeshiva in Slobodka, Lithuania, where he studied Talmudic analysis and *mussar* (character building). He studied for his *smicha* while simultaneously enrolled in the doctoral program at the University of Koenigsberg, the university nearest Slobodka. He completed both programs, earning himself the titles of rabbi and doctor—and he grew a beard. He was twenty-one.[26]

In Nitra and then during his studies in Slobodka, Solomon emulated his father's dedication to *Torah im Derekh Eretz*. In December 1933, with his *smicha* and Ph.D. in hand, Solomon returned to London to take over his father's pulpit at the Adas. His goal was to take over his father's roles as principal of the Jewish Secondary School, the Adas itself, and as presiding rabbi of the Union of Orthodox Hebrew Congregations.[27]

His term as substitute rabbi over, Eliyahu Munk went on to found the Golder's Green *Beis Hamedrash* and took many Adas members with him.[28] The young Solomon, inspired by his father's legacy and devoted to his spirit, was undaunted. He focused on enlarging and building upon his father's work in the Secondary School.[29] He eventually established four primary schools and expanded the Union of Orthodox Hebrew Congregations to include Hasidic *shtiblach* and the many new synagogues established after 1933 by refugees from Hitler's Europe.[30]

INFLUENCE OF RABBI MICHOEL BER WEISSMANDL

While Schonfeld's parents helped form his character and personality, Rabbi Michoel Ber Weissmandl, his teacher and mentor at the Nitra Yeshiva, was a very important influence on his thinking and the inspiration for much of his rescue work. They became close during Schonfeld's two stints at the yeshiva, and their relationship was strengthened during Weissmandl's three visits to England during the 1930s. They particularly bonded through their correspondence from 1938–45, in which Weissmandl urged Schonfeld to do what he could to rescue the Jews of Europe.[31]

Schonfeld first attended Nitra in the late 1920s, during his teenage years, when his teachers were Rabbi Shmuel Dovid Ungar, the Rosh Yeshiva, and Weissmandl. He went back to Nitra from 1930 to prepare for his *smicha*.[32]

Weissmandl was a leading Talmudic scholar, teacher and charismatic personality, considered by his peers to be a multi-faceted genius. In the pre-computer era, he discovered the now popular system of the Bible Codes (a system for deciphering hidden information in the Torah, following certain mathematical sequences).[33] During his research trips to Oxford, he published a critical edition of *Kikayon D'Yonah*, an early Talmudic commentary.[34]

When Weissmandl wanted to know about Polish Jewry, he visited Eastern Europe to see what Polish Jews were like and to meet some of the great Torah sages. In those days, there was little communication between Jewish communities because travel between them was expensive and uncommon, except for businessmen. Hungarian Jews were not familiar with Polish, Lithuanian or German Jewry, and vice versa. Hungarian Jewry was generally unaware, for example, of the great *halachic* work, *Mishneh Berurah* by Rabbi Yisroel Meir HaKohen, the *Chofetz Chaim* of Radin, Poland. In Hungary they studied commentaries on the *Shulchan Aruch*.[35]

The prejudices of one segment of European Jewry against another—German or Swiss Jews against their East European brethren; Hasidim vs. Lithuanian Jews; Sephardim against Ashkenazim, and so on—had negative consequences on rescue efforts. During the

Holocaust, when one group of Jews sought help from another, their historical prejudices militated against easy cooperation. These Jewish prejudices were a reflection of the host country's own prejudices— for example, Germany's prejudice against Eastern Europeans in general and East European Jews in particular. Weissmandl was one of a few, who, during the interbellum period, made it his business to acquaint himself with the different kinds of Jews living on the Continent.[36]

According to Marcus Retter, when Solomon Schonfeld went to study in the Nitra Yeshiva, he fell completely under Weissmandl's spell. Weissmandl's ability to gauge the individuality of each of his students is clear in an anecdote Retter tells about Schonfeld. One fine day, a teenaged Schonfeld was "caught" playing tennis with a girl. One of his fellow students came to Weissmandl to inform on Schonfeld and his flagrant violation of yeshiva standards. Knowing full well that British Jewish standards were not the same as those in Nitra or Pressburg, Weissmandl looked the informer in the eye and said in his inimitable Slovakian Yiddish, "*Zol a zah shtrick alleh muhl zayn tvishin zey.*" ("May there always be such a net between them.")[37]

Weissmandl visited England several times before the outbreak of World War II and often stayed at the Schonfeld home, reinforcing his influence on Solomon. He visited in 1935 and again in 1937 while doing research on *Kikayon D'Yonah* at the Bodleian Library in Oxford. His name is still in the library's register, where it is noted he had full run of the closed stacks in return for establishing the authorship of an unattributed ancient Hebrew manuscript.[38]

At the time, Retter reports, Weissmandl was attending a conference about modernizing the Hebrew language. Various Zionist spokesmen talked about how Hebrew should be streamlined. For example, the word *kelev* means dog. But there was no Hebrew word for puppy, so they suggested adding the diminutive "lav" to *kelev* and call a puppy "*klavlav.*" Weissmandl jumped up and said, "If we use this as a model, the Hebrew word "*melech*" (king) can be transformed to denote a prince by using the term "*meluchlach*" (which means filthy). The audience's laughter successfully squelched this attempt to modernize Hebrew and attracted the attention of Dr. Cosmo Lang, the Archbishop of Canterbury.[39]

Dr. Lang, a devotee of classical Hebrew, appreciated Weissmandl's quick wit and defense of the ancient language. The two became friends. Weissmandl's German probably enabled him to readily communicate with the Archbishop, and the two traditionalists, rabbi and cleric, found common ground in their defense of the holy tongue (*loshon hakodesh*).[40]

Weissmandl was also fascinated by physics and mechanics and worked on a perpetual motion machine and other inventions during his stays in Britain.[41] His brilliant and innovative mind made him the ideal rescue activist for the Slovak underground. While under fire, he developed and initiated many rescue schemes and tried to convince Jews in the free world to carry them out. Among those plans, some of which succeeded to some degree, were ransoming thousands of Jews in Slovakia and Hungary.[42]

In 1934, Weissmandl traveled to *Eretz Yisroel* with the Rosh Yeshiva, Rabbi Shmuel Dovid Ungar, and fell in love with the land, despite his later disagreements with Zionist ideology. After finishing his research at Oxford, he returned to Slovakia and married Brocho Rochel, Rabbi Ungar's daughter, with whom he had five children.[43]

From April 1938 until the end of the war, Weissmandl tried to alleviate Jewish suffering. He made several risky trips to Vienna to discuss the situation. Following the first of these trips, Weissmandl contacted Schonfeld and urged him to work on specific rescue efforts.[44]

On April 19, several weeks after the *Anschluss*, Weissmandl wrote to Schonfeld and asked him to make the free world aware of the terrible situation in Vienna. Tell the world, he asked, of the fate of the deported Jews of Burgenland. They were known in Jewish circles as the *Shevah Kehillos,* the Seven Communities—the first Jews to be dispossessed by the Nazis in Austria. Many arrived in Vienna and were cared for by its diminished Jewish community. Others were dumped in the no-man's land between Hungary and Czechoslovakia, including sixty rabbis who were placed on a boat and sent down the Danube, with no country willing to accept them. Weissmandl's good friend, the Archbishop of Canterbury, helped him obtain British visas for them.[45]

Julius Steinfeld, his son-in-law Charles Richter (both from the *Schiffshul*) and Rabbi Weissmandl tried to help as many Viennese Jews as possible, using *Aliyah Bet*, the illegal immigration to *Eretz Yisroel* and the *kindertransports* to London. As a result, the Burgenlanders, who used the *Shiffshul* as a refugee center, filled it to the rafters.[46]

In his letter to Schonfeld, Weissmandl described the terrible conditions faced by the Austrian Jews that included terrible beatings by Nazi thugs and savage hunger. He asked Schonfeld to find guarantors in London to get as many refugees as possible into Britain. He also demanded that Schonfeld focus solely on this tragedy, that he not tarry, that he alert the public and do everything possible. He told Schonfeld to make contacts in Parliament and to write a letter to the *London Times* to let the public know what was happening to the refugees. In frustration he wrote in bold letters, **"ARE YOU MADE OF STONE THAT YOU DON'T MELT!"**[47]

Weissmandl also enclosed an article from the *Prague Tagblatt* describing the situation. He added, sarcastically, that had this occurred somewhere in India or Africa, there would have been an outcry long ago.[48]

Weissmandl's entreaties and demands on his former pupil had their effect. We know that Schonfeld brought the plight of the Burgenland and Viennese Jews to the attention of Anglo-Jewry and made sure that publicity of their plight circulated widely among non-Jewish circles and in the secular media. He scrupulously followed Weissmandl's advice even to the suggested sequence of events.[49]

Weissmandl kept up his detailed reports of the sad situation in Europe throughout the war. At one point in 1938, while still in Vienna, Weissmandl found out from Steinfeld that the *Kultusgemeinde* evidenced an anti-Orthodox prejudice in the selection process for the *kindertransports*. He immediately suggested that Steinfeld get in touch with Schonfeld to arrange for separate Orthodox *kindertransports,* one of Schonfeld's more successful rescue plans.[50]

Schonfeld maintained contact with his teacher and mentor throughout the war via Weissmandl's former classmate, Boruch Meshulem Leibovitz, in Switzerland. And although it was illegal to receive mail from enemy-occupied territory via a neutral country, somehow HMG never put a stop to the correspondence nor reprimanded him. As a result, Leibovitz became the channel through which Weissmandl sent the Auschwitz Report and the plea to bomb the railroad tracks leading to Auschwitz and Birkenau.[51]

It was Weissmandl who inspired Schonfeld to establish Ohr Yisroel for the yeshiva students aged sixteen to eighteen who were ineligible for the *kindertransports*. Weissmandl wrote Schonfeld to bring them over and ". . . make sure they remain in yeshiva, rather than hanging around the markets of Whitechapel."

Weissmandl explained that bringing the students to England would "plant a tree of Torah" whose branches would spread far and wide. Retter speculates that Ohr Yisroel was intended to become the home for the Nitra Yeshiva—if it could be saved.[52]

On April 6, 1939, Weissmandl came to England again, this time on a rescue mission. He had a list of two hundred families from Nitra he wanted to send to Canada for safety.[53] With British help, he obtained Canadian approval for his plan. As Retter explained:

> I clearly remember that list because Schonfeld asked me to act as Weissmandl's escort and interpreter on his visits to the authorities in London. Though Weissmandl understood English, he did not speak it very well and wanted someone fluent to explain exactly what he wanted. Weissmandl wanted to organize a religious rural community in Canada similar to the post-war Yeshiva Farm Settlement in Mt. Kisco, New York. It was supposed to be a self-contained community, located away from the temptations of major cities. His list of two hundred families included a doctor, a rabbi and people who were trained in agricultural work.[54]

Inevitably, the war intervened, and among those two hundred families who never made it out were some in the first group to arrive in

Auschwitz in 1942. They were assigned to sort the clothing of those sent to the crematoria, and one of them sarcastically remarked, "So this is your Canada!" Thus did the sorting area become known as "Canada," a designation that passed into legend.[55]

On August 26, 1939, just eight days before the war began, Weissmandl went back to Slovakia, although the then-Archbishop of Canterbury, Dr. Temple, beseeched him to stay in Britain. If the war had broken out just three months later, Weissmandl, his family and the Jews of Nitra would all have been safe in Canada.[56]

Following the unsuccessful Slovak (and Jewish) uprising against the Nazis in the fall of 1944, Weissmandl's family and several thousand Slovak Jews were deported to Auschwitz. Weissmandl, who taught his students to cut through window bars with half a hacksaw blade and to jump from moving trains, managed to escape so that he could try to save Jews from the Nazis.[57]

Another influence on Schonfeld's life was Harry Goodman, the long-time member of the Adas. He was Schonfeld's mentor first and later became his partner in Jewish leadership and a close friend. On Goodman's fiftieth birthday in 1949, Schonfeld wrote to him:

> When I was twelve, a new *baal habayis* (congregant) at the Adas took the trouble to argue with me seriously about the battle of Orthodoxy. . . . You were our brother; we enjoyed your rows. When I was fifteen, you encouraged me in my first efforts at communal work and teaching, at public speaking and writing. When I was seventeen, you sponsored me as the potential rabbi. When I was twenty, you welcomed me to a position for which I was hardly equipped and you used your astute powers of influencing opinion in order to build up the name and authority of the rabbi of the Adas and Union, which you had assiduously nursed throughout. And for the last fifteen years, we have become partners in practically every field of Jewish life...[58]

Schonfeld was referring to the Weissmandl-inspired rescue efforts he and Goodman worked on together. In fact, Schonfeld tried to rescue Weissmandl many times during the war, but never succeeded. The two weren't reunited until the war was over.[59]

Weissmandl survived, but his wife and children did not. After the war, he settled in the United States, where he and Retter became close friends. He was a strictly Orthodox rabbi in the traditional Hungarian style and yet was able to establish working relationships with non-Orthodox Jews and non-Jews.

THE PRAGMATIC IDEALIST

Many prominent rescue activists worked hard for the larger community during World War II, but few were able to develop the kinds of personal relationships Solomon Schonfeld did. Whether they were Orthodox or not, he had a genuine interest in and compassion for the people he'd saved through the years. In the words of one who knew him, Rabbi Schonfeld

> . . . had the requisite capacity for leadership, and the religious beliefs, but he is not a contemplative man, nor has he ever had the patience to work with committees, except in the sense that he would give orders and he expected the committee to carry them out. His heroic decade was from 1939 [sic] to 1948. As the war clouds gathered, an emergency committee for the relief of European Jewry was formed under the aegis of Chief Rabbi J[oseph] H. Hertz, and Schonfeld, who shortly after was to become Hertz's son-in-law. . . . At once things began moving. To Schonfeld, an emergency was an emergency. He had no time for committees or budgets or precedents or permissions or red tape. He chartered ships and trains and moved into Europe himself to snatch whole families from under the very noses of the Nazis.[60]

The Home Office gave in to many of Schonfeld's requests, but far from all of them. He was not a sycophant who relied on empty flattery to get his way. Nor did Home Office officials "wilt at his approach." Officials recognized that he was a true humanitarian who did not seek recognition for his efforts, never sought the spotlight and was sincere about his purpose. In some departments he may have seemed like a nuisance—which he undoubtedly was. At other times, he served as the foil for Britain's standard policy of dividing and conquering Britain's Jewish community. But his persistence convinced the Home Office that he was solution-oriented and dedicated to the victims of war. This fostered an inclination to help him.

Furthermore, Schonfeld carried himself like an impeccable Englishman and gave an impressive appearance. His warm, personal approach in presenting the case for the Orthodox was direct and free of apologetics, and thus he often succeeded in cutting through bureaucratic red tape.

On the other hand, the forever-staid Anglo-Jewish establishment found Schonfeld's behavior "unimaginable," and kept its distance because it equated his "independence" from them as "irresponsibility" and his Orthodoxy as "un-English." Schonfeld's independence, at times, did throw their plans into disarray. Later, many survivors recalled that mentioning Schonfeld's name would get them prompt hearings at British agencies. But the "Anglo-Jews" rarely gave personal or financial assistance to any of his relief and rescue projects. The CRREC primarily fended for itself with the help of the Adas community built by his father and from sympathetic Jews of all stripes in the British Empire.

In December 1938, Schonfeld returned from Vienna and needed entry visas for three hundred youngsters he wanted to bring to England. He met with an official from the Home Office, who asked him for proof of temporary shelter to house the youngsters while waiting to be placed in Jewish homes or hostels. The official was insistent because the assimilationist Anglo-Jewish establishment, which did not want Orthodox children brought to Britain, informed the Home Office that Schonfeld had no place to keep them.

Schonfeld showed the official two empty schools—empty because the students had been dismissed for Chanukah vacation. The Chevra Ben Zakkai had cleared out the desks and classroom furniture and set up cots. The official noted the space could only hold 250 children because of precise governmental requirements. "Where," he asked, "would the rest of the youngsters sleep?"

Schonfeld took the official to the home he shared with his mother and youngest brother at 35 Lordship Park, and showed him rooms filled with cots—fortunately, his mother and brother were out of town at the time. "That's fine," said the official, "but where will you sleep?" Schonfeld took him up to the attic, where his own cot was located.[61]

That impressed the Home Office official, with whom he developed a cordial relationship,[62] making it easier for Schonfeld to ask for assistance without demanding concessions. In his first CRREC report, Schonfeld made it a point to thank the officials:

> A special expression of thanks has been communicated to the Home Office, voicing the gratitude of the Chief Rabbi and his collaborators for the prompt and sympathetic consideration given to the applications placed before them, and for the example they have set to other countries in giving temporary asylum to this class of refugees. Despite the extraordinary pressure brought upon the Department, matters were dealt with through *the superhuman efforts of the officials, through the nights and uninterrupted weekends*. It is felt that this spirit of charity and helpfulness deserves **every possible recognition** [emphasis added].[63]

Schonfeld maintained amicable relationships with all of HMG's departments and officials, although some were less forthcoming than the Home Office.[64] This is evident in a letter from an official in the Colonial Office who noted that he was transferring to another department and would no longer deal with Schonfeld personally. He wrote: ". . . Allow me to take this opportunity of thanking you for your invariable courtesy and co-operation while I was at the Colonial Office. It was a great pleasure to be able to work together on these difficult problems."[65]

Schonfeld's practicality in these matters was in sharp contrast to his older contemporary, Professor Selig Brodetsky, a major Zionist leader, a sympathetic personality and head of the Board of Jewish Deputies. Brodetsky, like virtually all of the other Zionist leaders in the United States and Britain (other than the Bergson group), was unable to detach rescue plans from his exclusive messianic, ideological focus on the *Yishuv* as the sole haven for refugees. Brodetsky could never drop the demand to "Open the Doors to Palestine" from any of his rescue plans and dealings with HMG.

HMG remained adamant in sticking to its policy of refusing to allow more than 75,000 Jews into Mandate Palestine. Its priority was to maintain good relations with the Arabs and not endanger their access to Arab oil. That is the reason the British White Paper, strictly limiting Jewish entry to the *Yishuv*, was issued in 1939.[66]

Brodetsky and the other Zionist leaders never understood that their insistence on using Mandate Palestine as a refuge doomed any of their rescue plans or efforts, even if the issue was only vaguely addressed. Schonfeld realized the pointlessness of using the *Yishuv* as a refuge,[66] as there was no way to convince HMG to reverse its Near East policy. As a result, he intentionally omitted any mention of Mandate Palestine as a possibility from all of his plans. In October 1942, he even developed a plan to rescue European Jews by transferring them to the British island of Mauritius in the Indian Ocean, and wrote to Lord Cranberry of the Colonial Office:

> "I much appreciate the various schemes involving the transfer of refugees to *Palestine*. I did not approach you in the first place *concerning that country, as I was aware of the limitations that do exist* as well as of the schemes carried out." (Emphasis added.)[67]

In the same letter, however, Schonfeld discusses a scheme to exchange Jews under Nazi occupation for Germans in Mandate Palestine.[68]

Arguably, Schonfeld faced even greater obstacles to his relief and rescue schemes from another source, i.e., the assimilation camp. By this we mean those Jews who acquired wealth and even knighthood, whose highest priority was to fully integrate into and be fully accepted by British society any particularist "Jewish" concerns such as kashrut, or the interest in locating Jewish homes for refugee children, would, in their mind, impede such acceptance. Most detrimental to their goal were the Orthodox, whose very garb and specific Jewish traditions made them the least assimilable, and therefore the most troublesome.

During the interbellum period, the assimilationists were satisfied with the much weakened state of Orthodox Jewish life in England. The issue of the Orthodox functionaries was but one of many instances where the Chief Rabbinate would come to Schonfeld's political rescue. When Sir Robert Waley-Cohen (Lord Woolton), a major proponent of assimilation, vice president of the United Synagogue and vice president of the Board of Jewish Deputies, said that bringing in religious functionaries was a communal matter in which the Chief Rabbi had no say, Rabbi Hertz contentiously replied, "Only the Chief Rabbi may determine if and how many clergy and teachers are necessary for English Jewry."[69]

Thus, the Agudah's Emigration Advisory Council (the EAC) and the CRREC were created to serve distinct needs not addressed by the major British Jewish establishment organizations most of whom were headed by assimilationist Jews. The Anglo-Jewish establishment neglected the Orthodox, whether they were rabbis, laymen or children.[70]

FINANCES

The CRREC was chartered under the British War Charities Act of 1940, and required to provide annual reports and audited accounts., and in all, Schonfeld raised and spent $2,000,000 in England and abroad on behalf of the committee. Generous "overseas" Jewish communities, including the United States and the Dominions, were the primary source of the monies. The U.S. chapter of the CRREC was particularly generous, especially for the campaign to bring Jewish orphans out of Poland in 1946. After his third trip to Poland, Schonfeld wrote a successful direct mail appeal that raised $200,000. It read:

I am asking you for £1 ($5 U.S.) per month to maintain orphans now in Poland whom I have arranged to take out from there.

In order to enable me to bring from Poland my fourth transports of up to 100 Jewish orphans, I will require 1,000 persons, each of whom promises to pay £1 per month for a period. My first three transports totaling over 300 children have [been] brought to England. This time the children are to be accommodated in Clonyn Castle, near Dublin, a large mansion that has been put at our disposal and specially adapted for this purpose. The Irish Authorities have extended every facility and we hope that, under the favourable conditions existing in Ireland, the children will grow up healthy in mind and body, and eventually emigrate to Palestine and other overseas countries.

Many of the children in our previous groups have relatives who can and are looking after them. These kiddies have no one, except you, if you will agree to be one of their guardians. I do not stress the worthiness of the cause—unless it speaks for itself, words will be useless.[71]

CREATIVE APPROACHES

Solomon Schonfeld looked for ways to solve problems, whether they were of an educational nature, concerned rescue operations, relief or refugee needs. The spiritual and physical welfare of the children and their education were always a priority. And even in times when men preferred women to stay at home, particularly if they were pregnant, Schonfeld showed extra sensitivity and respect for women.

While she was headmistress of the Hasmonean Secondary School, a co-educational establishment, Dr. Judith Grunfeld, discovered she was pregnant and told the rabbi that she would have to resign because it would be inappropriate to face the male students. After a moment, Schonfeld said: "We will purchase a girls' school and make the Hasmonean into two schools, one for boys and one for girls." He asked Dr. Grunfeld to get into his car and drove her to a non-Jewish girls' school, where he sought out the headmistress and asked if she would like to sell the building. After the stunned headmistress regained her wits, they came to terms. Thus was the Hasmonean Girls' School established.[72]

CHAPTER 2

PREWAR RESCUE

REFUGEE SITUATION DURING THIRTIES

After Hitler came to power in 1933, German Jews sought safe havens in Western Europe. They logically assumed that—despite being forced into a shrinking legal and economic framework by anti-semitic legislation and the brutal behavior of SS thugs—life would eventually return to normal.

In 1933 no one could conceive of "Planet Auschwitz." German Jews had contributed so much to Germany's image they could not believe they were being rejected as enemies of their Fatherland. From 1933 on, German Jews and Jews elsewhere published books citing Jewish contributions to civilization—in music, art, journalism, literature, drama, law, medicine, physics and chemistry. Such contributions were extraordinary, considering that the German Jews constituted, at most, only one percent of the 60 million people in Germany.[1]

German Jews rationalized that even Hitler's most devoted followers would realize the value of the Jewish people to Germany and Jewish greatness. They believed they would not be persecuted because of the cost to the country. (A large number of outstanding German Jewish physicists, including Albert Einstein, fled to the United States and became primary players in the development of the atom bomb.)[2] The apologists didn't understand that what bothered Hitler and his cronies were those very same Jewish achievements and influences. Jews were not regarded as contributors to German culture—they were labeled alien usurpers who had taken over the rightful German role in all fields of endeavor.[3]

Instead of recognizing the accomplishments of Karl Marx, Sigmund Freud or Einstein, the Nazi propaganda machine portrayed these outstanding thinkers as destroyers of society: Marx destroyed the social fabric, Freud destroyed the "mind"—the psychological world, and Einstein destroyed the physical world they had found comforting.[4] The number of Jews involved with Bolshevism also exacerbated antisemitic Nazi propaganda. The false image seemed credible because some Jews played a disproportionately large role in the leadership of the Bolshevik revolution in Russia in 1917 and in the interbellum, bloody and failed Bolshevik revolutions in Germany, Hungary and Poland. Ironically, however, the overwhelming majority of Jews in those countries were vehemently anti-Communist.[5]

The Protocols of the Elders of Zion, a forgery written and published by the Czar's Secret police at the turn of the century, and widely disseminated in augmented editions after World War I, became the bible of the antisemites. It accused the Jews of ruling the world through Communism, capitalism and "nefarious" means. As proof, the authors accused the Jews of successfully transforming Western Civilization by engineering the downfall of three centuries-old Christian dynasties within a single year: the Romanovs of Russia, the Hapsburgs of the Austro-Hungarian Empire and the Hohenzollerns of Germany.[6]

German Jews never dreamed that Hitler's *Judenrein* Germany (made possible with the complicity of most Germans) would become reality. According to his son, Jacob Rosenheim was hounded into fleeing Germany in 1935 and still could never fully absorb the fact that "his" Germany could descend to such levels of inhumanity.[7] Thousands of former refugees returned to Germany during several brief periods in the 1930s when things quieted down, especially during the 1936 Summer Olympics. The situation deteriorated rapidly after the *Anschluss*, when Nazis began victimizing Jews on a mass scale. *Kristallnacht* (The Night of Broken Glass, November 9–10, 1938) convinced an overwhelming majority of German Jews they would not survive even in a restricted Germany. There was a massive movement to leave and there were thousands of Orthodox Jews among the tens of thousands looking to flee.[8]

Eleven days after the *Anschluss* in March 1938, U.S. President Franklin D. Roosevelt called for an international conference on refugees in July 1938 to be held in the French resort town of Evian. At that conference the word Jew was never mentioned. Roosevelt announced that the United States would not loosen its quota, but it would open a fairly large combined quota for Greater Germany (Germany-Austria). Britain did not allow Mandate Palestine to be put on the agenda. Only the Dominican Republic, under the dictatorship of Rafael Trujillo, made a better offer: it would grant large tracts of land to as many as 100,000 Jewish farmers, because it wanted to develop the island.[9] No other country offered the Jews refuge. This disregard for the Jewish refugees at Evian sent a clear message to the Germans (noted in *Goebbel's Diaries*): The Western nations might shed crocodile tears for the Jews, but they had no more interest in them than did Germany.[10]

Then, after March 1938, England became the asylum of choice for hundreds of thousands of Jews seeking safe haven. Despite Britain's adamant stand vis-à-vis Mandate Palestine and the difficult world-wide recession from 1933–1939, England accepted about 50,000 German-Jewish refugees. (Proportionately, that was far more than America did.) Any Jew with a legitimate job offer or a personal or organizational guarantor was permitted to enter England.[11]

The Anglo-Jewish community, via the Board of Jewish Deputies (a representative body established in 1836 and dubbed the "Jewish Parliament" and the Anglo-Jewish Association, representing the old oligarchy known as the "Cousinhood,") provided HMG with a guarantee for each refugee who made it to England. These guarantees meant that the organizations were responsible for the full mainte-nance of any refugee who could not earn a livelihood and it meant mobilizing the Jewish community's resources. As a result, approxi-mately 330,000 Jews in England (from 1933–1939) raised almost £3,000,000 sterling ($15 million U.S.), an enormous sum, to help their brothers and sisters in Europe.[12]

Until mid-1941, after the invasion of the Soviet Union, Germany's concept of *Judenrein* did not mean the physical extermination of the Jews—it meant their expulsion from Germany. Thus, Jews in Greater

Germany (not those in occupied Poland) with end-visas to countries willing to accept them were permitted to leave, albeit with very few possessions and just a few Deutsche marks in their pockets.[13]

Thousands of Jews lined up at embassies and consulates hoping to get visas to any place that would accept them. Amazingly, it was Hitler's Axis partner, Japan, that welcomed thousands of German and Austrian Jews in the six months following *Kristallnacht*. All a family needed to get a husband or brother out of a concentration camp was a ship's card to Shanghai, partially under Japanese control this "exotic" place 8,000 miles away.[14] As a result, more than 16,000 German and Austrian Jewish refugees found safety in Shanghai. Still, after May 1939, with one major exception in 1941, this haven, too, was virtually closed.

Such was the plight of the refugees and potential refugees from Austria and Germany as the war approached. Thousands of Orthodox Jews among them faced the same problems as all the rest of the refugees, but their lives were further complicated by their unswerving commitment to their religious obligations.

CHALLENGES FACING ORTHODOX IMMIGRANTS

German-Austrian Orthodox immigrants to England were at a disadvantage in several respects. It was hard for them to find jobs as domestics, since there were so few *Shabbos*-observant homes.[15] The assimilationist English Jews—who controlled the Anglo-Jewish establishment relief and immigration organizations—had no interest in furthering a more intensive, Orthodox Jewish life, so they had no interest in bringing Orthodox rabbis and teachers—or even Orthodox children—to England. This created a situation where cooperation between the Zionist elements in England and the Zionist element in the overall Viennese *Kultusgemeinde* conspired to favor Zionist youth and worked against the Orthodox. By design, *Kultusgemeinde* policies excluded most of the non-party Orthodox youth.

There was an assumption that Zionist youngsters would be trained in *hachsharot* (training farms) in England and sent to *Eretz Yisroel* as *chalutzim* (pioneers). Thus they would emigrate from England, whereas non-Zionist Orthodox youth were more likely to remain where they—in particular—were least welcome. The discrimination involved even those few who sought to go to *Eretz Yisroel* under the small quota allotted by the *Sochnut* (the Jewish Agency) to non-party Orthodox (i.e. Agudah). Thus, when the Agudah tried to arrange for a group of 10 youths to work on a farm in Britain, to create a small *hachshara*, they were frustrated by Waley-Cohen, then chairman of the Agricultural Committee, who refused to fund the project.

Waley-Cohen wanted to know whether the *hachshara* "would be Orthodox," and "whether it is practical." He expressed concern about financial support for the small project and its sanitary conditions. He thought the group was too small to be successful and was particularly perturbed by the fact that the youths would not work on *Shabbos*. Finally, he questioned the "suitability" of Orthodox youth for agricultural work.

In his appeal for support from the Chief Rabbi and Rabbi Schonfeld, R. W. Oppenheimer, secretary of the EAC (Emigration Advisory Council), responded to Waley-Cohen's concerns.[16] First, Oppenheimer noted the Council for German Jewry had already allocated the necessary funds. Second, if the small size of the project was a problem, he would be delighted to add at least another five or ten youths. Oppenheimer said he had intentionally kept the project small in order to facilitate its acceptance. As for the sanitary conditions on the farm, they were part of the general supervision already in place by the Council's Agricultural Committee. Nor did observance of *Shabbos* pose a problem, since the farmer-owner himself had approved that stipulation.

Oppenheimer could not fathom Waley-Cohen's contention of the unsuitability of Orthodox youth for agricultural work. He pointed to one thousand German Jews brought over by the CRREC who had adapted well to all kinds of situations in Britain and overseas, including those who immigrated to *Eretz Yisroel*. Hundreds of German Orthodox youngsters made *hachshara* in Germany or the Netherlands and had successfully applied their new skills in the *Yishuv*.[17] Oppenheimer also pointed out that if the *Sochnut* had not required people to have agricultural training prior to coming to the

Yishuv, many more youths could have been sent directly there. Despite his on-target response, it is clear Oppenheimer was unaware of the ideological basis for Waley-Cohen's obstructions.

Another problem for the Orthodox was created by the British refusal to allow Jews to immigrate to Mandate Palestine. This affected all the Jewish refugees who wanted to go there, but made it particularly difficult for non-Zionist Orthodox Jews. British immigration restrictions were in place, to some degree, since 1920 and were increased when the Passfield White Paper (1930) was issued in response to the Arab riots of 1929. This document essentially repudiated the Balfour Declaration and the British Mandate that promised the Jews a national homeland. The devastating White Paper in 1939 limiting Jewish immigration to 75,000 was issued by HMG following the Arab riots in 1936 and the Partition Plan of 1937. By 1944, the British terminated *all* Jewish immigration to *Eretz Yisroel*.[18]

British Zionist leadership, however, insisted on limiting their own rescue schemes and readily scuttled others, including Schonfeld's, if they ignored "the Palestine solution."[19] The Zionists even opposed several of Schonfeld's rescue attempts. In 1943, for example, although 277 members of Parliament backed it, the Zionists forced them to shelve the Schonfeld-initiated British Dominions rescue plan.

Aliyah Bet was the Zionist reaction to these restrictions and it began as early as 1936 in response to the Nazis in Germany and rising antisemitism in Poland. Two radically different ideological groups, the Labor (socialist) Zionists and the Revisionist (New) Zionists participated in *Aliyah Bet.* But from the early 1930s–1939, it was the Revisionists who were primarily involved. The *Sochnut* and the rest of the Jewish Zionist establishment were not ready to buck the British—with whom they hoped to collaborate in the creation of a Jewish homeland. So until 1939, with few exceptions, the Zionists in New York and London actively opposed *Aliyah Bet.* One Zionist leader, himself a German refugee, sarcastically dubbed the leaders of *Aliyah Bet* as "The Jewish Admirals" in command of overcrowded, leaky ships.[20]

The Orthodox faced the greatest difficulty from the Labor Zionists, who had a socialist, inherently anti-religious and anti-

Diaspora ideology and a highly selective immigration policy that focused on idealistic and ideologically correct pioneering types. They trained youngsters in the *hachsharot* and created "New Jews," the *Ish Chadash*, the new man, the heroic *kibbutznik*, as opposed to the stereotypical downtrodden, subservient "unproductive" *Golus* Jews (Diaspora Jews).[21]

After the issuance of the 1939 White Paper, the Orthodox negotiated with the *Sochnut* (which controlled 90 percent of the Palestine Certificates) and received six percent of the available certificates for the Agudah's other non-party Orthodox. This "quota" remained fixed throughout the Holocaust, even when rescue, not refuge, was involved. As a result, Orthodox Jewish leaders from the Agudah, with Weissmandl in Bratislava and Steinfeld in Vienna, collaborated readily with the Revisionist Zionists and organized illegal transports to Palestine from Vienna, Prague and Budapest.[21]

Another difficulty facing Orthodox refugees was the issue of *Shabbos* observance, a major priority for them unless it involved *pikuach nefesh* (a danger to life). For the assimilationists, such observance had little or no priority. For example, a *kindertransport* from Germany was supposed to leave on September 12, 1938, a *Shabbos*. Waley-Cohen demanded that the transport leave that very day, though the rabbis in Germany, in contact with the CRREC, agreed with Schonfeld that this was not a case of *pikuach nefesh* and that there was no reason to violate *Shabbos*. In angry correspondence with Chief Rabbi Hertz, Waley-Cohen castigated the Orthodox for their obstinate religious stance.[22]

FOUNDING OF THE CCREC

Even prior to the creation of the CRREC. Jacob Rosenheim, president of World Agudath Israel, and a member of Schonfeld's Adas congregation, had fled Nazi oppression to England in 1935, was thus aware of the problems of refugees and immigration. By 1937, he alerted Agudah and Zeirei branches in Vienna, Berlin, Frankfurt, New York and London, to address the problem which affected thousands of Orthodox Jews who sought desperately to leave Germany, and after March 1938, Austria and Czechoslovakia as well.[23]

By mid 1938, Agudah had established a separate organization called the Emigration Advisory Council which opened an office in London, to deal with the thousands of inquiries concerning the possibilities for immigration to Britain from Germany, in search for English relatives (to provide the necessary guarantees), procurement of positions as domestics in kosher homes, and providing kosher food on boats. At about the same time in New York, Mike Tress, president of Zeirei Agudath Israel created a similar office that focused on obtaining visas and affidavits to aid potential immigrants and refugees desiring to reach the United States. In both Britain and the United States these early moves by Schonfeld and Tress were to have a profound effect on their later rescue efforts during the Holocaust.

By early 1938, Rosenheim came to the realization that immigration had become an insurmountable problem for the small London Agudah and recommended that a separate organization under the auspices of the Chief Rabbi should be created to raise funds thereby permitting Agudah to focus on its other work in England and Eretz Israel. Rosenheim discussed this issue with Harry Goodman, Dayan Isidore Grunfeld, and his rabbi, who, in characteristic fashion, quickly reacted positively to this idea.

After consultation with Viscount Sir Herbert Samuel and the full cooperation of Chief Rabbi Joseph Hertz, they developed the Chief Rabbi's Religious Emergency Fund, quickly changed to the Chief Rabbi's Religious Emergency Council for German and Austrian Jews. Within a few months this title was shortened to the Chief Rabbi's Religious Emergency Council [CRREC] or simply the Council.[24]

Rabbi Schonfeld was content to have Rabbi Hertz serve as the nominal head, while he, in his official capacity as executive director, was both the driving force, as well as the one who personally oversaw virtually all the CRREC's rescue and relief efforts. The fact, that unlike his father, Solomon Schonfeld always respected Rabbi Hertz as the sole chief rabbi of the British Empire, smoothed the way for a close cooperative venture. This was true despite the fact that Schonfeld's standards for Orthodox Judaism were stricter than those of the Chief Rabbi and the United Synagogue. Moreover, this cooperation continued even where occasionally they did not see eye to eye on certain rescue or ideological issues. Moreover, their personal relationship was cemented, when on January 1, 1940, Solomon married Judith Hertz, the Chief Rabbi's eldest daughter.

Although for more than a decade, he was to be fully pre-occupied with matters of relief and rescue, for which he personally raised several million dollars, Schonfeld lived solely on the meager salary as rabbi of the Adas, and as presiding rabbi of the Union of Orthodox Hebrew Congregations.

While the Chief Rabbi was the Chairman of the CRREC, Schonfeld, who had already been active since mid 1938 was the executive director. It was after Kristallnacht in November that the CRREC became the primary Orthodox rescue vehicle while Agudah, still involved to some degree, faded into the background. This situation was reinforced by Agudah's joining the Consultative Committee, with the World Jewish Congress, and the Board of Deputies, thereby reducing its freedom of action. On the other hand, Schonfeld retained his independence throughout and was able to accomplish much more.

THE CRREC'S FIRST MISSION:
BRINGING GERMAN CLERGY TO ENGLAND

The two major obstacles to Schonfeld's rescue work—beyond the Allied and British policies that worked against him—were those placed in his way by the Zionists and the assimilationist leadership of the Anglo-Jewish establishment. The assimilationists' primary objective was to be fully accepted as equals in English society. Anything that might cast the slightest doubt on their total loyalty to Britain and its interests was anathema—including saving the Jews of Europe. The assimilationists assumed that if they saved Jews, particularly those who looked "un-English," it would prevent their full acceptance into British society and foster antisemitism. No matter

their wealth, social or political station, this attitude in the assimilationist community was a manifestation of their insecurity and fear of
rejection.

Orthodox Jews were seen as old-fashioned, alien and too Jewish
in dress, customs and thought to be unassimilable. And, if this was
true of Orthodox laymen, the image of Orthodox rabbis and teachers
was even worse. They were accused of foisting their Jewishness on
English society by raising issues of providing kosher food and Jewish
homes to refugee children.[25]

The same assimilationists had no difficulty accepting Jewish scientists and academic refugees fired from their university positions in
Germany in 1933. The British government formed an organization
called the Academic Assistance Council, later changed to the Society
for the Protection of Science and Learning, which was non-denominational and headed by Lord Ernest Rutherford, a Nobel laureate in
chemistry. The objective was to provide positions in British universities for as many of these refugees as possible and to support them in
their research.

A second, somewhat similar organization, founded by Jews, was
called the Jewish Academic Committee. Headed by the Nobel laureate, microbiologist Dr. Ernest B. Chain, and later known as The
Professional Committee, it first brought out Jewish scientists and
academics. Later it concentrated on bringing out professors of Jewish
Studies. The Central British Fund (CBF)—the major Jewish relief
organization in England, similar to the American Joint Distribution
Committee—supported this second committee. Neither committee
had any interest in rabbis, cantors, teachers, ritual slaughterers or
other religious functionaries.[26]

By 1935, Jacob Rosenheim found refuge in England and two
years later, he alerted the Agudah and Zeirei branches in Vienna,
Berlin, Frankfurt, New York and London to address refugee and
immigration problems. The Agudah in England focused its efforts on
its Emigration Advisory Council. By 1938 it was dealing with thousands of inquiries about immigration to Britain from Germany. The
staff searched for English relatives to provide the necessary guarantees, procure positions for refugees as domestics in kosher homes and

provide kosher food on boats.[27] At about the same time in New York, Michael Tress, president of Zeirei Agudath Israel, created a similar office to obtain visas and affidavits for potential immigrants and refugees to the United States.[28]

Otto Schiff, director of the German Jewish Aid Committee, a primary figure in creating refugee policy, strongly opposed the creation of Agudah's EAC, as well as the CRREC, seeing them as competitors for funding and separate from the British Jewish community. In addition, Schiff had no problem sending Jewish children into non-Jewish homes.[29]

This opposition to the EAC and the CRREC was analogous to objections from the American Joint Distribution Committee when, in 1939, the Vaad Hatzalah, the Orthodox Rabbis Rescue Committee, was created to save the yeshivas of war-torn Europe. Both the American and British Jewish establishment organizations feared competition for funding and both claimed to represent the interests of all refugees, not merely the Orthodox.[30]

Working with Marcus Retter, Henry Pels, secretaries and volunteers, the first group Schonfeld and the CRREC focused on rescuing in mid-1938 were the religious functionaries from Germany. They needed guarantees from private individuals or sympathetic organizations, but no one came forward except Schonfeld.[31] A week after *Kristallnacht*, Schonfeld brought out 45 rabbis of all denominations who had been inmates in concentration camps and their families (200 souls).[32] By December 22, Schonfeld brought out an additional 112 rabbis, 26 cantors, 150 teachers and 130 youths over the age of eighteen. Within four months his total rose to 505.[33]

By the time war broke out on September 1, 1939, Schonfeld had brought 1,300 rabbis, teachers and other religious functionaries and their families to England.[34] The British Jewish establishment accused him of discriminating against non-Orthodox clergy and Schonfeld proved the charges were false.[35]

To make the arrival of numerous rabbis palatable to the Anglo-Jewish establishment and allay their fears and those in the Home Office, Schonfeld tried hard to get jobs for his functionaries throughout the Empire and in the United States. To a degree, he succeeded. When an American organization, the Committee on Refugee Jewish Ministers, asked for Schonfeld's help in bringing clergy to the U.S., he gladly complied.[36]

Unlike the large transports from Vienna, Schonfeld's German transports consisted of small groups traveling separately—in families, in pairs and groups of three or four. Ernie Mayer, an Israeli journalist who came to Britain from Germany as a youngster, recalls a few such groups from Germany. He remembers Dr. Erich Klibansky, director of the Yavneh High School in Cologne (founded by Rabbi Dr. Emanuel Carlebach), who, after *Kristallnacht,* shuttled back and forth between Germany and England as the go-between, between the Gestapo and Schonfeld.

Klibansky's goal was to transfer Yavneh's student body of several hundred to London. In London he met Dr. Louis Rabinowitz, a member of the CRREC, who contacted Schonfeld. Mayer remembers Sir Herbert Samuel assisting in the matter. But time was not on their side. By the time the war broke out, Mayer had only been able to transfer approximately one hundred children under the age of sixteen to London. The school in Cologne functioned for another eighteen months, until the summer of 1942, when Klibansky, his family and all his charges were deported and killed.[37]

A secondary objective of Schonfeld's rescue campaign was to strengthen existing Jewish institutions and create new ones by sending refugees to towns in Britain, the United States or the Dominions. For example, he brought over Rabbi Moshe Szneider, who once headed a Lithuanian-type yeshiva in Frankfurt, and helped him reestablish *Toras Moshe,* his yeshiva, in London. Teachers and rabbis who were sent as internees to Australia became the founders of the first day school and other religious institutions there.[38]

The natural results of Schonfeld's rescue efforts were felt years later, when Britain's Orthodox community was radically transformed by the proliferation of Orthodox people, institutions and religious intensity.[39]

KINDERTRANSPORTS

Political and religious differences among Jews were the basis for the discrimination Orthodox children faced in the selection process for the *kindertransport*. The assimilationist *Reichsvertretung* in Berlin and the *Kultusgemeinde* in Vienna, the two umbrella Jewish organizations in Nazi Germany and Austria, handled the operation. Among those 50,000 refugees accepted by Britain, 10,000 were children, 9,000 of them Jewish.

The slots were offered to the Jewish community in the fall of 1938—perhaps as a token of regret following the debacle of the Munich Agreement, wherein Prime Minister Neville Chamberlain appeased Hitler by handing him Czechoslovakia. The *Reichsvertretung* and the *Kultusgemeinde* selected the children who left.[40] When the Orthodox were neglected, the CRREC created a refugee children's department, headed by Judith Hertz, the Chief Rabbi's eldest daughter.

It began with a phone call from Steinfeld, shortly after *Kristallnacht*, begging Schonfeld to help organize an Orthodox transport for children ignored by the *Kultusgemeinde*. Schonfeld immediately called a meeting with the Agudah's Rosenheim and Harry Goodman and made his way to Vienna the following day. In the meantime, his two congregants arranged further meetings and formed committees.[41] Schonfeld made practical plans with Steinfeld in Vienna and prepared a *kindertransport* of close to three hundred Orthodox youngsters, primarily from the *Schiffschul*. Steinfeld followed up with several trips to London to meet with Schonfeld to plan bringing more Orthodox Jews out of Europe.

Meir Eiseman, who lived on the same street as Schonfeld's Secondary School in London, remembers Hanukkah 1938, as they prepared the building for the first *kindertransport* from Vienna.

A group of volunteers, including myself . . . had been asked to clear out the whole school building. All the desks and classroom furniture were stored in the backyard, and the schools—

the one in Northfield, the one in Stamford Hill and the one in Amhurst Park—were converted into hostels.

It was a pretty cold winter, with lots of snow. I believe that these children landed in England on a *Shabbos*. Dr. Schonfeld attempted to convince the mayor of Harwich to allow the children to stay there over *Shabbos* so that they would not have to violate [the *Shabbos*] by traveling. Unfortunately, he wasn't successful, so the children boarded the train and arrived in London just as *Shabbos* ended. Rabbi Borenstein, the rabbi of the *Beis Medrash* (study hall) at the Jewish Secondary School, and I waited at the school until the first refugee children and staff walked in with their knapsacks, about an hour after nightfall. Since it was Hannukah, I lit the candles for them. Afterwards, many of these children became my very good friends.[42]

For all the administrative details he had to juggle, Schonfeld never lost his personal touch. Anecdotes are legion. A little girl sheltered in his house awakened him one night with sobs of homesickness. He distracted her by taking her and another little girl on a drive around London. Another woman remembers Rabbi Schonfeld's first question to her, "*Hast du Taschengeld?*" ("Do you have pocket money?"), as if he didn't already have enough to worry about.[43]

CHAPTER 3

PREWAR-DOMESTIC

CHILDREN IN NON-JEWISH HOMES

The largest bone of contention between the assimilationist Jews and Schonfeld was the placement of refugee Jewish children in non-Jewish homes. This began before the war started and continued through the post-war era. Thousands of Jewish children were affected, especially by the organization, The Care of Jewish Children from Germany Movement (the Movement). Woburn House, whose costs were defrayed by the Council for German Jewry, placed other Jewish youngsters in non-Jewish homes and schools.[1]

Placing Jewish children with non-Jewish families, where they might lose their Jewish identities, suited the assimilationists just fine. Their attitudes were exemplified by Anthony de Rothschild of the Anglo-Jewish Association and Sir Robert Waley-Cohen. Waley-Cohen was only interested in developing "English Jews [who] were entirely British in thought, aspirations interests and zeal."[2] To the assimilationists, the less one stood out by being different, by making waves by raising Jewish issues—even those of refuge and rescue, *kashrut* and Jewish homes for Jewish children—the better. According to them, raising those issues was a source of antisemitism.[3]

Assimilationist Jews in a position to help Orthodox Jewish children often did not do so, using legalisms and insistence on adherence to bureaucratic detail, even when children's lives were at stake. The dispute came to a head in December 1938, when the Movement reacted to Schonfeld's independent attempt to bring over the *kindertransports* from Austria and Germany by telling him the accommodations he wanted to provide for his close to three hundred children were "quite insufficient and would in any case not be ready for the children's reception."

58

After consulting with members of the Movement and phoning Vienna, they cancelled the children's departure to London. They had concluded that, "When suitable accommodation is ready to receive them, we shall be only too glad to authorize their departure from [Greater] Germany." [4]

From the beginning Schonfeld accused the Movement of intending "to make these children forget all their past, to send them as ambassadors into the homes of Christian foster parents where they could assimilate and create Christian/Jewish goodwill." [5] When the Movement discovered that Schonfeld brought the children over without their help, they, like Waley-Cohen, called the Home Office and reported him, but after their inspections, the Home Office overcame any doubts it may have had and let him continue in his work.[6]

The Movement and other well-meaning individuals lacked Schonfeld's sensitivity and so concentrated on the condition of accommodations instead of *pikuach nefesh*. They persisted in their obstructionist efforts, and several months later complained, this time to the Chief Rabbi, that conditions were "appalling . . . overcrowded and unsanitary . . . and [that] it was found necessary to send a qualified person to investigate." They concluded by stating that they did not "discriminate against the Orthodox."[7]

The Movement frustrated Schonfeld when they placed Jewish children in non-Jewish homes. A Major Langdon in the Movement said he would "vehemently oppose" placement in Jewish homes, positing that doing so would encourage antisemitism. Another member "refused to allow the Jewish children to be moved from a non-Jewish home." [8]

The Movement also claimed that there weren't enough Jewish homes available and was not interested in looking for them. Schonfeld said there were plenty available, and if not, hostels could be organized. He was sure he could deliver both, and he did. He felt the assimilationists' attitudes gave non-Jews the impression that the Jewish community was ready to abandon its children. He felt such perceptions would encourage antisemitism.[9]

Schonfeld was being realistic. In one instance, a child placed in a non-Jewish home was taken to church and created a disturbance during Sunday services. She threw down her prayer book and yelled, "I am a Jew." After the ensuing tumult, the child was immediately placed in a Jewish household. In another case, a Christian woman requested non-Jewish children for a hostel. When none were available, she asked for Jewish children who had no previous religious training. Once the children arrived, however, a number of them refused to eat her food because they were raised Orthodox.[10]

Matters were further complicated by terminology. What meant one thing on the Continent meant something else in Great Britain; in Germany, the word Orthodox referred only to the ultra-observant, the term *konservative* referred to those not much less observant than that, and the term Liberal applied to Jews who still observed *Shabbos* and *kashrut*. The term Liberal in Britain meant Reform, not traditional, and the term Orthodox in Britain usually described people who were less observant than their European brethren. Because of this confusion, the Movement treated fully observant children as non-observant.[11]

Adding to the confusion, the Movement told parents in Europe it would be difficult to have their children placed in Orthodox homes. Parents anxious for their children to get out of Germany didn't always put the word Orthodox on their application forms, and most of them had hoped to rejoin their children as soon as they could. When the war started, that became impossible and many observant children were stranded in non-Jewish homes in England. Yet the appeals made in every British synagogue were for funding for placement in Jewish homes, not non-Jewish ones.

The Movement was obstructionist throughout the war and wrapped requests for placement in Jewish homes in red tape while impeding the development of Jewish hostels.[12] They also prevented European volunteer rabbis and teachers from tutoring or giving religious training to Jewish children and refused a member of the CRREC permission to join their sub-committee on religious education.[13]

These conflicts were exacerbated in 1939, when Schonfeld pleaded with HMG to allow the CRREC to provide facilities so he could transfer the children from non-Jewish homes. If they could not be moved, he accurately predicted that there would be additional losses to Judaism. The truth of this came to light in a booklet, *The Child Estranging* [*sic*] *Movement: An Expose on the Alienation of Jewish Refugee Children in Great Britain from Judaism: "Defend the Religious Rights of Jewry's Orphans,"* published by Schonfeld's Union of Orthodox Hebrew Congregations in January 1944.[14]

The booklet was an attempt to affect a decision in Parliament concerning the Guardianship Act, whereby the Home Office would determine the guardianship of the thousands of Jewish orphans then stranded in non-Jewish homes. The booklet demanded that Jewish authorities, particularly the Chief Rabbi, be recognized as the Jewish orphans' guardians. It didn't work.

To complicate matters even more, the Movement tried to keep their files on the children secret, making it difficult to investigate specific problems. In one case, an Orthodox boy's Orthodox uncle removed him from a non-Jewish home. The Movement called the police, who forcibly removed the boy from his uncle's care and, against his will, returned him to his Christian foster parents.[15]

In another incident, a young observant girl was clandestinely removed from her Christian home to a Jewish hostel. Three of her siblings, who were placed in three different non-Jewish homes, were forbidden to join her there.

Worst of all, perhaps, the Movement would do nothing to prevent non-Jewish foster families from converting their charges to Christianity.[16] Thousands of Jewish youth were lost to Christianity in Great Britain from 1939–1949, and recriminations for that still resound in the Jewish community.

CHAPTER 4

WARTIME (DOMESTIC)

INTRODUCTION

Once the Germans invaded Poland on September 1, 1939, it was no longer possible to bring over large-scale *kindertransports* or groups of adults. As a result, Schonfeld shifted his focus to two fronts. The first was the refugee community in England, where he concerned himself mostly with the needs of the Orthodox Jews in Britain. The other focused on small-scale rescue attempts. Ever the pragmatist, Schonfeld never challenged HMG's decrees, rules and regulations on ideological grounds. Instead he sought to make the best of a bad situation, meeting each challenge with vigor and dedication.

When the war began, 550 Orthodox children had to be immediately evacuated from London with thousands of other youngsters. By necessity, they were brought into the non-Jewish environment of Shefford and several other villages in the London countryside. In May 1940, Schonfeld had to cope with the internment of thousands of Jewish refugees of every stripe as enemy aliens, and he was, for a long time, the only person in Anglo-Jewry to help them.

The mass deprivation of the civil liberties of so many Jews came after a scare about a Fifth Column inside England, after the quick fall of France and the British evacuation of Dunkirk. True to form, Schonfeld never argued about the moral injustice of internment with HMG; instead, he obtained permission to inspect the camps and informed them of problems that required attention.

While the war raged on, rationing was the rule in England. Still, Schonfeld and his congregants took portions of their own rations and presciently collected cans of kosher meat for eventual distribution to the survivors in Europe. When Waley-Cohen found out about

Schonfeld's food collection campaign, he reported him to HMG for performing an "unpatriotic act." Schonfeld, however, convinced HMG that his action was in the British interest and fully consonant with Jewish tradition. HMG and the Ministry of Food allowed him to continue, and he was thus able to provide services to Displaced Persons in Europe after April 1945.

In the meantime, Schonfeld still needed to find employment for hundreds of refugees and to provide education to Orthodox refugee youngsters who were not evacuated to Shefford. He was able to employ most of the rabbis and teachers in *yeshivos* and schools in the cities and evacuation centers, and later used many of them as chaplains on the Continent after the liberation. In addition, there were more than one hundred elderly or sick rabbis who required full time maintenance because they could not work.

As part of its responsibilities, the CRREC had to provide kosher food for the canteens in all the Orthodox youth hostels and, in wartime, supply Orthodox Jews in every city and evacuation center in Britain and the Dominions with religious articles—prayer books (*siddurim*), prayer shawls (*taleisim*) and other ritual objects, including *shmure matzoh* (specially supervised matzoh for Passover). Schonfeld also had one of "his" rabbis make sure that there was homegrown wheat for *shmure matzoh.*

Schonfeld also provided some 25,000 Jewish British servicemen stationed at home and overseas with the required ritual objects and kosher food packages. The servicemen's group included Orthodox Americans stationed in Britain. He tried hard, and was partially successful in helping Jewish servicemen keep *Shabbos* and Jewish Holy Days. With Goodman, Schonfeld even prepared a series of uplifting and patriotic BBC programs for broadcast to Jewish communities and servicemen throughout the far-flung corners of the Empire. The CRREC also acted as a publisher of prayer books and Bibles.[1]

SHMURE MATZOH

Producing and distributing *shmure matzoh* for Passover in wartime was a challenge. Retter remembers that before September

1939, the matzoh came from Antwerp, Belgium. Now the British
Jewish community had to grow its own wheat. On behalf of Kedassia,
the kosher supervision service, Rabbi Eli Munk of Golder's Green
Beis HaMedrash and the London Bet Din asked some farmers about
40 miles from London to grow the wheat. (The Adas was also
involved.)

Two German Jewish refugees who were chemists, Drs. Bloom and
Wertheimer, served on the Kashrus Committee. They checked the
wheat to determine if it had gotten wet and cracked, which would
make it unusable for *shmure matzoh*. That first spring, when they
examined the wheat under a magnifying glass, they thought the
wheat might be unfit. Retter then asked Lord Wedgewood, his contact in HMG's censor's office, if he would be kind enough to send a
200-word cable with the details about the homegrown wheat to Chief
Rabbi Herzog in *Eretz Yisroel*. Once Retter explained the religious
significance of the problem, Wedgewood gladly accommodated him.
Rabbi Herzog's short reply arrived forty-eight hours later. He wrote,
in Hebrew, "The Torah was not given to angels. . . . EAT . . . Have a
Kosher and Happy Passover" (*Lo Nitno Hatorah leMalachei
Hashores . . . ichlu . . . chag kosher vesomeac*).[2]

They did.

EVACUATION TO SHEFFORD

After September 1, HMG ordered the voluntary evacuation of
most school children in London to the countryside, where they were
supposedly safe from anticipated German bombings. Some parents
kept their youngest children with them in London,[3] while others left
for outlying villages on the first Friday of September 1939. The children were billeted in the homes of the local populations, who were
responsible for supplying them with food and lodging. The arrangement was obviously unsuitable for Orthodox Jewish children, and so,
once again, Schonfeld faced a challenge. Provincial as they were,
most of the villagers in the towns surrounding London had never seen
a Jew before, nor had they heard of the Jewish dietary laws.

Schonfeld and his colleague Judith Grunfeld devised an education plan for their evacuated students. The children, including those whose parents were still trapped in Europe, would still live and study in a Jewish environment, though they slept in non-Jewish homes. At first, however, the children had to take meals at their assigned homes. So to help them avoid eating non-kosher meat, Schonfeld asked them to tell their foster parents that they were, as he ingeniously put it, "fish-eating vegetarians"—until a few weeks later, when his school's kosher kitchen was opened.

Grunfeld tells the story about life in the cluster of villages around Shefford and Bedfordshire during the Blitz in her book, *Shefford*. During the day, the children ate, studied, prayed and played in a building known as the "White House." In addition to the kitchen there, the CRREC established kosher canteens in three evacuation centers and four hostels. All the teachers and rabbis in Schonfeld's schools were provided for by the CRREC.[4]

Though Schonfeld stayed in London, he was the guiding spirit in the lives of the evacuees and those who cared for them. He visited Shefford frequently, speeding the 40 miles from London in his little car, which was often filled with kosher treats like salami and sausage.[5]

One of his former students remembers how, at the train station in London, she was separated from her five-year-old brother. Afraid she might never see him again, she began crying. Schonfeld, in the midst of supervising the evacuation, promised her he would reunite them. As soon as he arrived in Shefford, Schonfeld leapt into a car and drove through the countryside until he found the boy and delivered him into his sister's arms.

Schonfeld introduced himself to those who volunteered as foster parents and developed an instant rapport with the local clergy. He, Grunfeld and the staff explained Jewish customs and tradition to them, helping them understand the children and appreciate their religious heritage. To the villagers, Schonfeld presented an unexpected image of the traditional Jew—he radiated pride in his Judaism and carried himself well. Together, he and Grunfeld created an atmosphere where the villagers came to look upon their charges with special affection and respect for their religious traditions, creating relationships that endured long after the children returned to London.

For the youngsters, Shefford became a novel, highly constructive Jewish experience instead of the disaster it might have been. Schonfeld's rapport with the townsfolk set a wonderful example of Judaism in practice and behavior that glorified God's name.

A Story of Shefford
from the book SHEFFORD by Dr. Judith Grunfeld[6]

"Village Life and the Children of Israel"

Back to the market square we drove and there we found Dr. Schonfeld, who had just arrived in his car from London. We see him, a tall and handsome figure, with a smile that charms old and young alike, in hilarious conversation with the Billeting Officer. It is obvious that they are getting along fine together. Talking to this young rabbi, the Billeting Officer obviously gets the impression that Jews are optimists and charming conversationalists, that they are, after all, not so different from other people and that with sunshine from above and with smiles in abundance, life is worthwhile. The Billeting Officer now looked rather animated and amused. The young Rabbi seemed a practical man indeed, well versed in Holy Writ, and with common sense and practical ideas, equal to any emergency.

He had just quoted the biblical reference to the dietary laws and had bewitched the salesman in the Gas Company showroom . . . He had already secured the consent of the vicar to allow this large number of children the use of this well-kept, well polished hall, the apple of the eye of the community. He had unloaded from his car one huge box of Vienna[s] [sausages], four large mess saucepans, a hamper with plates and cutlery, all this to give the hungry crowd of children a kosher Sabbath meal, cooked and served by our own management. And there he was, shaking the hand of the Billeting Officer, Gas Company Manager and Village Parson, laughing across the barricade of our religious restrictions, radiating friendliness and receiving trust in exchange.

And this master of emergency, leaving sausages, saucepans, gas-stove and goodwill behind, jumped back into his car to be in London in time for Sabbath, to give solace to the pining parents who had entrusted their children to the fanfare of the "Pied Piper" early that very morning. Everywhere I could see my pupils. One waved to me from the front garden behind the fence, some boys were walking in groups, getting acquainted with the geography of the village, there a girl went shopping with her new foster-mother. Some of our senior boys were busy in the St. Michael's Hall helping Miss Dym fill the huge saucepans with water, wipe the plates clean of dust, count the cutlery and arrange tables and chairs. Some boys had the Scroll of the Law [Torah] open in front of them and prepared the *leining* (reading of the Torah) for tomorrow's service. One was reading from the Torah; the other *Chumash* in hand, corrected him. . . .

War, evacuation, or whatever else was storming the country and creating an upheaval in the world, these boys were singing the *nig-gunim* (tunes) that came from beyond the border of time on the wings of Jewish tradition... while the girls prepared the scanty Sabbath meal ... Teachers and helpers told me of the great difficulties our children had encountered when they arrived in the foster-homes. Everywhere a welcoming meal and with some especially nice things had been prepared for them. Foster parents and their own families had been eagerly watching the new additions to their household and had joy-fully anticipated how they would relish the first meal, a ham omelet, that token of welcome that had been so lovingly prepared for them. And everywhere it had been the same story. The children, shy and tired, had not touched the meal, had shaken their heads and hardly sipped a few drops of tea. They had shown signs of embarrassment.

Some had been able to say a few words of "thank you" that obvi-ously came from their hearts, but they had all succeeded in creating in these village homes an atmosphere of disappointment and frustra-tion. What on earth was the matter with these children? Were they just awkward, ungrateful and troublesome? At the Baker's, over the garden fence, at the fishmonger's and at the post office, neighbors exchanged tales about the unappreciative evacuees. This tale was confirmed everywhere. Disappointment, annoyance and anger were gradually gathering momentum all around. But this was only the beginning—there was more yet to come. It was getting darker and shadows fell. They gathered round the innocent heads of our sleeping children and formed dark clouds there.

Our teachers heard about this wave of disappointment and had decided that they would visit the houses, one by one, and speak to the villagers and explain the situation to them; explain to them that these were Jewish children and that they were brought up to obey the "Law of Israel," that they had been taught to observe the dietary laws according to the Bible, that some of them had just come over from Nazi persecution, could not speak English and consequently were unable to explain why they had to refuse the truly delicious meal which had been so thoughtfully, nay, so lovingly, prepared for them, but that they were, nevertheless, truly and sincerely grateful for all the kindness shown to them.

The streets of the village were shared out among the teachers on that first Friday afternoon, Ampthill Road, New Street, Northbridge Street, etc. To each street one or two teachers were allotted the task of going from house to house to try to explain the situation and to clear away the misunderstandings. They went on their rounds. They found courtesy and a calm acceptance of their words. But how many families they succeeded in enlightening about the underlying motives of these children's behaviour on that day we do not know. The villagers tried their best to see the point—but it remained disturbing in spite of all that the nice young schoolmaster said.

Night fell, the Sabbath Queen had arrived. She made her glorious entry for the first time in world history into the small villages of Bedfordshire and she was welcomed by hundreds of young voices singing in the dimly lit St. Michael's Hall: *Lechu Nerannanu* and *Lecho Dodi* (in welcome of the Sabbath). The boys were the cantors, the readers (*baalei koreh*), the beadles (*gabbaim*), and they had even formed a choir. The blessing over the wine was recited, and the "amen" coming from the chorus of children was one to lift the roof.

The meal was served, consisting of one sausage, one piece of bread per head and an abundance of *Zemiros* (hymns). Perhaps there were some signs of homesickness, perhaps under their shirts . . . some tears and doubts of faint hearts.

But the community spirit that would become so strong during the coming months and years had already started to weave its magic net and this net was to become even firmer, enveloping these evacuated children who were clinging to each other and to the living Tree of Torah life during those fearful years of war.

Thus passed our first service in evacuation. After the prayers and the meal they went home—home to their village houses. "Johnny switch the light on just on your right while I hold the bucket" the farmer would call out from the stable to the evacuee whom he wanted to show his cows. "Sonny, I have to go over to the greenhouse, you can come with me and carry the torch for me;" "Jackie, will you put the kettle on the fire, please, Grannie fancies a cup of tea." "Here, are two shillings, run over to the pub and get me a packet of cigarettes."

Our dear precious Jewish children were confronted, surely for the first time in their lives, with the painful situation of being anxious to please but unable to comply. "I am sorry, sir, but it is my Sabbath today," perhaps some of them were just able to falter. But not many of them knew the English language well enough to find the polite way of phrasing . . .

The complaints mounted; they don't speak English, they won't eat with us. Strange ways they have, poor kiddies, but what about those big ones, foreigners in every way. At the Rector's house, at the Vicar's, there were continuous phone calls too, conveying complaints and bewilderment. The Vicar himself was disappointed. He had hoped to fill his Sunday School and find new members for his church choir.

Neighbors called each other and early next morning, with the postman, the milkman, at the butcher's, at the baker's, there was one topic all through the village and they all agreed that they would not take this lying down. They had been cheated in the fulfillment of their national duty. They had wanted to take little evacuees to their houses, to their hearts, to their churches and Sunday Schools. They had intended to make them a part of their own family. But with these children this was simply unthinkable. They were so totally different from what they had expected them to be, and some of the little ones cried all the time.

They could not communicate but had the look of hunted animals. The bigger ones, many of them charming and polite, spoke and laughed in a different language and did not eat anything but bread and drank only lemonade. They did not join in prayers, they had strange books in their luggage, had strange cotton squares with fringes under their shirts. It all seemed such a big mess. "We shall have to organize their exodus back to London in exchange for children of our own brand and faith." "Tomorrow we shall contact the Billeting Officer in Biggleswade, put the entire case before him and we shall see that it will all be changed and rectified. They cannot force us to keep these children."

And while the villagers were angry, the little children, unaware of all the annoyance they had caused, slept peacefully in all the homes where the revolt was brewing. The *siddurim* were lying by their bedside, *Arba Kanfos* were dangling from the chair, *yarmulkes* were on their sleeping heads. They were blissfully ignorant of the plan that concerned them so much.

"But behold, the Keeper of Israel neither sleeps nor slumbers." The next morning the sun rose and the children awoke. Some of them, being rested, had a captivating smile, some took a fancy to the little dog or to the canary, some had a lovely way of saying "Thank you very much" and looked so pathetic that one's heart could melt. They were very clean, and surprisingly well mannered: some liked to play with the baby in the pram (carriage); some of the boys liked to watch and help the old man in the shed. Although they were so young they had a way of looking after themselves and after their younger brothers and sisters. Their habits were immaculate; they never asked for anything.

It was very strange. One could not even say what caused it or how it came about, but it is a fact that soon enough Mrs. B. told Mrs. H. that her little evacuee had settled down so very well and Mrs. H. retaliated by praising her own little girl. The Rector and his wife, the

Reverend and Mrs. A. McGhee, took their seven evacuees for a treat to Wipsnade Zoo and felt proud of themselves to own such well-mannered young men. And while they treated them to toast and lemonade in the Wipsnade Restaurant, they encouraged them not to be shy but to put on their 'ceremonial skull caps,' realizing that that they would not start eating without them. They had already understood that this was essential when partaking of a meal. It is a fact too that not long afterwards freshly-washed *Arba Kanfos* (fringed garments) were seen dangling from the washing line in Mrs. K's pretty garden, and Moss, the village grocer, got in a supply of kosher margarine because suddenly so many customers asked for it so "that Jackie (or Freddie or Bernard) could have a piece of bread with margarine instead of eating the bread dry all the time."

The fact is that Mrs. B. helped Annette to tie her handkerchief round her wrist on Friday night before Annette went out to join the service and Mrs. F. went upstairs to switch the light off in Simon's bedroom, because "I know the boy will sleep all night with the light on if I don't do it for him as it is his Sabbath."

All this is a mere recording of facts. Slowly and surely these Jewish children, firm and sure in their loyalties to their upbringing, captured the hearts of their hosts, their foster-parents, as they were called. Slowly the relationship developed, and pride grew in the hearts of those kind-hearted people who came to consider the children as their own evacuees, respected them and respected the whole crowd of them for their steadfastness and loyalty to their own religious tradition, loved them in spite of all differences between them, and kept them in their cottages for six long years.

It was something inexplicable. I remember today how a farmer's wife came to my office. It was two years after the events just related took place. She cried bitterly and appealed to my sense of fairness and asked me to stop Leo from leaving her house because they had all grown so very fond of him. I should stop him from going to—"what do you call it –a *Yeshiva*," she said. "He is one of ours, how can he go away just like that after all this time? It will break my husband's heart and mine. Please don't let him go." (Leo was a refugee from Vienna and 15 years of age when we decided to send him to a *Yeshiva*).

It was also reported to me that at a meeting of the Church Ladies' Guild, when they discussed the date for the annual Whist Drive, which was to raise funds for the church, Mrs. W. objected to the date being fixed on Tuesday, because that Tuesday she said "was the only day when her evacuee was allowed that month to have his hair cut" (Tuesday was Lag B' Omer) and for that haircut she had to take him to a good barber in Bedford, and this was important enough for her.

For six long years we stayed in Shefford with these people in their homes, and in their Church Halls, and when in the year 1945 the time for parting finally came there was a friendship, affection and blessings when saying goodbye. In those six years the evacuees had been taken to their hearts, had grown in size and in maturity under the care of the kind Shefford population.

* * *

Sir Immanuel Jakobovits, the Chief Rabbi of Great Britain, noticed the long-range impact of Schonfeld's actions on behalf of the Jewish refugees. Jakobovits and his immediate family were among the thousands rescued by Schonfeld from Nazi Germany. Sir Immanuel arrived in London in 1936, lived for a year in the Northfield boarding school and then was enrolled in the Jewish Secondary School in Aberglaslyn. In his memoirs he recalls his school uniform and the excitement of the evacuation to Shefford and surrounding villages, where he witnessed, "the magic transformation of a sleepy little Bedfordshire town into a spiritual fortress throbbing with Jewish life." Never before had there been such a concentration of Jews and Jewish life in Britain.

That intense Jewish life lasted for six years and influenced thousands of people for decades to come. "Hundreds of former Sheffordians—and indirectly by now, thousands of their children—were to look back on this experience as a nostalgic event evoking the most deeply cherished reminisces, and as the most formative influence on their lives, their commitments, their ambitions and their friendships, sometimes indeed on the choice of their life partners and even on their decision to settle, or at least study, in Israel."

Sir Immanuel also recognizes the extraordinary contributions of Grunfeld, who "governed the schools' destiny during difficult and challenging years." Her students, he noted, called her "…the Queen, and she truly ruled over her scattered juvenile empire with regal dignity and sovereign authority," inspiring her "subjects" and uniting them in loyalty to the schools' ideals.

Sir Immanuel noted that the only Jewish schools to survive the war were Schonfeld's, and that those schools evolved into the Jewish Secondary Schools Movement. He concluded that this was a result of the "perseverance of a solitary, frequently derided pioneer, whose triumph far transcends [his] success…"

THE BLITZ AND THE ORTHODOX

The Blitz targeted London and no one was safe, but during 1940–41, the bombings caused the dispersion and loss of congregations and jobs for rabbis and other religious functionaries. As always, Schonfeld made sure that these people were supported in a discreet and dignified way.[7] Jews were hiding in air raid shelters with everyone else, but Schonfeld made sure that Passover 1941 could be observed by having the CRREC distribute *matzoh* to 1,200 Jews trapped in shelters in London. The Agudah Report from fall, 1941 notes that study sessions (*shiurim*) continued unabated, even during the Blitz.[8]

CHAPTER 5

WARTIME DOMESTIC

INTERNMENT

For the first six months after the outbreak of war, as the Jewish refugees struggled to establish themselves in their new surroundings, they developed a false sense of security. In fact, an early governmental tribunal evaluating the refugees considered the vast majority of them "friendly aliens," and little was done to disturb their status quo. Many of them found jobs, went on to higher education or made arrangements for immigration to the United States or elsewhere.

Things didn't stay uncomplicated for long. When Hitler's *Blitzkrieg* overran Denmark, Norway, Holland, Belgium and France, Britain was virtually isolated. At the beginning of June, 340,000 British and French forces without weapons, and some refugees, evacuated Dunkirk on the northern French coast. At that point, Churchill tried to rally a despondent populace with his classic words, "We shall defend our island whatever the cost may be. We shall fight on the beache... we shall never surrender!"

Despite Churchill's words, by mid-1940 Britain was gripped by fear of imminent invasion. British civilians were recruited for the homeguard and xenophobia was rampant. The paranoia was reinforced when it was discovered that German "Fifth Columnists" collaborated in the fall of Western Europe. Those in England who spoke German became targets, especially the Jewish refugees from Germany.

The invasion of the Low Countries and France in the late spring of 1940 brought new anguish to many Jewish refugees in England when HMG carried out the wholesale internment of refugees from Germany and Austria because they were suddenly considered "enemy-aliens." Unfortunately, HMG made no distinction between the Nazis and the refugees from Nazism, and often quartered them near each other. Those in category A (most dangerous enemy aliens), had already been incarcerated for being linked to the Nazis.[1]

HMG locked up approximately 30,000 mostly German-Austrian Jewish refugees in internment camps, the majority of them males aged 16–60 who were previously classified as category B (refugees hitherto restricted but not interned) and category C (refugees hitherto exempt from internment and restriction).

The refugee community was in chaos. The sudden move broke up families and removed the breadwinners. There were 10 internment centers on the Isle of Man and in other isolated areas in Britain. Relatives couldn't find their husbands, sons or brothers. Many internees were elderly and too sick to withstand the primitive conditions in the camps and began to die. Six months later, HMG made matters worse when they deported 8,000 younger male refugees, including German Nazis—deemed most dangerous—to Australia and Canada.[2]

Internment of "enemy-aliens" was British policy during the First World War. Prisoners from Germany and Austro-Hungary were interned on the Isle of Man, when Avigdor Schonfeld, Solomon's father, worked hard to alleviate their plight. During World War II, Britain again implemented this policy, but was not the only Allied power to do so.

The United States government also interned enemy aliens, inflicting far greater injustice and racial discrimination in America than did Britain, when it created the War Relocation Authority (WRA) in 1942. At President Roosevelt's command, the Army and WRA forcibly moved 110,000 Japanese-Americans from the West Coast to the interior because the U.S. feared a Fifth Column would collaborate on a Japanese invasion. Of the 110,000 aliens, the WRA deemed 15,000 persons "most dangerous"—those who refused to sign an absolute loyalty oath to the United States. Those internees were taken to a particularly harsh location near Lake Tule in northeastern California. Food and shelter were provided and wages were paid to those who wished to work, but living conditions were poor and the inmates soon rioted.[3]

The last internment center at Lake Tule was closed in March 1946. Japanese-American internees lost over $400 million in property, and the U.S. Government was severely criticized for depriving citizens of their civil liberties.[5]

The Americans also treated Jewish refugees badly. In one incident, 80 German Jewish refugees were interned as "enemy-aliens" with a larger number of German and Japanese civilians transferred from South America to various POW camps in the South. It took the JDC and the National Refugee Service more than a year to reclassify them as "internees-at-large" and get them permission to live outside the camps.

During Roosevelt's fourth term as President, almost one thousand Jewish survivors liberated in Italy in 1944 were brought to an old army camp in Oswego, New York, where they were housed in wooden barracks surrounded by barbed wire fences. Orthodox organizations, like Young Israel and Zeirei Agudath Israel, provided the internees with kosher food and other religious amenities. However, the internees in Oswego were not in much better shape than the Jewish internees in Britain.[4] The majority of the American internees remained incarcerated until after December 1944.[5]

When one compares the dangers facing America's West Coast to the dangers facing England, there is surely no comparison. The virtually unarmed British were separated from Hitler's Panzer Divisions only by the 20-mile-wide English Channel. More than 6,000 miles of Pacific Ocean separated Japan from the well-armed United States.

* * *

Everyone in the Anglo-Jewish community, including Schonfeld, accepted HMG's decision to intern the refugees. The International Refugee Joint Consultative Committee (RJCC) known as the Coordinating Committee for Refugees, on which all the Anglo-Jewish organizations were represented, agreed that matters of general policy toward the refugees were matters strictly for HMG to decide.

But Schonfeld began following the *halachic* dictates of *pidyon shevuyim* (ransoming captives) and went right to work. In two days he managed to obtain a pass from the Home Office to visit all the camps. During his first inspection tour, he obtained the speedy release of sick persons and brought back reassuring reports to anxious wives and others. Families whose sole providers were interned received financial support from the CRREC. The Council set up synagogues and kosher kitchens in the camps and supplemented the camp diet with extra groceries, gifts and pocket money for needy internees. The Council even established the first Jewish cemetery in Douglas, on the Isle of Man, where hundreds of Jewish refugees were interned.

HMG took Schonfeld's reports about the camp conditions seriously because they were objective and accurate. Schonfeld's intervention with the Home Office allowed a number of special hardship cases and individuals whose services were required by the English Jewish community to be released. Internees who wished to enroll in Canadian and Australian yeshivos or universities were shipped to Canada or Australia.[6] Schonfeld also facilitated the release of aged clergy, yeshiva students and refugees of Polish and Galician origin (many of whom had lived in Germany). Because they were not German citizens, they could not be considered enemy aliens.[7]

In all, under the sole sponsorship of the CRREC, Schonfeld helped obtain the release of about one thousand people. In this and in several other rescue and relief schemes, Goodman at the Agudah helped him get the necessary sponsorships.[8] Internees could also be released by volunteering for the Auxiliary Military Pioneer Corps. Though they weren't permitted to join the military,[9] two thousand young men released from the camps on the Isle of Man performed yeoman tasks for the British war effort. Schonfeld also helped internees in Canada who were university students or enrolled in Rabbi A. A. Price's yeshiva in Toronto.[10]

Schonfeld often gave his personal attention to cases that were hardly a priority for the social workers. For example, one young groom-to-be on the Isle of Man held a visa for Cuba, but he did not want to leave without his future bride—who was free but could only

leave if they were married. Schonfeld got permission from the Home
Office and the camp commander to arrange for the bride to be flown
to the camp from London. The marriage was held in front of five
thousand internees, with the camp commander as a witness. After the
celebration, the newlyweds met in London and flew off to Cuba.[11]

COMMUNITY REACTION

The Anglo-Jewish establishment community's patriotic response
was surely based on fear of a German invasion. *The Jewish Chronicle*
reflected this in an editorial: "In a life-and-death struggle for national survival, the Government justifiably claims the right to interfere
drastically with the freedom of the individual."[12]

Brodetsky, the Zionist and head of the Board of Jewish Deputies,
agreed "that in view of the war situation, the Government's policy in
regard to internment should not be opposed." The Under Secretary of
the Home Office noted universal Jewish acceptance of internment,
but added: "There was some criticism of the manner in which it has
been carried out."[13]

While there were some suggestions to improve conditions for the
thousands of internees, the Anglo-Jewish establishment hardly provided practical help. Again, they feared that raising the issue at this
delicate juncture would cast suspicion on their patriotism. It wasn't
until six months after the tragic sinking of the SS Andora Star, filled
with internees on their way to Canada, that there was even the slightest criticism of HMG's policy.

Schonfeld, in the meantime, was the only Anglo-Jewish leader
who showed a personal interest in the internees and their physical and
spiritual concerns. His CRREC was the sole Jewish authority to concern itself with their welfare. In typical pragmatic fashion, he fully
supported the government's policy *per se*, as he worked behind the
scenes to improve the situation. A year after it was implemented,
Schonfeld justified internment in an article, writing that given the
circumstances, it probably benefited the refugees' safety. Internment
". . . was a rush undertaking, no less than the overrunning by the
German hordes. Accommodation, as well as official instructions, had

to be improvised. And releases were slow and for many months a cumbersome procedure."[14] Schonfeld noted that "There was a sincere determination all around to see 'fair play'—wrongs redressed and improvements carried out . . ."[15]

Schonfeld's article noted occasional errors, unpleasantness and avoidable hardships in individual cases. The gravest among them was that previously mentioned deportation of 8,000 internees to Canada and Australia as "prisoners of war."

Precisely because Schonfeld accepted the inevitable and did not attack HMG directly, he was able to accomplish a great deal on behalf of all the internees, not just the Orthodox. He, not the Anglo-Jewish establishment, voiced concern for all the internees after conducting four of his five inspection tours. As the sole Jewish representative on the Joint Committee for the Welfare of Internees (headed by Reverend Dr. W. Paton of the Church's Commission), Schonfeld improved conditions in all the camps.[16]

Schonfeld's first project was to set up kosher kitchens and synagogues in each internment camp. At first, the United Synagogue even refused to provide funding for kosher food, and Schonfeld was forced to look elsewhere to pay for this basic Jewish requirement. Waley-Cohen and some officers felt bringing in kosher food for Jewish internees during tense times would create antisemitism.[17]

The same reasoning stood behind the Anglo-Jewish establishment's silence vis-à-vis the placement of thousands of Jewish children in non-Jewish homes. The establishment did not want to make waves, even if the Jewish "aliens" couldn't eat kosher food or hold services. And when Brodetsky criticized HMG's treatment of the enemy aliens after the SS Andora sank, he did not do so on behalf of the Jewish victims.[18]

While inspecting the internment camps, Schonfeld served as a post office, taking messages, letters and first-hand reports of reassurance to anxious wives and other family members. At first, many refugees confused the British internment camps with German concentration camps, but the rabbi vehemently opposed these glib comparisons. He pointed out that, "In the camps, [with two notable exceptions, which were shortly closed down] there was no manhandling, forced labor or unnatural deaths; neither [did the internees wear] prison garb nor receive unusually harsh treatment as prisoners of war."[19]

The CRREC purchased kosher food, *siddurim*, religious books, radios and newspapers for distribution in all the camps and delivered personal packages to the internees. Schonfeld's warmth and concern showed them that they were not being treated with condescension. His most appreciated efforts were those that allowed inmates to see their spouses.[20] A former internee said, "I felt that he was someone to whom you could always come for help, advice and guidance. Rabbi Schonfeld never patronized us as 'refugees.' He treated us as equals. So many of the English Jews in those days looked down upon us, but Dr. Schonfeld made us feel worthwhile."[21]

Schonfeld's concerns also extended to thousands of British internees in the Dominions. They, too, required intercession. For example, at first, the Jewish refugees were mingled with Nazis aboard transport ships and in camps—a situation that led to violence. In Canada, the Canadian Jewish Congress helped him, as did some of the rabbinic leaders of the North American community, who provided kosher meat.[22]

In Canada and Australia, Orthodox internees organized Jewish seminars on all levels, daily prayer services and services for *Shabbos* and holidays. After almost eighteen months, most of the Canadian and Australian internees were released and, in their new locales, contributed to the rebirth of Orthodox Jewish life. Former internees were inspired to found the first Jewish day school in Australia in Melbourne[23] and served as the rabbinate and faculty. In Toronto, others helped create an advanced yeshiva and a day school. Some contributed to the Jewish community in other ways and many of them joined Allied military forces.[24]

Overall, while internment was unpleasant, its results were not catastrophic. Still, it was another example of how differences in ideology and practice in the Anglo-Jewish establishment affected the refugees' quality of life.

JEWISH SERVICEMEN

In addition to all of his activities on behalf of the refugees, Schonfeld was concerned about the spiritual care and kosher feeding of all Jewish young men, including the Orthodox, in the Allied armed forces. Jewish men had enlisted in unprecedented numbers in Britain, and many American Jews in the U.S. Armed Forces were stationed in England after the first week in December 1941, when the Japanese dragged the U.S. into the war by bombing Pearl Harbor.[25]

Schonfeld tried to ease military restrictions so the men could observe Shabbos and keep *kashrus*. By March 1941, the CRREC successfully organized a parcel drive for the soldiers, and provided kosher salami and cans of other kosher foods to each one. Although food was rationed, Schonfeld had permission from the Ministry of Food to send CRREC parcels to the Jewish troops. Later the approval also covered CRREC packages for Jewish British troops in Occupied Europe. Schonfeld also tried to arrange for Jewish American servicemen to spend *Shabbos* with local families.[26]

Every spring during the war, Schonfeld sent out special Passover parcels containing items for communal *Seder* celebrations, including special foods, Haggadahs (the printed service) and wine. In 1944, he sent 25,000 pounds of *matzoh*, 500 pounds of meat, 15,000 pints of wine and 5,000 Haggadahs. During the war years, he sent out nearly 200,000 cans of kosher food and 70,000 pounds of kosher meat. The CRREC also shipped out prayer books (*siddurim*), prayer shawls (*taleisim*), phylacteries (*tefillin*) and scholarly works. Some books, like Chief Rabbi Hertz's *A Book of Jewish Thoughts* and the special edition of Adler's holiday prayer books (*machzorim*), were published by the CRREC for just that reason. Jewish British soldiers around the world, even in places as remote as the Faros Islands, Lagos, the Dutch West Indies and Singapore, received these packages, as did all Jewish boys about to become bar mitzvah.[27]

HMG noticed Schonfeld's distribution network was well organized and well established, and they asked the CRREC to serve as the central importer of *esrogim* (citrons), *lulavim* (palm fronds) and other

religious articles from *Eretz Yisroel,* a trade route they tightly controlled and closed to commercial trade. Top priority for *esrogim* and
lulavim went to the synagogues in Britain, followed by the youth hostels and camps, and then the troops. As soon as peace was restored,
the CRREC gave the import business back to the dealers who handled it prior to war.[28]

THE ANGLO-JEWISH ESTABLISHMENT
OPPOSITION TO FOOD COLLECTION

When Schonfeld heard about the mass murder of two million Jews
in Poland from Rabbi Stephen S. Wise's press conference in New
York (November 24, 1942, as reported on the BBC), he pressed
ahead on two fronts. One was to rouse the British public to the dangers facing European Jewry and the other was to initiate rescue
efforts. To this end, and with the help of Lady Eleanor Rathbone, MP,
Schonfeld organized the Committee Against Nazi Terror that included many prominent non-Jewish personalities, among them the
Archbishop of Canterbury. All of them lobbied to make the British
public aware of the mass murders in Europe and to get the public to
act.[29]

Schonfeld and his supporters wanted immediate practical action to
save Jewish lives, even if it had to be done via a Parliamentary resolution that ignored the most logical haven for the Jews—Mandate
Palestine. Long-term solutions would not serve.[30] As an acrimonious
debate raged, Parliamentary proponents of a resolution suggesting
Mauritius as a refuge were drawn into a dispute about Mandate
Palestine and solved their political problem by permanently shelving
it.[31]

When Schonfeld looked beyond the war, he focused on the survivors. He created a Post-War Reconstruction Department for the
CRREC which became part of the Council of British Societies for
Relief Abroad, known as COSBRA or COBRA, the official non-
denominational British umbrella organization for relief efforts.[32]
Schonfeld's first project was to prepare a stockpile of canned kosher
meat, although meat was still rationed in England.

Waley-Cohen continued to disrupt Schonfeld's efforts. The British Lord convinced HMG to reverse its approval for Schonfeld's relief plans and forbid him to carry them out.[33] In HMG's view, Jews were considered citizens of their countries of origin, and those countries were responsible for their well being. If the host country said their Jews had no problems that settled the matter, even if this was not the case. Moreover, "any individual relief effort, [such as Schonfeld's] might be construed as part of some international Jewish organization—that is, a veiled attempt to bolster the Zionist cause."[34]

Thus, the staunch Zionist, Norman Bentwich, was prevented from becoming a member of the United Nations Relief and Rehabilitation Administration (UNRRA). The assimilated Anglo-Jewish leadership was afraid that calling attention to the Jews would differentiate *them* just as they were melding into British society. Singling out Jewish refugees for rescue, championing a supra-national view of Jews— such as Zionism—ran the same risk.[35]

When the Jewish Committee for Relief Abroad (the JCRA) was established in January 1943, under the chairmanship of establishment Jews like Dr. Radcliffe Salaman and Leonard Cohen, it came as no surprise that they readily accepted HMG's restrictions. Ironically, the committee's main task was to recruit, train and equip teams of volunteer workers to care for Jewish survivors after the Holocaust.[36]

Despite a challenge from Zionist leader Selig Brodetsky, Leonard Cohen declared that, "Jews are citizens of each country and the objective of the JCRA is general relief, including Jews equally with everyone else."[37]

Cohen said aiming first at relief of Jewish suffering was "too narrow and insufficiently humanitarian."[38] Schonfeld refused to accept this. Although it was not easy, he eventually convinced HMG that "Jews had been persecuted as a religious group no less than as a racial entity" and that a proportion of the Jewish population regarded the strict observance of Jewish food regulations as an essential part of their faith.[39]

The Ministry of Food then permitted the CRREC to begin collecting kosher canned food.[40] Once again, Schonfeld had Waley-Cohen to contend with, since he was the advisor to the Ministry of

Food on "The Jewish Food Question."[41] Waley-Cohen again "informed" on Schonfeld, and circulated a letter (dated September 1, 1943) to members of the CRREC, accusing Schonfeld [and the Chief Rabbi] of initiating an unauthorized project inimical to the public interest. The British lord added that "such a food collection would force consumers to reduce their consumption . . . [and] it would have a bad effect on this nation's war effort."[42]

This action placed Schonfeld's project on hold for three months, until the fall of 1943, when he convinced the Ministry of Food to reverse its negative ruling. In a strongly worded letter to G. H. C. Amos of the Ministry of Food, with reference to Waley-Cohen, Schonfeld wrote:

> I must warn you that that such underhanded dealing lays you open to libel and damages, [I demand that you] withdraw that letter, until the matter has been fairly considered . . . As for Sir Robert Waley-Cohen, I am puzzled to know where he comes in. He has nothing to do with the Chief Rabbi's Religious Emergency Council or the Council of British for Relief Abroad [COBRA]. He is supposed to advise you on Jewish (kosher) food in this country . . . Self-sacrificing Jews are depriving themselves of one small packet of food each month. This can hardly involve a reduction of their consumption to a lower level, nor could it create additional difficulties for other consumers. We are collecting food for European Jews after the war...There is no collection "on a large scale." . . . This misinformation makes your concern unnecessary.[43]

Schonfeld explained his appeal for kosher food, citing a letter written for the Chief Rabbi by Marcus Retter. It read:

> The Chief Rabbi has asked his flock to "fast" one fraction of a meal once a month in aid of a charitable cause. . . . It is not for you to express an opinion on the kind of appeals the Chief Rabbi should or should not issue to his communities, provided

they are legally in order. . . . Surely no layman or Christian would presume to dictate to him on such a matter.[44]

In a positive response to Schonfeld on October 19, 1943, the Ministry of Food pointed out that:

> Mr. Amos' letter of last September was in no way meant to cast any doubt upon the statement made in your appeal pamphlet to the effect that you had been assured by the Ministry that there was no legal objection to gifts by individuals of rationed food . . . provided that the individual has obtained the rationed food from a retailer for household consumption. Lord Woolton [Waley-Cohen] has decided that he will not ask you to withdraw the [food collection] scheme.[45]

Waley-Cohen, however, was not off the hook. Schonfeld wrote another letter to the Ministry of Food in the name of the Chief Rabbi, in which he condemned Waley-Cohen specifically. The letter maintained that the President of the United Synagogue, "misused his position [at the Ministry of Food] to intervene privately with the Hon. Officers of the Chief Rabbi's Committee, asking them to disassociate themselves from [the Chief Rabbi's] activities . . ." The letter also demanded that Waley-Cohen refrain from acting in "Jewish communal affairs outside his proper field of activity."[46]

Schonfeld's postwar relief effort was successful. His intelligent, sincere presentation of the true Jewish perspective to HMG was neither unpatriotic nor detrimental to anyone. In his postwar report, Schonfeld alluded to this negative episode with the words, "although not fully appreciated by the community at the time . . ."[47]

BROADCAST MEDIA

Through the CRREC, Schonfeld kept in touch with his constituents in England and abroad via cables, packages and letters. He also assured that a message reinforcing the Jewish way of life was sent over the airwaves. He arranged for regular radio broadcasts involving the then-Chief Rabbi, Dayan H. M. Lazarus, and other leaders of British Jewry. The first transmission of a Jewish religious service was arranged with the full cooperation of the British Home and Overseas Services, and such programs became a staple of the BBC.

Schonfeld's programming included themes on religious literature, appeals by the Chief Rabbi, reports about the CRREC's accomplishments and needs, and news about the refugees. Such information strengthened the links between Britain's Jewish communities and world Jewry and inspired overseas communities to donate money and supplies to the relief effort. In return, Schonfeld was able to send rescued religious functionaries to these same communities to serve their religious needs.[48]

CHAPTER 6

RESCUE EFFORTS

MAURITIUS

One of the most successful tools used by Schonfeld and other Orthodox rescue activists were "Protective Papers," i.e. visas or passports from neutral countries or Allied colonies that were recognized by the Germans. These papers provided a modicum of protection for the Jews that held them. Schonfeld used these in a number of rescue schemes, starting in 1942. Eventually, his efforts managed to save more than one thousand people.[1]

Mauritius is a small British colony of about 500,000 located on a tropical island in the Indian Ocean, about 450 miles east of Madagascar. The British had a number of internment camps on this island, where they mostly incarcerated Zionists who were caught trying to smuggle themselves into Mandate Palestine.[2]

Schonfeld's goal was to get visas to Mauritius from the Colonial Office. Each visa would be good for a Jewish family in Nazi-occupied territory and would enable its holder to get transit visas to nearby neutral countries, such as Turkey, Spain or Portugal. At first, Schonfeld focused on thirty rabbis interned in the U.S.S.R., but the issue became larger as names were added to his list. He never expected to get Palestine Certificates for these rabbis and their families; he just wanted to get them out of harm's way.

A prerequisite for getting to a neutral country was for the refugee to have an end-visa to a country willing to accept him/her in the first place. Schonfeld assumed that if the British issued Mauritius end-visas to these rabbis, they could eventually get to a neutral country. Meanwhile, the Mauritius visas would serve as protective papers. Along similar lines, Schonfeld tried to convince the British to permit

Jewish children to go to Mauritius or any other British colony—anywhere but Mandate Palestine.

On August 28, 1942, Schonfeld asked the Colonial Office for an appointment to "discuss with you a proposal concerning a limited number of oppressed Jews" and made it very clear that *"the proposal does not concern Palestine but refers to any other part of the Colonial Empire"* [Emphasis added].[3]

On September 2, 1942, Schonfeld wrote to Lord Cranborne of the Colonial Office: "I appreciate the various schemes involving the transfer of refugees to Palestine. I did not approach you in the first place concerning that country, as I was aware of the limitations that do exist, as well as of the schemes which are carried out."[4] Through Schonfeld's persistence and politic way of doing business, in 1943 the thirty rabbis and their families (about a hundred people) got their visas.

HMG did not want the scheme to get any publicity, since it might become too much for them to handle. Schonfeld was forced to raise money for the project privately, and when the Zionists discovered that Schonfeld was perfectly satisfied to send refugees to Mauritius, J. Linton, the Jewish Agency representative in London, sent a letter to the CRREC, including a cable from South African Zionists. It read: **"PERTURBED PRESS REPORTS MAURITIUS VISAS FOR REFUGEE RABBIS THROUGH HIAS-ICA LISBON STOP WHY NOT PALESTINE"** [Emphasis in original].[5]

Rabbi Hertz defended CRREC's Mauritius scheme and compared it to the Palestine-centric Zionist perspective:

> The Mauritius scheme was organized as an additional outlet for refugees who might escape from the Nazi terror. It was felt that besides the larger scale schemes of the Jewish Agency, efforts should be made to explore the possibilities of more limited schemes. The Mauritius visas were useful in providing an ultimate destination. It was not necessarily expected that any of the refugees able to reach a neutral country should proceed to Mauritius.[6]

One theory posits that HMG approved Schonfeld's Mauritius scheme in order to mitigate criticism of restrictions on refugees. If the Chief Rabbi advocated sending Jewish refugees to Mauritius because it was a good location, permission from the Colonial Office could prove it was not obstructionist. Even the governor of Mauritius had no objection to the arrival of the Jewish refugees, as long as they lived with the other internees.[7]

Hellholes they may have been, but the internment camps in Mauritius were infinitely better than Auschwitz, Treblinka and the other death, labor or concentration camps on the Continent. At least these European Jews were rescued from certain extermination. All told, Schonfeld was able to obtain 340 Mauritius end-visas and saved about one thousand souls, thus convincing a number of neutral countries to provide their own end-visas. He assured the issuers that the papers would be used solely as transit visas. This pragmatic approach to Jewish rescue compelled him to accept the poor conditions on Mauritius and explain British policy to the refugees.[8]

Conditions in the camps improved slightly whenever HMG got complaints from the Zionists and the Americans, to which it was exquisitely sensitive.[9] Many inmates in those internment camps had come from Poland and been exiled to Siberia. After the war, some of them immigrated to *Eretz Yisroel* via Teheran, Iran. Among the almost one hundred souls saved in this way was Rabbi Elchanan Sorotzkin, the well-known Rosh Yeshiva who went to the *Yishuv* after the war.

WEISSMANDL'S PLEA TO BOMB AUSCHWITZ

Schonfeld always tried to devise new solutions when rescue schemes failed, and in his decade-long pursuit to help his fellow Jews, the rabbi was never deterred. In history and in Jewish tradition, Jews are responsible for making the effort. The success of those efforts is up to the Almighty.

Among Schonfeld's greatest failures was his inability to convince HMG to bomb the railroad tracks leading to Auschwitz and the gas chambers. In April 1944, soon after the Nazis occupied Hungary, Rudolph Vrba and Alfred Wetzler, two Slovakian Jews, escaped with the help of the underground in Auschwitz from Auschwitz, where they had worked in the camp's registry office. They had memorized important details of the deportations and genocide of close to 2 million Jews between April 1942 and the beginning of April 1944. Sometime early that month, they managed to reach the underground "Working Group" in Slovakia headed by Weissmandl and Mrs. Gizi Fleischmann. They were interrogated for 24 hours and a 33-page document, known as the Auschwitz Protocols, was written based on their testimony. Vrba gave a copy of this report to Rudolph Kastner, head of the Rescuc Committee of the Sochnut in Budapest., but Kastner never showed this document to anyone other than his close friends.[1]

Weissmandl also prepared a five-page summary in Hebrew, which included his plea to bomb the railroad tracks, as well as other suggestions to the Allies. On May 15, 1944 the Nazis began mass deportations of Hungarian Jews to Auschwitz—at the rate of ten to twelve thousand per day. Weissmandl immediately sent copies of both reports to representatives of all the Jewish organizations in Switzerland. Within 24 hours, Natan Schwalb, head of Hechalutz, the socialist-Zionist pioneer group, had translated both Auschwitz documents into German and typed them on his own stationery, dated May 17, 1944.[2]

Schwalb had the best courier system in Switzerland and within 48 hours copies of the "Auschwitz Protocols" reached all the Zionist organizations in London, New York, Jerusalem and Istanbul. Yet none of them made the information public or followed up quietly. In addition to the pleas in the Protocols sent by Schwalb, Weissmandl sent another series of urgent cables pleading for the tracks to Auschwitz to be bombed. He noted that the same tracks were used to transport Axis materiel and troops to the Eastern Front.[3] Recha and Isaac Sternbuch, primary Orthodox rescue activists and the Vaad Hatzalah's representatives in Switzerland, sent copies of Weissmandl's pleas to the Vaad Hatzalah in New York City, and by June 18, Rabbi Avraham Kalmanowitz had brought them to the attention of the War Refugee Board.[4] Schonfeld received his copies of the Protocols and the plea via Boruch Meshulem Leibovitz in Switzerland.[5]

The Allies ignored the plea, claiming that only war-making facilities were the proper targets of their limited resources. However, they did manage to bomb the Buna synthetic rubber factory five miles from the Auschwitz compound that was staffed by Jewish inmates.[6]

George Mantello, the Jewish First Secretary of the El Salvadoran Consulate in Geneva, circulated Weissmandl's report and a brief report in Hungarian to all the newspapers and churches in Switzerland. The British and American intelligence services assisted him in spreading this news, because they owed him for help he had given them in the past. He also had the help of two major Swiss theologians, Paul Vogt and Karl Barth.[7] By June 23, 1944 most of the Swiss press broke the horror story on page 1, and the churches rang with sermons condemning the Nazis inhumanity at Auschwitz and the Hungarian complicity. The publicity in Switzerland generated an international response that pressured Hungary into stopping the deportations. On June 30, Chaim Weitzmann, Britain's leading Zionist, approached HMG with Weissmandl's plea and, like Schonfeld before him, was ignored.[8]

Schonfeld also helped 500 yeshiva students and rabbis—who fled from Poland to Vilna in 1940–41—escape to Japanese-occupied Shanghai, where they survived and continued their Talmudic studies. He raised funds to provide for them and tried to get them to countries like Sweden or Mexico. Sweden agreed to take the students, but first they had to get there. The only possible route was by train through Siberia, but Schonfeld failed to get the Soviets to issue transit visas.[9]

VITTEL AND LATIN AMERICAN PROTECTIVE PAPERS

Schonfeld took another opportunity to use "Protective Papers," passports and citizenship papers sold by Latin American consuls, especially in "neutral" Switzerland. Other organizations, like the World Jewish Congress, followed his example. However, some

Jewish organizations and leaders, like Saly Mayer, the JDC representative in Switzerland, refused to use what he called "fraudulent" papers.[10]

Eli Sternbuch, Recha Sternbuch's brother-in-law, discovered the system of "Protective Papers." He learned that a Polish Jew living in Warsaw with a legitimate Swiss passport did not have to wear a yellow star and was permitted to live outside the Ghetto. He purchased a Paraguayan passport in October 1941 from a Mr. A. Hügly, the Paraguayan counsel, who was in close touch with the Polish legation in Bern. In October 1941, Eli Sternbuch sent the passport to his intended fiancee, Guta Eisenzweig, who was living in Warsaw. To expand the rescue network, Eli soon handed the project to Dr. Julius Kuhl, head of the Jewish Division of the Polish Legation, and the noted the humanitarian, Ambassador Alexander Lados,[11] head of the legation. Paraguay was the first country to sell such passports—for profit. The consuls of other Latin American countries in Bern soon followed suit, and prices skyrocketed to an average 700 Swiss Francs each. The only consul to give away citizenship papers on a humanitarian basis was George Mantello. The Germans chose to recognize these papers, though they knew full well they were bogus. This is because thousands of Germans lived in Latin America with German papers. If the Nazis refused to recognize the Latin American papers, the Latin American countries issuing them could retaliate by refusing to recognize German papers.

Abraham Silberschein, a member of the World Jewish Congress and head of RELICO (a relief organization for Polish Zionists), used the papers to rescue Labor Zionists in Poland. In late 1942, the Nazis brought approximately two hundred holders of such Latin American papers (including Sternbuch family members) to Vittel—a detention camp located in a former hotel compound in France—where they were treated quite decently until December 1943. On the first day of that month, however, fearing an influx of Jewish immigrants, Paraguay suddenly withdrew recognition of its passports.[12]

Once Paraguay rescinded its recognition, so did other Latin American countries. When the Germans discovered the papers were no longer valid, they withdrew their own recognition of the

"Protective Papers," endangering the Jews in Vittel and thousands of other such paper-holders in Nazi-occupied territory. In Berlin, the Spanish Ambassador wanted Germany to retain its recognition of the papers, but failed to convince them to do so. When the "protective" status of the papers was rescinded, Recha Sternbuch, and her colleague Rabbi Shaul Weingort, who had managed to stay in touch with the inmates through the International Red Cross, raised the alarm and cabled the Vaad Hatzalah in New York and Schonfeld and Goodman in London. She warned them that the inmates in Vittel would be deported, and many soon were.

All the concerned parties tried to convince the American and British governments to intervene with the Latin American governments and ask them to renew official recognition of the "Protective Papers." They were also asked to assure the Latin American governments that the bearers of the "Protective Papers" would not settle in Latin America after the war. They did not succeed. In the case of the Vaad Hatzalah, the U.S. State Department broke its promise and never sent the message to the Latin American countries involved.

On Passover, April 5, 1944, Recha Sternbuch sent all three Orthodox rescue activist organizations another urgent cable. The inmates would be deported, and unless immediate action was taken to send that message to the Latin American embassies, their lives might be lost. Again, all three tried desperately to intercede on behalf of the Vittel inmates, but failed. They were deported to Auschwitz.

On the day they received the cable, April 6, the second day of Passover, Rabbis Abraham Kalmanowitz and Shabse Frankel of Brooklyn and Baruch Korff of Boston traveled to Washington to see Henry Morgenthau, Jr., Secretary of the Treasury and head of the War Refugee Board, a U.S. governmental agency created by President Roosevelt in January 1944.[13] The young Korff—a speechwriter for Congressman John McCormack, later Speaker of the House, and Senator James Mead of New York—was the most audacious of all. He told Morgenthau that Drew Pearson, the scandal-mongering newspaper columnist, would expose the Roosevelt Administration's lack of interest in rescuing the Jews of Europe. Rabbi Frankel pleaded, Rabbi Kalmanowitz cried and fainted, Rabbi Korff threatened, and, on the spot, Morgenthau called Secretary of State Cordell Hull to explain the situation.

Morgenthau told the Secretary that he was under intense pressure from the rabbis and noted that for months the State Department had lied about sending cables to Latin America. He wanted a different result that very night, and would not take no for an answer. Hull gave the order to send out cables to each Latin American embassy requesting official recognition of the "Protective Papers." At the end of a long day, Morgenthau wrote to his colleagues:

> Nothing has pleased me more than being able to get the State Department to send out this cable in regard to Camp Vittel. It just shows if we put enough heat in the right place it can be done, and believe me, we have put plenty of heat on Mr. Hull proper. When these things are out and nothing happens, they must ask themselves, "Well, after all, what is all this fighting [the war] for?" The fact is that the March 16 cable went—of course in the room I can say it is a tragedy it didn't go on March 16.

Approximately 250 people were murdered because the memo didn't go out that day, including immediate members of the Sternbuch family.[14] While the American Vaad was not successful in rescuing the inmates of Vittel, they did end up saving many thousands of Jews who held Latin American and other "Protective Papers."[15]

Just three inmates from Vittel managed to elude deportation by hiding in Vittel's bakery ovens. They were Dr. Hillel Seidman, the noted historian and journalist from Warsaw, Guta Eisenzweig and her mother. All three possessed Eli Sternbuch's Paraguayan papers and managed to stay hidden with the support of several other prisoners. Two others managed to escape to Switzerland before the deportation.[16]

Vittel also held several thousand non-Jewish prisoners, most of them British civilians and soldiers who were candidates for prisoner exchanges. In the fall of 1944, a British nurse and several officers

were exchanged and returned to England, and Dr. Seidman, who authored *The Warsaw Diary*, wrote a message to Goodman on the lining of a jacket belonging to one of them. The message included a list of names of people Seidman hoped would intercede to rescue them.
The message, written in Hebrew, read:

> Save the remnants of Polish Jewry. Don't delay! I am a lone survivor! The only hope is an exchange of German nationals in the Near East and Jews with Palestinian Certificates. Sister Chana Horowitz Seidman, Tel Aviv, and my cousin Anshel Fink, Brooklyn. Get in touch with [Dr. Abraham] Silberschein [of the World Jewish Congress in Zurich] and [Dr. Ignacy] Schwartzbart [of the Polish Government-in-Exile in London], [Yisroel Chaim] Eis, Zurich, [Yitzchok] Sternbuch, St. Gallen.[17]

Goodman could not respond because the cryptic message aroused the suspicions of Scotland Yard, and he was summoned for questioning. Schonfeld was in no position to convince HMG to respond to the plea. In the end, however, as the Allies swept across France, the three survivors were liberated.[18]

THE PARLIAMENTARY RESOLUTION

On December 17, 1942, the United Nations Declaration responded to press reports released in November 1942 that more than 2,000,000 Jews had been murdered in Europe. This inspired Schonfeld to attempt a relatively large-scale rescue effort, applying the concept of "Protective Papers."[19]
He discussed his ideas with a number of high churchmen and members of Parliament and organized Parliamentary-wide support for a motion that asked HMG to make a declaration along the following lines:

> That in view of the massacres and starvation of Jews and others in enemy and enemy-occupied countries, this House asks

H.M. Government, following the United Nations Declaration read to both Houses of Parliament on 17th, December, 1942, and in consultation with the Dominion Governments and the Governments of India, to declare its readiness to find temporary refuge in its own territories or in territories under its control for endangered persons who are able to leave those countries; to appeal to the Governments of countries bordering on enemy and enemy-occupied countries to allow temporary asylum and transit facilities for such persons; to offer to those Governments, so far as practicable, such help as may be needed to facilitate their co-operation; and to invite the other Allied Governments to consider similar action.[20]

Within 10 days, two Archbishops, eight Peers, four Bishops, the Episcopate of England and Wales and 48 members of all parties signed the notice of meeting to consider the Motion. Eventually the number of members of Parliament in support of the motion rose to 177.

The Zionists deeply resented the omission of Palestine as a safe haven, considering that omission a cardinal sin—even though including it meant the British could not rescue trapped Jews.[21] Selig Brodetsky spearheaded the opposition with his mentor, the veteran Zionist leader, Lavey Bakstansky. They tried their best to sabotage the motion by canvassing members of Parliament, asking them not to support this rescue effort.

What galled Schonfeld about this was that he had offered the Board of Jewish Deputies' Consultative Committee the option of co-operating or making the motion *their* project, and would have been glad to give them credit for the idea. In this case, however, he condemned their obstructionism, especially since they had no proposal to offer in its place. What was worse was the unfortunate impression this sectarian battle left on the members of Parliament who were trying to save Jews. It made them weary at best and disgusted at worst,[22] so the House of Lords shelved the resolution and it never again saw the light of day.

STRANGER'S KEY

Schonfeld's failures, no less than his successes, demonstrated his creative approach to rescue. At one point during the war Schonfeld even asked the Colonial Office, "If I may invite anyone to my house, is it possible to invite someone to one's island?"

He was told he could and so solicited and received a £10,000 donation from a philanthropist to purchase Stranger's Key, an island in the British Bahamas. His objective was to provide safe haven for Jews by getting HMG to issue entry visas to different areas of the British Empire. Such papers included Palestine Certificates, the Latin American "Protective Papers" and especially Salvadoran citizenship papers—all recognized by the Germans.

Schonfeld was going to issue visas to Stranger's Key, which some punster suggested he rename "Solomon lsland." The visa would entitle the holder to protection from the powers in various belligerent countries, in the same way "Paraguyan Protective Papers" helped the inmates at Vittel . . . until they were invalidated by Paraguay. The Stranger's Key rescue program failed because another department in HMG refused to go along with the Colonial Office and Schonfeld's idea. [23]

CHAPTER 7

POSTWAR

INTRODUCTION

Schonfeld was prepared, two years in advance, for the challenges presented by war's end. He did it by going up against Lord Woolton and collecting cans of kosher food and other items that Jewish Displaced Persons (DPs) would need in order to rebuild their Jewish lives. Only the survivors knew how horrible the Holocaust really was, and few people knew what would be needed to provide even minimum relief to the refugees.

When he realized the enormity of the destruction, Schonfeld focused on the ever-increasing need to feed the survivors in DP camps or in their unfriendly hometowns. (Many survivors went to their old homes to seek out family members.) For almost a year, the Allied Occupation Forces did not permit any private relief organizations to serve the camps, and the non-denominational UNRRA that did was hardly sensitive to concerns directly affecting the Orthodox survivors under their care. They had no interest in providing kosher food, religious articles, constructing *mikvos* or synagogues or helping rebuild other important institutions throughout the multi-denominational Jewish community.

At the same time, Schonfeld tried to bring as many Jewish orphans as possible out of Eastern Europe, where the Communists were taking over and making Jewish life difficult, if not impossible. At one point, he wanted to bring 150 orphans out of Warsaw, few of them Orthodox. But none of them had passports or other identifying documents.

Schonfeld traveled to Warsaw and discussed the problem with the First Secretary of the British Embassy there who agreed to issue British visas for the children. But where would they place the visa stamps? The quick-thinking rabbi recalled the internationally recognized Nansen Passports (named for the Norwegian explorer who later worked for the League of Nations and handled the post-World War I refugee problem), and issued photo ID cards authorized by the CRREC. These cards were then presented to British embassy officials for stamping.[1]

With his youthful entourage following him around as if he were the Pied Piper, Schonfeld went to Gdansk (Danzig). Anxious to get the youngsters out of Poland, he bought a boat, filled it with the150 orphans, all of them minors. Other than the captain and a small crew, Schonfeld was the sole adult aboard. After their arrival in London, he sold the boat and settled the newcomers with Orthodox Jewish families. Some of the families who took them in were those he'd brought to England before the war that were only too happy to help him.

THE DISTRESSED PERSONS SCHEME

Schonfeld obtained HMG's approval for the Distressed Persons Scheme, an idea he broached to Home Secretary Baron James Chuter-Ede. The rabbi wanted to unite survivors on the Continent with their loved ones in Britain, and he would provide families with assistance before their arrival and after reunification. HMG refused, so the rabbi changed the request to permit the entry of Jewish children.

Schonfeld succeeded in organizing another transport of Czechoslovakian Jewish children in 1945 that arrived in England just before Passover. He wheedled and cajoled the owners of some of the finest kosher hotels in Bournemouth into taking the youngsters in as guests for the week—even though the resorts were already full.

Shortly after the war, when air travel for civilians was rare, Schonfeld arranged for a flight to Poland, with a departure time slated for right after *Shabbos*. To get to Heathrow Airport (16 miles from London) on time, he had to leave while it was still *Shabbos*, so he arranged for three pairs of shoes and clean socks to be strategically placed at three equidistant locations along the road to the airport. He spent most of that *Shabbos* afternoon briskly walking to the airport and caught the flight without compromising his Torah observance.[2]

Schonfeld wanted to airlift survivors out of the liberated areas in Europe, and asked the Air Ministry if he could buy surplus airplanes, but none were available. They suggested he take the issue up with COBRA, but nothing happened.[3]

GERMAN AUTONOMOUS REGION

About four months after the war ended, tens of thousands of Holocaust survivors were streaming into DP camps in northwestern Germany. Conditions in some of them were not much better than in some of the concentration camps. Schonfeld's goal was to provide all of the survivors with kosher food, religious articles and a psychological boost. He went to Ernest Bevin, the antisemitic British Secretary of State for Foreign Affairs, and proposed the creation of a temporary autonomous area in northwestern Germany, site of a number of DP camps. This would be a temporary, mini-Jewish state, replacing the DP camps, allowing the survivors to recuperate under circumstances without German or British Army authority hanging over them. Schonfeld noted that German inhabitants did not need to be evacuated from the area,[4] but did not take into account the fact that Jewish DP population would increase several-fold. In any case, Bevins brought the idea to the Foreign Office. They said no.[5]

At the time of his request, Schonfeld was probably not aware that Britain and the United States were already pursuing a benign policy toward Germany because of the brewing Cold War and the role Germany would play in it. This prevented Britain from exhibiting films showing German atrocities—namely the liberation of the concentration camps—films taken by official army photographers. This convergence of political necessity and the fate of the Jews resulted in the failure of Schonfeld's creative plan to truly "liberate" the Jews of Europe.

MOBILE SYNAGOGUES

The survivors who filled the DP camps came from concentration camps or were among those returning from Central Asia and captivity in the Soviet Union. Tens of thousands flooded the Allied Zones immediately after the war, where private relief organizations were not allowed to assist the DPs. The Allies, in their bureaucratic wisdom, chose to use UNRRA to handle all relief efforts. Unfortunately, UNRRA wasn't equipped to deal with the survivors and especially not with the particular needs of the Orthodox.[6]

After the war, Schonfeld implemented one of his most successful ideas, the synagogue ambulance, or mobile synagogue—after HMG announced that any relief organization providing its own transportation would be allowed to conduct relief activities immediately following liberation. Making use of this idea, Schonfeld used the moving vans to dispense kosher food, medicine and religious articles to the DPs in the British Zone, while the Vaad Hatzalah and the Zeirei Agudath Israel in America handled the needs of the Orthodox Jews in the American Zone.[7]

BACKGROUND

When HMG created COBRA in 1943, it was decided that when the war was over, COBRA would oversee relief work. The Jewish organizations represented in COBRA were the Board of Jewish Deputies (in the form of a new organization called the Jewish Committee for Relief Abroad [JCRA]) and the CRREC. Normally COBRA required private organizations to contribute money, services and goods on a non-denominational basis. The assimilationists were right there to laud the universal perspective and disdained any particularist or direct help for the Jews. Leonard Cohen, Vice-President of the JCRA, maintained that, "to take as a first aim the relief of Jewish suffering was 'too narrow,' and insufficiently humanitarian."[8]

In early March 1943, the CRREC established the Postwar Religious Reconstruction Department. At the time, Schonfeld, and Chief Rabbi Hertz began the canned food collection campaign authorized by COBRA and the Ministry of Food that so infuriated Waley-Cohen. The objective was to have a kosher supply of food ready as soon as Nazi-controlled areas were liberated, food to be available to the survivors even before private Jewish relief organizations could get there.[9]

Schonfeld's prescience about food collection made it possible for him to stock the mobile synagogues immediately. And while he would have been pleased to let other Jewish relief organizations take over the burden of feeding and spiritual care of the survivors, most of them had neither the supplies nor ability to operate as freely as he did during the first few months after the war.

The first to make use of Schonfeld's far-sightedness, ironically, was the Board of Jewish Deputies, the same group that originally refused to get involved in the food campaign. In February 1945, several months before the war ended, the JCRA sought permission from the Ministry of Food to provide Jewish survivors in liberated France and Belgium with kosher meat. The Ministry approved the use of 10,000 tins for each country, which the CRREC gave the JCRA from its collected stock.[10]

In March 1945, Schonfeld requested permission from the Ministry of Food to give approximately 120,000 cans of kosher meat to various Jewish organizations for distribution in France, Holland, Czechoslovakia, Greece and Egypt (for Jews in Tripoli). Those organizations included the JDC and OSE (the French Jewish children's relief organization). Some of the food was quickly shipped to Europe with UNRRA's permission. The Ministry of Food insisted only that all the food distributed in the Netherlands, Belgium and France be sent via the respective national Red Cross chapters and not through the British Red Cross.[11]

Schonfeld would not accept "trickle down" methods of providing for the Jewish survivors because he knew secular relief agencies did not understand specific Jewish needs. He worked hard to convince COBRA and the British military authorities that Jews, "have been persecuted as a religious group, and one must take into consideration the strict observance of Jewish ritual food regulations as an essential tenet of their faith." Getting the powers that be to understand this principle was one of Schonfeld's greatest accomplishments.

Postwar Europe was in chaos because of the extensive Allied bombing of Europe's infrastructure. Postal services and public transportation were either erratic or nonexistent. But as soon as parts of the British Zone were liberated in 1944, Schonfeld put the mobile synagogues together. Each van held enough religious, medical and food supplies for 500 people. In addition to the phrase *Shalom Aleichem* (Peace Unto You), each was emblazoned with gold lettering in English: "Synagogue Ambulance," followed by "Presented by the Hebrew Congregation of . . ." with the name of the congregation that paid for it.[12]

Marcus Retter often acted as a proxy for Schonfeld on visits to the Isle of Man and on missions to the DP camps, and that included bringing mobile synagogues to the DPs. He drove the first van— funded by a congregation in Melbourne, Australia—to Holland. (Australian Jews and Jewish New Zealanders were generous donors to many of Schonfeld's appeals. They took 500 tons of food worth £50,000—bought and packed in Britain—and shipped it to the Continent.)[13]

Retter and the mobile synagogue were part of a convoy of twenty trucks organized by the Dutch Government-in-Exile in London. The convoy assembled in South London and drove to the coast, where it boarded an LST—a landing craft that looked like a flat-bottomed barge—and sailed for Europe. Retter was the only non-military person aboard. He was treated with respect because of the items he was carrying; the mobile synagogue was treated as a sacred shrine.

He arrived in Antwerp, Belgium on a Thursday night and remained for *Shabbos*. Concerned about security for the mobile synagogue, Retter appealed to the Dutch Consul, who sent two soldiers to guard the truck and stay with him until he reached the Dutch border.

Since regular bridges had been destroyed during the war, Retter drove his van across whatever was available, even pontoon bridges. He finally arrived at the Jewish Hospital in Amsterdam, where the elderly Chief Rabbi Tal and his young assistant eagerly greeted him. A few Agudists were also there, and Retter promised to help them reestablish their congregation.[14]

A few weeks after Retter's arrival in Europe, the CRREC sent five railroad cars loaded with food, clothing, medicine and the remaining mobile synagogues through Switzerland via Vienna to Budapest, where it was the first relief convoy to arrive for the Jewish community. All told, the CRREC sent twenty-three trucks into the British Zone and around Europe. Then each mobile synagogue, accompanied by a chaplain, visited several locations.[15]

Retter needed to find Orthodox leadership to establish a committee to distribute the supplies, and did so within two weeks. One of his more complicated tasks was to negotiate a peace agreement between the elderly chief rabbi and his more modern assistant.

Schonfeld drove a mobile synagogue to The Hague, where Retter joined him and helped reestablish an Orthodox *kehillah* there. What was worth even more than the supplies was the respect they were shown by the British Army and HMG. This treatment gave the Orthodox Jews status and a much-needed psychological boost.

Retter next drove one of the mobile synagogues to the German border, where he handed it over to two chaplains and received permission to return to England by air—thanks to COBRA and the British Occupation Forces.

A few weeks later, Retter returned to Holland where he worked to bring harmony to a community split between descendants of the Spanish-Portuguese Jews (*Sephardim*) and the rest of the European Jews (*Ashkenazim*). Since each used different *minhagim* (traditions) in their prayer services, they spent a great deal of time fighting over procedure. Retter spoke from the pulpit and told the story of nineteenth-century Jews in Pressburg, who fought the same battle now being fought in Amsterdam. Their leader at the time was Rabbi Moshe Sofer, the Chasam Sofer, who told them the following story:

> There was once a rich man who married off his two daughters, for whom he provided full support for life. While he had no problem supporting both, there was only one problem. One son-in-law always ate dairy, while the other restricted himself to meat. One day, unfortunately, the father-in-law lost his wealth, and could no longer afford to supply his sons-in-law with their sumptuous, individualized meals. Instead of fancy meat for one, and heavy cream and fancy dairy dishes for the other, he gave them each potatoes to eat. The dairy person

cooked his potatoes in his dairy pot, while the meat person cooked his in the meat pot. They were still estranged so they didn't speak to each other.

When the father-in-law realized this, he told them, "When things were wonderful and I could afford to give each of you what you desired, you could afford to eat totally different types of meals. Now, that you're both eating the same potatoes, why do you need two different types?"[16]

Retter added: "When times were good, and there were many of you, you could afford all kinds of prayer groups. Now that we underwent the tragedy of the Holocaust and lost most of our people, why can't you all pray the same way?" Thus he succeeded in creating a single congregation.

On this same trip, Retter drove another mobile synagogue to Germany, and dropped it off at Bergen Belsen in the British Zone. Then he traveled to Hannover, Frankfurt and Berlin.[17]

In the end, one truck was sent to Paris, another to Prague; six went to the British Forces in Germany and two to Belgium; two went to Amsterdam, four to Poland; three went to Hungary, including one to the Jewish Hospital in Budapest; one went to Bucharest and the last three went to two Jewish chaplains in Italy and the Jewish community in Rome. Nine were used for Jewish servicemen's religious needs. Dayan M. Gollop and Rabbi I. Brodie (who later became the Chief Rabbi of Great Britain) headed that chaplain corps.[18]

Chaplain Reuven Monheit, a student of Weissmandl and a French Army captain, made the most use of the mobile synagogue assigned to him. He frequently came back to base, "refilled" it and drove it back to Paris—often with thirty or forty survivors who lacked the papers to allow them into France. He brought hundreds of survivors to France, where they were processed by the Agudah or Vaad Hatzalah and sent via the *Bricha* (illegal immigration) to the *Yishuv* or to North America.[19]

Monheit once took a mobile synagogue from Bregenz, Austria to Tournan, France, with a group of Agudist survivors from

Transcarpathia. When they arrived at the confiscated Chateau Des Boulayes, they established a small DP camp and established Rabbi Weissmandl's Nitra Yeshiva there.[20]

Usually one chaplain or CRREC member accompanied the mobile synagogue, but two or more were sent if there were large Jewish centers. For example, four chaplains took a mobile synagogue to the liberated British Zone in Germany. They were Rabbis S. Baumgarten, Eli Munk, J. Vilensky and Rev. A. Gruenbaum, who went to the Bergen Belsen DP camp near Celle. In and around Bergen Belsen, they established a congregation with many religious and welfare activities, including prayer services, Hebrew classes, kosher kitchens, *shechita* (ritual slaughter), *mikvos* (ritualaria) and other institutions of Jewish life.[21]

One reason Schonfeld was so successful was that he looked like a military man of top rank and acted like one. Whenever Schonfeld went to Europe, he wore a uniform he designed himself. As a member of COBRA, he had an aura of authority that lifted the spirits of the pleasantly surprised survivors. Schonfeld made good use of that power and ran the CRREC like a one-man show.

One observer wrote:

"He was [dressed] in a military uniform, in which he looked a good deal more natural than with a *talis* over his head. People were not too sure about his rank, but he acted as if he were Chief of the General Imperial Staff. He gave orders right and left, set up soup kitchens, synagogues and study rooms and commandeered whole transport fleets." [22]

The chaplains also created a private mail service for the survivors, who were anxious to inform relatives and loved ones in the free world that they were still alive and needed help.

BERGEN BELSEN DIARY

Schonfeld arranged a fact-finding trip in July 1946 for a delegation of four rabbis sent to the Bergen Belsen DP camp. A large number of Jews lived there, including Orthodox groups who had barely survived their recent liberation. The rabbis reported on the conditions and suggested improvements. Rabbi Shlomo Baumgarten wrote:

Time is of the essence and one can write hundreds of pages. One can do more *mitzvot* here during one day than in a lifetime in London. I arrived here shortly before *Shabbos*. Soon after my arrival two girls came to me crying bitterly. Their mother had just died. All they asked for was a separate grave for their mother, rather than her being dumped in a mass grave. I went to the Burial Officer and pleaded for the fulfillment of this last wish. Today at 11:30 am the funeral took place and I spoke a few words . . .

You walk through the camp: people come toward you from all sides:

Rabbi, *Sholom Aleichem*, Where are you from? In a few minutes hopes are aroused, and people wish to discuss their personal matters with you. Everybody wants encouragement and advice . . . . My *tefilin* are in use from morning to night. I wish I had hundreds of pairs here.

How can I describe this last *Shabbos*? I was asked to speak and about two hundred people came. I said goodbye to the Czech group. They tell the story of the Jews of Slovakia and Bohemia. I cannot control my emotions. One *kehillah* after another was sent to Auschwitz and a few hours later were destroyed. Each one of those who have survived is a separate *nes* (miracle).

In the face of these heroes we should be ashamed of our petty troubles . . . . These survivors had been a fortnight without bread, without a drop of water; an ordinary event. Children of six years fasted for days and gave their slice of bread to their mothers. Hundreds are unhappy that they must leave the camp without at least a *siddur* . . . . I have visited the children's home, and have arranged for a *bris*; the first in Bergen Belsen. In the evening I am speaking to the Beth Jacob Group, which has been active here since liberation...

In the children's home a girl of about ten came up to me: "*Rebbe*, I have a *Zeide* in London, I know his name. Can you find him?" I asked the child where are your parents? "They were thrown into the *offen* [oven]," was the reply. Indeed, the same reply was given to me by very many children. At least I should have a piece of chocolate for each child. All they ask for is a small mezuzah or Magen David [Star of David]. It is so little, yet so much . . . .Tell the Agudah to send as many Jewish newspapers as possible. The people yearn for news. [Bergen Belsen] is a camp full of tragedy. I hear the story in a hundred versions. Now I understand what we were told about.[23]

Schonfeld put in equal efforts on behalf of Western European Jews, who had also suffered in the Holocaust. Immediately after liberation, he established the Comité Central Israelite in Brussels and financially supported its numerous activities to reconstruct Jewish life.[24]

RELIGIOUS ARTICLES

Schonfeld assumed that giving the mobile synagogues to key people would help reestablish the Jewish communities. He began the food campaign in 1943, and had also asked British Jewry to donate spare *tefilin, mezuzahs, taleisim, siddurim, machsorim, chumashim, shofaros,* folios of the Talmud and other items.[25] Although the response was generous, by 1944 he realized that the need was far greater than anticipated.[26] He reached an agreement with the JCRA to purchase larger quantities of religious articles, paid for by the Central British Fund. Appeals were made to Jewish communities in Britain and the Empire to donate Torah scrolls. By the end of 1946, the CRREC sent more than 100,000 religious articles and a large number of Jewish books to the Continent. The *tefilin, mezuzahs* and *shofaros* were purchased in *Eretz Yisroel*; the *taleisim* and books were purchased in Britain.

The CRREC printed approximately 20,000 prayer books. For *Sukkos* in 1945, sets of *Arba Minim* [palm fronds, myrtle, citron and

willow] were distributed on the Continent for the first time since the
beginning of the war. All these items arrived via the mobile synagogues.[27]

POSTWAR TRIPS
Poland

Schonfeld's first of five trips to Poland took place in October
1945. His twin objectives were to rescue Jewish orphans and to help
reconstruct struggling Jewish *kehillos* (communities) and Jewish life.
The latter consisted primarily of Jews returning from concentration
camps and many more who came back from Siberia and Central Asia.
This aroused great opposition among the Communists in power—
especially the Jewish Communists—who were creating a new
"order" to solve Europe's economic problems. Solving these, they
assumed, would automatically resolve the "Jewish Problem"—antisemitism.[28]

In addition, Schonfeld helped organize a movement of an
unknown number of Jews returning from Siberia to *Eretz Yisroel* via
Germany. Here too, Jewish Communist opposition reared its ugly
head.[29] To bring the Polish children to England, Schonfeld worked to
obtain block exit visas for larger groups. Schonfeld helped hundreds
of adults and children leave Poland with the help of HMG and the
Polish government.

As part of his campaign, Schonfeld paid large sums of money in
order to get Jewish children out of Christian homes and institutions.
Whenever he gained custody of a child, he placed them in the hostels
he organized in England, and from there, many of the children went
on to *Eretz Yisroel*.[30]

On his first trip to Poland, Schonfeld found the few survivors disorganized, dispirited and lured to the lives of the radical Jewish sec-
ularists. Initially, Schonfeld gathered the few surviving religious
leaders in some of the towns and villages—to help them establish the
nucleus of *kehillos* in their locations. Within the *kehillos*, he helped
establish synagogues, Talmud Torahs, kosher kitchens and orphanages or childcare centers where Jewish orphans were "collected."

To do this, the rabbi drew on his experience in establishing the Union of Synagogue Communities in Britain. By the time he completed his fifth trip to Poland, he had helped to create 78 *kehillos*, all under the umbrella of the Union of Synagogues. To garner financial support for these projects, Schonfeld made a fundraising trip to the United States in December 1945. There, he aroused the interest of the Orthodox Vaad Hatzalah and other Jewish groups, who began related missions to offer relief to the Jews in Poland.[31]

Because he couldn't do everything at once, Schonfeld assigned the second Polish mission to Retter. As usual, it was a mission with a dual nature: to help strengthen/reconstruct Orthodox Jewish communities and to bring out as many youngsters as possible. Some children had been hiding in the forests, but most were hidden in private homes, convents and other institutions, and a great deal of money was needed to reclaim them.

Instead of bringing out the (mostly orphan) youngsters in one large group, as Schonfeld did, Retter worked with the Polish authorities to bring out the youngsters in small groups of four or five. This was most likely done to avoid the publicity that would be generated by a large exodus. Once exit visas were obtained, John P. Russell, First Secretary of the British Embassy in Warsaw, provided the children with entry visas to Britain. Retter convinced Russell to provide certificates. They gave him the certificates and when Retter showed them to the Polish authorities, they provided the requisite exit visas. Hundreds of children were brought out in this way.[32]

After the Kielce pogrom in 1946, it was clear to most of the tens of thousands of refugees that there was no future for Jews in Communist Poland. Poland's Chief Rabbi Dr. David Kahane was the first Chief Chaplain of the Polish Army and now as the Chief Rabbi, warned Retter that Poland was still dangerous, especially for Jews. He told Retter that Schonfeld had been the target of an assassination plot during his first trip to Poland but that Schonfeld had shrugged off the threat, saying, "If the Almighty wishes me to carry out this task, He will take care of me."[33]

It took Retter almost four months to get the tickets and visas for the children. Retter was also a Communist target and the longer he stayed, the more dangerous it became. Kahane was so worried about him, he said: "I am *gozer* (giving an order based on halachic grounds) that you leave immediately to Prague, even if you have to travel on *Shabbos*. The authorities might call you for an interview and you may never return."[34]

Retter managed to get to Prague about two hours before Shabbos. When he got there, an officer approached him and told him that Rabbi Victor Vorhand was waiting for him. Schonfeld, who had come to Prague earlier, arranged with Vorhand to help move the children through France to England.

Retter writes:

Schonfeld wanted to remove all orphaned Jewish children from the countries formerly occupied by the Nazis, particularly Poland. This included orphans hidden in non-Jewish homes during the war and those who spent the war years in orphanages, monasteries or convents. After the war, the Polish government found lists of Jewish children placed in orphanages. The CRREC had lists of its own, with thousands of names supplied to us by Polish Jews living in England. We turned the lists over to the Polish government, that is, to Szajnawski, but it was still difficult for us to identify the children, because 95 percent of them had changed their names. Professor Michael Zylberberg, of the office for the official Jewish community in Warsaw, helped us track them down.

Zylberberg called himself professor because, before the war, he was a high school teacher. When we met, he was director of the office of the *kehillah*, the official Jewish community. Zylberberg was not observant but was from an Orthodox background, and in the post-war period worked with Rabbi Dr. David Kahane.[35]

The second *kindertransport* from Poland contained approximately 150 children. The third left early in 1947, with roughly two hundred youngsters. In each case, the transports left on military aircraft because consumer airline tickets were unavailable. Tickets were allocated by the British Foreign Office, which instructed the Royal Air Force to assign a block of seats to an individual named Marcus Retter. This was possible because Schonfeld had maintained excellent relations with various British government officials.[35]

Schonfeld saved people first and later worried about finding the money to feed them. Things in Britain were better for the Jewish community after the war, and most of the Orthodox Jews who had made it to England before the war began were now established. Some were even financially successful. Before long, all the children were placed in Orthodox homes—even Retter and his wife took in a little girl.[36]

Last Rescue-Czech Group[37]

Schonfeld arrived in Prague in the spring of 1948, just after the arrival of Soviet troops. He put together his last children's transport of approximately 150 youngsters, ranging in age from six to seventeen. The children were gathered in Bratislava and Prague, just as the Communists were dropping the Iron Curtain around Czechoslovakia. As soon as Schonfeld arrived, he contacted Vorhand. Vorhand knew how to make good use of the freer atmosphere in Czechoslovakia immediately after the war.

After the Soviets released the Polish Jews they sent to Siberia in 1941, Prague became the postwar center for tens of thousands of these refugees. From Prague, the Jews were helped to get into Western Europe, especially France. (After an agreement with the Polish General Wladyslaw Sikorsky, a large proportion of those in Siberia were allowed to travel to Soviet Central Asia, i.e. Tashkent and Samarkind.)

Even in Prague, however, a refugee needed citizenship papers to be accepted in France or other countries. Dr. Yaakov Griffel, an Orthodox rescue activist in Turkey, partially solved the problem by obtaining one thousand signed Salvadoran citizenship papers from George Mantello, the Salvadoran diplomat in Switzerland. When he left his diplomatic post, he took the signed papers with him. Each was good for an entire family.[38]

Although Schonfeld was told he could bring only orphans back to England, he didn't refuse parents who asked to have their children sent out. He also went to a convent and asked for the Jewish children who had been abandoned there. The Mother Superior told him that there were no such children in the convent, and so Schonfeld asked to say goodbye to her charges. As he toured the dormitories, he slowly chanted the *Shema* and several small voices joined in. Those children left the convent with him.

Schonfeld needed to be clever around the authorities as well. Older youngsters were told to curl up to make themselves appear younger, and since the British consul allotted him only 148 visas for 150 children, Schonfeld had the children run around to confuse the counting. The children were also told not to speak Czech and to pretend not to understand it, since Czech youngsters were not permitted to leave.

Years later, when a British Home Office official was asked to provide a visa for the parent of one of these children, Schonfeld was held to task because he had claimed that the children he brought to England were all orphans. The official asked him: "How could you, a man of God, state that these children were all orphans?" Schonfeld replied: "After all they have gone through, would you deny a child his mother?"

Once again, as he had during the war, Schonfeld temporarily cleared out his schools and used them as dormitories until all the refugee children were placed. About a third of them were placed in various hostels and with some families who had themselves been Schonfeld charges.

About eighty younger children and twenty older ones who helped care for them sailed across the Irish Sea to Dublin and were greeted by the ladies of the Dublin Jewish community, who had no idea how deprived the children had been. When they offered the children tea with lemon or milk, the children took both, tasted the brew and thought they were being poisoned. The children were so traumatized during their years in hiding that they could not help thinking in warped ways. When sirens went off or a police officer was present, they were terrified. Older "brothers" or "sisters" took care of the

younger children and relationships developed into lifetime friendships.

The children sent to Ireland were housed in Clonyn Castle, an
imposing Gothic pile on the edge of Delvin, a small village. It was
surrounded by gardens, fields and woods and was purchased to house
the children by a benefactor in Manchester, England. Rabbi Israel
Cohen and his wife were the benevolent leaders of this little community, and Schonfeld's influence was everywhere. Under the Cohens'
tutelage, the castle became a wonderful place where the youngsters
regained their humanity and dignity and their pride in Judaism.

As in Britain and the United States, there were assimilated Jews in
Dublin who resented the influx of this group of young survivors, fearing that they would inspire antisemitic reactions in a completely
Catholic area. As usual, the predicted antisemitism never material-
ized. The survivors openly practiced their devout Orthodox Judaism,
and relations with their neighbors and shopkeepers were excellent.

Cyprus

One of the more interesting missions carried out by Schonfeld and
members of his staff, was commissioned by the Colonial Office.
Survivors after the war were anxious to get out of Europe and to *Eretz
Yisroel,* legally or not. The Sochnut, the "unofficial" government of
the *Yishuv,* channeled this desire into the *Bricha,* the movement of
survivors across the Continent, and encouraged them to immigrate to
Eretz Yisroel en masse. According to the British White Paper of 1939,
however, only 75,000 Jews were to be admitted. This illegal route to
Eretz Yisroel was known as *"Aliyah Bet."*

All the various parties in the Jewish Agency sent hundreds of
emissaries to the DP camps to organize and prepare the survivors for
their trek across Europe—especially to France and Italy—from
whence they boarded leaky old boats to the *Yishuv.* Many of the
Agency's emissaries were former members of the Jewish Brigade,
who fought the Nazis under the British flag. Others came directly
from the *Yishuv.*[39]

Her Majesty's Navy was no longer busy fighting a war with Axis powers. Instead, from 1945–48, they focused on capturing small, unseaworthy ships in the Mediterranean, overcrowded with survivors, and preventing their entry into Mandate Palestine. At times, the boats were captured close to shore, or even while passengers were disembarking on the beach. Sometimes the British would fire across the bows of these pathetic vessels. If they refused to stop, the British would fire at the hull, heedless of the already tormented lives aboard. Then the ships would be sent back to the ports they came from.[40]

By August 1946, the British had imprisoned 52,000 Holocaust survivors—illegal immigrants—in several primitive detention camps on the Mediterranean island of Cyprus, just 200 miles from the *Yishuv*. Conditions were deplorable. Weeks later, in mid-September, the Colonial Office sent a delegation from the CRREC to Cyprus on a fact-finding mission. The delegation included Dayan Rabbi Dr. Isidore Grunfeld, and his wife, Dr. Judith Grunfeld. While Dayan Grunfeld was involved in many of Schonfeld'S rescue attempts, he also served as a rabbinic judge and representative of the CRREC on various missions. His wife's varied career and experience proved useful for the critical mission to Cyprus.

During the 1920s, she served with Dr. Leo Deutschlander as a primary pedagogue for Soroh Shenirer, founder of the Beth Jacob Teacher's Seminary in Cracow, Poland. It was the training ground for the teachers of the first Orthodox girls' school movement in Poland. Judith came to Poland from Germany in 1923, at the behest of Jacob Rosenheim, president of World Agudath Israel. That same year, his organization had adopted the Beth Jacob girls' school movement and its Teacher's Seminary at the First Knessiah Gedolah (international conference) held in Vienna.[41] This educational movement for women was part of the World Agudah's program to create stronger Orthodox Jewry internationally during the post-World War I era. The religious girls' schools were to act as a foil to rising secular Jewish ideologies attractive to many Orthodox youths.

Judith taught two generations of Beth Jacob teachers and later, its principals. After she married Rabbi Grunfeld and settled in Britain,

she was headmistress of Schonfeld's Hasmonean Girls' School and
retained that position for years.

* * *

The CRREC mission arrived on Cyprus by plane on September
25, 1946, about a month after the British set up the camps. It was the
eve of Rosh Hashanah, and the Grunfelds remained there until
October 23, *Hoshanah Rabbah*. The mission's objective was fact
finding—to inspect the primitive conditions and improve them as
much as possible. They discovered that the British treated the survivors like prisoners of war and surrounded them with barbed wire.
The average incarceration on Cyprus lasted approximately a year.

Among the thousands of inmates there were all shades of
Zionists—from the radical socialist left to the religious Zionist
Mizrachi and Poalei Agudath Israel on the right. There were between
eight and nine hundred Orthodox inmates from across the spectrum,
and a large contingent of former Beth Jacob students and graduates.
Dayan Grunfeld's first order of business was to arrange for High
Holy Day and *Sukkos* services. He convinced many of the non-observant inmates to join a religious service that brought back memories
and warm feelings within their embittered hearts. Many of them had
forsaken all connections to the faith of their parents and
antecedents.[42]

The Orthodox assumed the Grunfelds represented their enemy—
the British. The coldest reception Judith Grunfeld got came from the
least likely source—former Beth Jacob girls and young Orthodox
women. She used her Beth Jacob experience to form a bridge to these
bitter souls by invoking the name of Soroh Shenirer and talking about
their close association. Finally, she broke the ice. The songs she sang
with the girls reminded them of the songs their teachers taught them.
The relationships Judith Grunfeld formed that day lasted her lifetime.

In later years, Judith Grunfeld relished telling the story of a young
Orthodox couple's wedding in the Cypriot camps. Friends sacrificed
their rations to create a beautiful wedding cake and used extraordinary ingenuity and skill to create a wedding dress from scraps of tent

cloth. At first glance, it was not obvious that the beautiful bridal bouquet of white roses was made from scraps of rationed toilet paper. The wedding was an outstanding affair that made up in spirit, song and dance for whatever it lacked in material goods. The Grunfelds even convinced the British authorities to enhance the festivities by giving them extra rations of various items.

The Grunfelds eased the lot of the inmates by setting up a post office connecting them to the rest of the world. The CRREC donated money for food and for consignments of clothing for the internees. In a note of gratitude from the Jewish camp authorities in Cyprus, a request was made of the CRREC to maintain its rabbinic office there, and later, other CRREC delegations continued the missions to Cyprus.

Just prior to taking leave of hundreds of new friends, Judith Grunfeld was presented with a heart-shaped box made with great ingenuity and embroidered in different colored threads from the inmates' tents. This expression of love and admiration was one of her most prized possessions. Years later, when she visited Israel, she renewed many of the friendships begun on Cyprus.[43]

STATISTICS

The sheer number of projects the CRREC undertook by the end of the war is amazing, despite the fact that except for a few volunteers and a few paid staff members, it was essentially a one-man operation. Schonfeld's personality enabled him to deal with Jewish leaders, governmental agencies and non-Jews of every stripe. He remembered and kept track of every child and adult.

Schonfeld was behind most of the fundraising that supported the CRREC's numerous relief, rescue and rehabilitation projects. He raised large sums for relief, rescue and rehabilitation, but never took a penny more than his meager salary as the head of the Adas and the Union.

In all, he raised half a million pounds, not including the various subsidies he received at different times from Jewish organizations and HMG. This is equivalent to $2,500,000 U.S., (a huge sum at the time, when average workers earned $25–$30 per week in the U.S.) Not all the money was raised in Britain. Large contributions came from Jewish communities in the Dominions, and after the war from the Vaad Hatzalah in the United States. He also received some assistance from The Central British Fund, the primary financial arm of the Anglo-Jewish establishment.[44]

CONCLUSION

Schonfeld was more than a thorn in the side of the Anglo-Jewish establishment. In addition to being the "outsider" who turned into a competitor for rescue and relief funds, and whose rescue efforts frequently proved successful in ways and in places where others could not prevail, his long-range impact proved to be far more "dangerous."

Schonfeld greatly strengthened British Orthodox Jewry with sheer numbers, adding about four thousand Orthodox Jews to the community when he rescued them. In addition, the large number of rabbis, teachers and religious functionaries he brought to England were catalysts in strengthening existing Jewish institutions.

Another long-range impact of Schonfeld's rescue efforts was the creation of new institutions such as the Yesodei Hatorah Hasidic Educational System in Britain, founded by one of "Schonfeld's Boys"—Rabbi Shmelke Pinter, and the establishment of the first Jewish Day School in Australia.

Because Schonfeld had the ability to open doors, he frequently obtained the assistance of HMG, members of Parliament and the Anglican clergy without the intercession of the Anglo-Jewish establishment, including the Board of Jewish Deputies. Schonfeld created a self-confident, sometimes militant, independent British Orthodoxy that made the former secular lay leadership more irrelevant than ever.

After Prof. Selig Brodetsky scuttled the Schonfeld-inspired Parliamentary Rescue Resolution in January 1943, he said of the rabbi:

The intervention of an unauthorized individual, however well-intentioned, in a situation to this sort, naturally brings confusion and may have damaging effects.[45]

Furthermore, no citizen has the right to set up his own War Cabinet and run the war as he thought fit.

The Board . . . [has] enjoyed the advantage of accessibility to the British government on matters affecting Jewry inside and particularly outside this country. Any interference with this power would mean the diminution of the power of British Jewry to act on behalf of Jews and would be a crime against Jewish interests.[46]

Eventually, a time came when Schonfeld set down his thoughts in writing. Selections from his essays, addresses and articles were collected in *Message to Jewry* (1959) and *Why Judaism?* (1963). His *Universal Bible: Being the Pentateuchal Text at First Addressed to All Nations* (1955) and *A New-Old Rendering of The Psalms* (1980) represent a creative effort to acquaint the non-Jewish world with the spirit of traditional Judaism. His edition of the *Daily Prayer Book* with a lineal set of references (1973) contains an English translation that is, in places, unusual and profoundly moving.

Rabbi, educator, rescuer, negotiator, counselor, writer—Rabbi Dr. Solomon Schonfeld was one of the most engaging, creative, productive and forceful personalities to be produced by Anglo-Jewry in the modem era.

Shefford children most of whom came from the "Kindertransport."

Young persons' post-war Transport.

Childrens' Transport from Czechoslovakia.

Post-war Polish children. Center, Ruth Linzer an organizer of the Childrens' Transport.

Rebitzin Judith Grunfeld during the period of the Second World War.

Post-war Poland from Childrens' Transport.

Childrens' Transport from post-war Poland.

Childrens' Transport from post-war Poland.

Post-war Childrens' Transport.

Post-war Poland.

Childrens' post-war transfer.

Inauguration of the First Synagogue Ambulance. Chief Rabbi Hertz, center, Rabbi Schonfeld on left. Donated by the Jewish Community of Melbourne, Australia.

Inauguration of the Synagogue Ambulance with installation of a new Sefer Torah. Donated by the Cairo Jewish Community.

Post-war Poland.

Chief Rabbi Joseph P. Hertz.

Judith (Hertz) Schonfeld.

Shefford

*The story of a Jewish School Community
in evacuation 1939–1945*

Illustrated by Daniela S. Grunfeld

VIGNETTES
PART TWO

Part I of this book is about Rabbi Solomon Schonfeld's family background and personality, the influences on his life and the description and analyses of his numerous rescue efforts. Part II personalizes these experiences through the eyes of the people who were rescued by or worked directly with him.

TRIBUTE

AN APPRECIATION OF RABBI SOLOMON SCHONFELD ON THE OCCASION OF HIS 70TH BIRTHDAY, 1982
BY LORD JAKOBOVITS, z"l,
CHIEF RABBI of GREAT BRITAIN

There are few individuals whose achievements leave permanent marks on an entire community. There are even fewer whose single-handed efforts saved thousands of Jews—who multiplied into tens of thousands. Rabbi Dr. Solomon Schonfeld is an Anglo-Jew who did both.

As the principal driving force behind the growth of the Jewish Secondary School movement in England—when such schools encountered hostility and contempt—Rabbi Schonfeld sparked a revolution by changing communal attitudes and transforming the Jewish educational environment. All Jewish day schools owe much of their popularity to Rabbi Schonfeld's pioneering efforts and to the standards he set. The phenomenal expansion of the movement's schools and all day school networks, which encompass some twenty-five percent of all Jewish school children in the country, can be credited to him.

Equally significant has been Rabbi Schonfeld's impact on the regeneration of Jewish life in the British Isles. It was made possible by Holocaust survivors who benefited from the rabbi's monumental rescue work before, during and immediately after WW II. Unlike earlier waves of immigration that were soon absorbed into the secular community, the survivors recreated dynamics and institutions that reflected the vibrancy of European Jewry before it was destroyed. Their continuing proliferation, in size and influence, has already changed the religious contours of Anglo-Jewry beyond recognition, though not without accentuating their polarization. The infusion of this fresh blood of an altogether new type has contributed much to render the formerly acute question of Anglo-Jewish survival hypothetical in the extreme.

Such massive practical achievements are but rarely accompanied by literary creativity as well. It is a measure of Dr. Schonfeld's versatility, no less than his inexhaustible energy, that even at the height of his super-active career he found the peace of mind to produce a variety of books and articles, all of them of great originality.

To a man with such an incomparable record of dedication for the advancement of our faith and our people, on reaching his 70th birthday, it is a privilege to pay homage, in a communal as well as personal capacity, especially as one whose own life and early education owes much to his enterprise. May he live long and in good health to enjoy the rich fruits of his labor, sustained in tranquility by the affection of the community he has done so much to save from the tempests of spiritual and physical destruction and to revitalize through the seeds he helped transplant and cultivate for renewed growth.

A TRIBUTE TO RABBI SOLOMON SCHONFELD
ON THE OCCASION OF HIS 70TH BIRTHDAY, 1982

BY DR. SOLOMON GAON, z"l

Chacham, World Sephardic Federation, Director Sephardic Studies Program, Yeshiva University, New York, NY, U.S.A

I am delighted to join in the tribute to my distinguished colleague, Dr. Solomon Schonfeld, on the occasion of his special birthday. Throughout his life, Dr. Schonfeld has been a man of conviction and deep-felt principles that he never hesitated to proclaim, and for which he fought tirelessly—often at the risk of his personal health.

After the death of his pioneering father, Solomon took up the work of establishing Jewish day schools in London, where he encountered great opposition from many Jewish leaders who felt this special education would tend to isolate the Jewish child from the modern world. But Dr. Schonfeld undauntedly continued to expound the thesis of *Torah im Derekh Eretz* (lit. Torah and the ways of the land—i.e., combining secular and Jewish worlds). The Jewish day school, he believed, has a crucial contribution to make to the survival of Judaism in the modern world, and that conversely, the modern world would have a great deal to gain from the concepts of Torah Judaism.

When Nazism cast its shadow over Europe, Dr. Schonfeld was one of the first to see that Hitler was not merely a transient phenomenon. He embarked on a one-man, whirlwind, cloak-and-dagger venture to save Jewish lives. Thousands owe Dr. Schonfeld their physical and spiritual existence. Many men and women who are prominent leaders in world Jewry today owe their achievements to the fatherly love and guidance that Dr. Schonfeld gave them in such large measure.

Dr. Schonfeld himself is the personification of loyalty to the Torah, and an intrepid fighter for the rightful place of Torah Judaism on the world scene. His courage, steadfastness and devotion to the highest ideals of Judaism are an inspiration to future generations.

May Dr. Schonfeld inspire us for many years to come as he has in the past.

IN GRATITUDE TO RABBI SOLOMON SCHONFELD
ON THE OCCASION OF HIS 70TH BIRTHDAY, 1982
BY DR. JUDITH GRUNFELD, z"l
HEADMISTRESS OF HASMONEAN GIRLS' SCHOOL,
LONDON

God has many messengers. And while we give thanks to Him, we must feel deep gratitude to those who were worthy of being His human agents. And so today, let us remember the rabbi, who, four decades ago, as a young man of 28, devoted every moment of his day to rescuing children and adults. He traveled several times to danger zones in Poland and elsewhcre to bring children to safety. He organized, collected, planned, equipped, petitioned, and used his influence and his God-given sparkling personality to save the lives of his unknown Jewish brethren in deadly peril.

Solomon Schonfeld did this in many ways, through many channels. With the spark of his ingenuity and the force of his personality, he could march through closed doors; talk to deaf ears; melt stubborn hearts; bend the iron rules and cut the red tape. His car could glide through the thickest traffic; his voice could penetrate through the most Anglo-Saxon stillness and stir it with the flash of his eye, his sparkling youth and his zest for life. His whole being was directed toward one aim: to bring just one more person over, to rescue just one more life.

The Chief Rabbi's Religious Emergency Council (the CRREC) was his organization, his instrument. Behind it, he was at work, quick as lightning, sharp, intent, unrelenting, demanding. There was unabashed hope in his approach. He was untiring, even forgetful of the strain under which he and others labored throughout the day, throughout the night, to place one more name among the chosen ones, to chose one more for life on the slippery, treacherous road to safety, to carry one more child into the haven of freedom and future—one more, more, and still more.

So many of the little children we see skipping and dancing so gracefully, so comforting to our hearts, filling the Jewish schools, the *chadorim*, to overflowing, are *neshamos* (souls) that he has, as it were, brought down to earth from the great heavenly storehouse of the Almighty. He did it by saving those to whom it was then given to build up true Jewish homes and families upon the ruins and ashes of the past.

When we look around and see flourishing *yeshivos*, *chadorim*, Jewish day schools and boarding schools in London and in the Provinces, we find that many of those who took a leading part in the establishment of these schools and gave them their lifeblood were once names on Dr. Schonfeld's list. Through his initiative, these people regained life and meaning through his agency, becoming active in Jewish life, multiplying life and blessing.

These few lines mirror the feelings of so many. A great debt of gratitude is acknowledged, and words of blessing are sent out from all corners of the world to Rabbi Dr. S. Schonfeld, who served *Hakadosh Baruch Hu* (G-d) by dedicating his time, energy, strength and youthful vigor to the rescue of his fellow Jews.

CHAPTER 8

KINDERTRANSPORTS - VIENNA

WITH CROOKED TEETH, SMILING
by Frieda Stolzberg Korobkin

We are walking to the river, Papa and I. In reality, I am not walking, but gliding over water, sailing on air. The pavement is liquid beneath my feet, which have no momentum of their own. My arm has forgotten to ache from being suspended at Papa's side, and my hand, which he has clamped tightly between his long, thin fingers, is numb, entirely without feeling. There is no feeling in any part of my body, except in my chest where a joyous constriction reaches right up to my throat and threatens to choke off my breathing. I am completely weightless, without substance.

Papa soars besides me, above me. In his free hand he holds the thick tome that accompanies him wherever he goes. For once, it arouses no jealousy within me. It is enough to be at his side. Today I have no brother, no sister and no mother. There is just Papa and me. Papa, in his black coat and hat with his dark red beard attached to his lean, ascetic face, his forehead marked on either temple by fine, thin veins which nevertheless stand out like auxiliary roads on a country map.

I, in a long-sleeved, faded cotton dress which once was bright with clusters of spring flowers when my sister first wore it; and on my feet the cracked brown shoes which look more and more like the faces of two nonagenarians; shoes which lace right up past my ankles and have known two other pairs of feet before mine.

We are floating along in the direction of the park that leads down to the river. Why am I not in school? Is it because my kindergarten teacher has reported that I spat into my classmate's spinach the day before? Nothing has been said. I get up in the morning and there is

Papa, in a good mood, folding his prayer shawl and wanting to know whether a certain young miss would like to accompany her father today? Except he does not say "accompany" but uses a less formal phrase, something like "tag along." One would never suspect that only the night before he and my mother exchanged harsh words; words which assaulted me in my half-sleeping, half-waking state and which, as always, concerned Die Kinder; words which left my mother weeping. In recent months there have been either sigh-filled silences between them or voices, once quiet, raised in unaccustomed anger, or, perhaps, in pain.

We are sitting on the grass verge that slopes down to meet the not-so-blue Danube. (Why can't the song tell the truth?) The water makes gentle, musical sounds as it washes against the shore. I open the bag that I have brought with me, scoop out a handful of salt and carefully begin to sprinkle the river with it. Somewhere I have heard that salty water keeps people afloat even if they are unable to swim and I am determined that the Danube shall be buoyant for non-swimmers like myself. A pleasure boat cruises up the center of the river on an early summer outing.

Music blares from the boat and carries to the spot where we are sitting. Papa looks up from his book, his thumb frozen in midair as it comes up from its nosedive over the open page, his other hand arrested in the act of caressing his beard. He is staring across the water, not seeing; his lips move as if not sure of the words. This pose of his, one I have seen before and with increasing frequency of late, has the power each time to shred my insides into ribbons of anguish. I continue my activity but the joy has gone out of it. Small gray waves swish up in quick, frenzied motions from the boat's wake and reach almost to our feet.

Papa's voice. I turn quickly, gladly. He speaks slowly, still gazing out in the same sightless way over the water that now is empty and calm. Surprisingly, he is talking about genii. What, he wants to know, would I wish for if a genie were suddenly to appear? I do not have to think. This is easy. I laugh, delighted with the game. "Half-shoes, Papa. Oh! half-shoes!" Then I think to myself: I will be like the Ginzburg girls, the only girls on our street with "half-shoes." Papa's soft, brown eyes lose their dead, vacant look as they focus on me and come to life again.

He throws back his head and laughs with me, revealing his two crooked bottom teeth that overlap. I realize that I have not heard him laugh or seen that crooked smile in weeks. Then he pats me on the head and continues smiling.

Saying nothing, he just pats me on the head and smiles.

November. It is cold—a bone-eroding cold, outside and inside. There is no longer any heat in the flat. Papa sits, no, crouches over his book day and night, swaying to and fro, to and fro, his overcoat never leaving his back. He drinks endless glasses of hot tea and when his hands are not wrapped around the warm glass, they rub each other in a steady washing motion in his lap. My sister, my brother and I play our games in half-hearted fashion, desultorily. Even our squabbles are without enthusiasm.

There is little food left. They have closed our grocery store. First they broke all the windows and ransacked the shelves, then my parents are ordered to sweep up the broken glass and debris, then to kneel and scrub the pavement. I did not witness this indignity. The windows of our flat face the back courtyard and we younger children are not allowed downstairs anymore. Every morning my mother leaves the house with my sister, each of them carrying a saucepan. They line up outside the community center for the daily food ration.

Each day they creep home a little more weary and silent than the day before and climb fully clothed into one bed where they cling to each other for warmth. My brother and I climb in, too, fighting for a place next to our mother. Fighting to get on top of her, under her, inside her, back inside her womb.

"Nein! Nein! Nein! Josef. Nein!" my mother screams. Then her voice shatters into convulsive sobs. Their voices again insinuate themselves into my sleep. But this time only my mother's is raised. Papa speaks softly, resignedly, sadly. "Es muss so sein." A decision has been reached. It must be so.

Again my hand is in his. But this time I do not feel the actual flesh of his fingers, just the long, bony outlines, for my hands are protected by mittens attached to each other by a long string drawn through my coat sleeves and around my neck. His hands, too, are encased in gloves, but his grip is hard and tight, tighter than I can ever remember, as if he will never let me go. He has forsaken his book for an old brown leather suitcase miraculously held together by an apologetic piece of string and my mother's prayers. Again I am alone with Papa.

My brother and my sister, who trudge in the snow alongside us carrying paper bundles also tied with string, are mere shadows, nonexistent. It is nighttime. The streets are brightly lit and busy. Soldiers, civilians, people throng everywhere. It is some time since I have been outside at night and I look around, taking in the Christmas ornaments, the flags and the pictures that are everywhere. A strange-looking man with penetrating eyes and a funny mustache looks down on me at every turn. We are jostled by some soldiers. There is a flash of steel. Papa tugs at my hand. I look up. His beard is no longer there. Just a jagged red mess attached to his chin. Laughter. I cannot move.

My legs are frozen to the spot just as they were one afternoon a few months ago, when, on coming into our building after playing with my friends, I saw the Storm Troopers. The armbands with their compelling, invincible insignia have a hypnotic effect on me. I cannot take my eyes from them. I cannot move. Papa is thrown against the wall, jerking me after him. More laughter. Silently, we continue on our way. Not once has he uttered a sound. I peer up at him. His lip is bleeding; his face has taken on the hue of cold ashes. The yellow streetlights reflect ghoulishly in his eyes, which stare sightlessly ahead. My hand stays glued to his, his to mine.

Three days later, in sleeting rain, we arrive in London: my sister, my brother and I. We sleep in a large room, a dormitory filled with children. A family comes to adopt me. Temporarily. "For the duration." A husband and wife with two sons. They live in a real house with rooms both upstairs and downstairs, all of them heated. There is a bathroom upstairs with two taps, one for hot water, the other for cold. Downstairs there is even a separate lavatory with a sink and two more taps. Not at all like our flat with its one lavatory and cold water and wooden bathtub, which, on bath nights, was dragged to the center of the floor from under the kitchen table and filled with water heated on the stove.

These people must be rich. On the very first day they buy me new clothes; a dress, a skirt, some blouses and jumpers, new underwear. And two pairs of "half-shoes." One is for school, with laces. Black. The other pair, also black, is for "dress" with an ankle strap. It is to be worn with white socks that reach all the way up to my knees. It is much fancier than the Ginzburg girls' shoes. The shoes for "dress" are very glossy and smooth. Their shiny surface is like a mirror in which I behold my image as it slithers elusively about in ripply waves. I hold one shoe up to my face and peer into its black looking glass. A face peers back at me. His face: distorted, smiling, with crooked teeth.

MY FIRST HALF-CROWN
by Felicia Druckman

"*Hast du Taschengeld?*" ("Have you got pocket money?") asked the tall man with the red beard and the incredibly blue eyes which were fixed on my face as if he really wanted to know the answer.

It was a few days into January 1939. We were in London and it was cold and wet. There were no blue skies and no sun. I was part of a children's transport that arrived from Vienna and I felt doubly alien, for my parents did not belong to Agudath Israel. I found myself at Northfield, where a host of well-meaning ladies scurried hither and thither, asking questions, yet never had the time actually to listen to a reply. For days, no one had looked at me as an individual—I was just one among many, who had to be fed and accommodated and now, suddenly, here was someone actually asking me a question, wanting to know and waiting for an answer.

I shook my head, indicating "No," whereupon Rabbi Schonfeld handed me a half-crown, which became my first English *Taschengeld.*

The buxom lady standing next to him was one of the many members of the Jewish community who had been invited to open their hearts and homes to Dr. Schonfeld's children, and he was giving me a send-off into my new life with a sympathetic foster mother. There must have been dozens of children leaving Northfield that evening, yet it seemed to me as if he had all the time in the world for me and this was the only moment since I left Vienna that I felt someone really cared about me.

I did not come face to face with Dr. Schonfeld again until, after Shefford, I somehow landed in the office of the Chief Rabbi's Religious Emergency Council. I have always suspected that I got the job because I was "one of Rabbi Schonfeld's children," and he felt that a place had to be found for me. Whatever the reason, I am deeply grateful for the opportunity it gave me to work under his inspired direction. For was it not inspiration when he decided that mobile synagogues, which could be turned into ambulances, would be required as Allied troops moved further into Germany toward the end of the war?

It seemed to me then that the idea was born in one minute, crystallized in the next and executed in the third. For instance, there came the day when Dr. Schonfeld decided that a boat should be chartered to go to Gdynia (Gdansk) and get out all the Jewish children who were with non-Jewish families in Poland. He said, "Charter me a boat," and though the remarks were not directed at me, I sat there, opposite him in the big room at "86" and marveled at the implausibility of the order, for an order it undoubtedly was.

Three minutes later—or so it seemed—he was off to Gdynia and soon after that, practically the whole of his staff found itself at, I think, Brown's Wharf, watching the boat dock with its cargo of children. I believe Dr. Schonfeld himself had disembarked at Tilbury, so that he could be in London to meet the boat. I shall never forget the cheer that went up when the children caught sight of him.

Though I do not think I was aware of it at the time, I have now realized the extent to which Rabbi Schonfeld influenced my life merely by treating me as a person, rather than just another "refugee." There were many instances of this, and I think he might find it amusing if I recall just a very few of them:

The first unforgettable thing that happened soon after I started as an office junior at the CRREC, doing menial jobs such as making tea, licking stamps and attending to the filing, was when I came across some correspondence relating to my three months' course at Pitman's

College in Bedford. I had never been told that I was expected to repay
the tuition fee that had been advanced for me, so I was very surprised
and angered to read the remarks which the General Secretary (who
shall remain nameless!) had written in the margin and which injured
pride has etched ineradicably into my memory: "She will never repay
this."

I felt that honor naturally demanded that I repay the debt forth-
with; however, I lacked the means to do so. I took the first opportunity to speak to Rabbi Schonfeld and somehow stammered out my
suggestion that a shilling or two be deducted from my salary every
week. While I delivered myself of this suggestion, he slid further
down into his chair, stretched his legs and reached for the Royalty
cigarettes in the silver packet. There was a pause during which I
feared he would demand the whole amount. With hindsight, I now
think he was really laughing at me for being so pompous, particularly since he was well aware that I lacked the wherewithal.

But he just smiled and forbade me to raise the subject again. The
matter, he said, was closed and he did not wish me to repay the money.
I walked about for weeks afterwards hoping that the General Secretary
would challenge me on the subject, so that I could say to him, "Dr.
Schonfeld did not wish me to repay the money," but the gentleman
never raised the matter and so I never had my moment of glory.

Another incident I recall vividly came when we were all working
so hard in connection with the Bernadotte scheme [Mauritius??] and
Dr. Schonfeld was enlisting the help of prominent Members of
Parliament. The thunderclouds had gathered on his forehead, which
meant he was tired and worried, but I was totally unprepared when,
one *Erev* Shabbos, I found myself alone in the office with him and he
suddenly told me off for something about which I had been totally in
the dark.

I remember fury going through me like lightning at the injustice
of the accusation. In a moment of mental aberration, I stamped my
foot and actually shouted at him, "Don't you shout at me like this!"
The moment the words were out, I became aware of the enormity of
my *chutzpah* (gall). I stood rooted to the spot, expecting the wrath of
Dr. Schonfeld to strike me down, but nothing happened. The silence

became ominous and I wished I were dead. But as no chasm appeared in the floor to engulf me and put an end to the situation, I started to formulate an apology. However, no words came. I was literally paralyzed with fear. He reached for his Royalty, took a puff, stretched his legs and burst into hearty laughter! I cannot really remember much of what ensued, except that the Bishop of Chichester rang in person to speak to Dr. Schonfeld and I was so "shell-shocked" that I could not operate the switchboard!

He never told me off again. The rapport had been established—he teased me and I was cheeky. I did my work to the best of my ability, because I wanted him to see how much I appreciated the special understanding he showed me, of which the following is a further illustration:

A quarrel with my then current boyfriend brought about a break in the relationship and, in the way typical of the young I felt my world had come to an end. I once studied piano and thought that a headlong plunge into taking up the piano again would give some purpose to my "shattered" life. The piano teacher whom I approached offered me the use of her instrument on which to practice at 8:30 every weekday morning, as my foster mother's home did not have a piano.

If I took up the teacher's offer—and I desperately wanted to do so—It would mean that I could not start work on time. I explained my predicament and asked Dr. Schonfeld whether I might be permitted to come in a little later, provided I took a shorter lunch hour. I naturally expected a refusal, because it really was an impertinent request, but he said that if a young person wanted to take up music again, nobody should stand in the way of that ambition and I should go ahead. I persevered and—in spite of a conspicuous absence of talent—got as far as being able to play the First Movement of the Moonlight Sonata. Then I met Harold and, no longer suffering from a need to drown my sorrows in music, I promptly gave it all up. But Rabbi Schonfeld's ability to sense my unhappiness and help me get over it with so much understanding meant a great deal to me and has never been forgotten.

Nor have I forgotten the many happy hours I spent with Lord Wedgwood, to whom he sent me—first of all to help with some paper work—as he was one of our patrons. He and I got on well together, so he requested that I be allowed to work for him a couple of times a week. I spent frequent Sunday mornings working at his flat in Dolphin Square and many a weekday afternoon at the house. The first time I arrived at Westminster, I told the policeman on duty at the door I was Lord Wedgwood's secretary. They asked me in, called Lord Wedgwood to the telephone and passed on the message, which was "to send up his little ray of sunshine."

That was what he called me to his dying day, and so did Lady Wedgwood, with whom I remained in contact for years afterward. Lord Wedgwood was an ardent Zionist and often asked me why the Jews did not fight for their land, because he thought that was the only way that they could attain it. Sadly, he did not live to see the State of Israel established.

Being Lord Wedgwood's secretary made me feel rather important at a time when I was very much aware of my own insignificance. "Refugee Committees," though well intentioned, somehow aggravated that awareness and that is why Rabbi Schonfeld's personal attention to my problems meant so much to me.

So, on the occasion of Rabbi Schonfeld's seventieth birthday, this cheeky child of his, now somewhat old and gray and battered by life, would like to send him all good wishes and, above all, to thank him for everything; for saving my life, for Shefford and for my early working years with him. And—I almost forgot—thanks also for my first half-crown.

THE PIED PIPER
by Naomi E. Grunfeld
New York, NY

Reliving my childhood impressions, I see Dr. Schonfeld before me as I saw him then, a handsome, powerful personality who commanded respect and admiration. We looked up to him as our guide, our rabbi and friend, as the one who seemed to us able to solve all problems and bring good cheer into every dull assembly.

I remember clearly how one morning he strode into the school hall followed by a trail of shy, bewildered children who were unable to communicate because they had come to us from Poland. Most of them, we soon discovered, did not know the fate of their parents. Those who knew were still too shattered by the cruel separation to want to think about it. But their eyes were focused on one man: they were drawn to him as if searching for strength, support and guidance.

This was their "Pied Piper," and they followed him unquestioningly; he was their handsome hero, who promised them nothing, but had a magic power that imparted comfort and hope and drew the children around him with a magnetic force. How does a child instinctively know whom to trust? Not by any process of logic but by infallible intuition.

And so Dr. Schonfeld, young though he was, became father to them all. Those children whose parents were left to the cruel fate devised by the Nazis received new life and courage from this man's magnetic power.

I often meet many of these now grown-up children in the United States, South Africa and Israel. They are parents now and even grandparents. All of them are grateful and marvel at the pure moral courage of a man who, against all odds, risked his life over and over to help those teetering on the verge of disaster. No one asked him to do this and he asked for no reward. But posterity, where perspectives are fair, will record the blessed fruits of his endeavors.

I personally owe him an immeasurable debt of gratitude for an immortal lesson in courage. One is privileged if in a lifetime one gets to know even one man like Dr. Solomon Schonfeld.

THE STUDENTS HELP
by Yitzhak (Arnold) Loewe

As a former pupil of the Jewish Secondary School, I am happy to have an opportunity to express my gratitude to Rabbi Dr. Schonfeld and my admiration for his unique devotion to the refugees from Nazi Germany. I feel deeply indebted to him for all that he has done for me.

Two events from my association with Rabbi Schonfeld stand out with special clarity. One Friday afternoon—I think it was the Shabbos just before Chanukah 1938—we, a group of pupils of the top form, were just about to leave the school premises when Dr. Schonfeld's car pulled up. He leaped out of it and harshly commanded us:

"No one will leave this building now!" He signaled us to follow him into his office, where he explained in short and terse words what he wanted of us.

He had said he had just succeeded in obtaining, as he put it, a thousand visas from the Home Office, which would enable him to rescue a thousand children from Vienna. All personal data of these children had to be recorded on the visa forms from a list of children prepared by the Agudath Israel in Vienna.

"I need all the help I can get," said Dr. Schonfeld. "Each one of you must take part in this work. I must have the documents filled out properly at once, so I can take them back to the Home Office before Shabbos. I must urge you to be extremely careful when you copy the names and addresses of these children on the forms. Any mistake, any incorrect data will make the visa invalid and this will mean sacrificing a Jewish life."

These words so forcefully spoken by the Rav are still in my mind. We all felt we had been chosen for a momentous task and applied ourselves to it with great concentration. We completed the work half an hour before Shabbos. Dr. Schonfeld sped off to the Home Office with the big bundle of papers. By the time he arrived at the Home Office, of course, Shabbos had already begun. So he left his car parked wherever it was at the time and returned from Whitehall to his home in Lordship Park on foot. The great lesson in saving lives we received that day is still engraved upon my heart.

I recall *Sukkos* in Shefford during the war. Six other boys and I were billeted at the imposing mansion of the Rector of Campton. We explained to him the nature and purpose of a *Sukkah* according to Biblical law. The cleric immediately instructed his head gardener to cut some branches and help us erect a "Tabernacle" according to our wishes. He permitted us to open his garage doors and keep them open for eight days so we could use them as two walls for the *Sukkah*.

The villagers of Campton had never seen anything like it before. Our *Sukkah* in the rector's beautiful, much-respected house became a village event, because the villagers were impressed with us, a group of young boys away from home, who were trying hard to keep the laws of their religion in strange surroundings. We somehow aroused great admiration among the country folk, who had never been in contact with Jews before. Early every morning, they watched us march up the hill, no matter how cold the winter or how high the snow, to attend early morning services. Some boys had to walk three kilometers to be in time for the morning *minyan*. The villagers watched in amazement as they saw us conscientiously upholding our traditions, no matter what befell us.

Behind all this, ever encouraging, was the imposing and admired figure of Rabbi Dr. Schonfeld, whose care for us (including the provision of kosher food in those crucial war years) was always evident. These and similar memories helped us along the difficult path of rebuilding our lives.

THE *MOSSER*
by Rabbi Joseph Elias
Monsey

I was a teenager who came to pre-war London because I was accepted as a student in the Secondary School. I saw Dr. Schonfeld as a larger-than-life figure, who dominated all around him; and they, in turn, regarded him with awe and boundless admiration. I can still see him in my mind's eye, striding along at his hurried pace, towering over the lesser [shorter] mortals around him. He literally overflowed with energy and ideas, even when he was on the verge of total exhaustion.

One episode above all remains forever in my memory. Shortly before the outbreak of World War II, Dr. Schonfeld cajoled more and yet more visas from the Home Office for his children's transports.

The auditorium of the Jewish Secondary School and every other available nook and cranny in the building was filled with folding beds. An overly pedantic member of Rabbi Schonfeld's committee thought that this was insane and dutifully reported Rabbi Schonfeld to the Home Office, accusing him of not really having adequate facilities to accommodate the children.

Dr. Schonfeld was horrified that this one man's lack of understanding might force the Home Office to stop his rescue operations and thereby hundreds of Jewish children might be lost. Dr. Schonfeld rushed to the Home Office to undo the damage. In the mean time, the rescue committee was called into session and waited at the rabbi's home office in North London.

I was working as a volunteer, translating the flood of heart-rending letters that came from German and Austrian parents asking us to save their children. I was sitting in the front room when the door opened and Dr. Schonfeld strode in. He threw open the door to the room where the committee was in session. He stood in the doorway and drew himself up to his full height; looked around and then, saw the man he was looking for, and uttered these words, *"Mosser!* (Informer!) Out!"* There was dead silence as the man rose and walked out. When he was gone, the committee immediately continued to plan rescue attempts.

I did not see—did not really want to see—who the man was. That was not important. After all, this poor fellow was only one of many who did not understand that Hitler's threats were meant in earnest. What was important to me was that Dr. Schonfeld understood and demonstrated his unshakable determination to save Jewish lives, a determination that brooked no obstacles.

We can only wonder—with no little anguish—what could have been accomplished during the war if the Jewish world at large had displayed the same determination as our beloved rabbi. That determination was the basis of all that Dr. Schonfeld achieved and for this we will always be in his debt.

THERE CAME A RAY OF HOPE
by Miriam Schwartz, nee Goldschmidt
London

I was a refugee from Nazi Germany. My late father, Mr. Max Goldschmidt, was deputy headmaster and teacher at the *"Israelitische Volksschule"* in Frankfurt-am-Main. In 1938 we desperately wrote dozens of letters asking for help to many parts of the world, so that we might be able to emigrate. My father was still headmaster of the school, but for how much longer could he continue? The answers from abroad were all disappointing.

Relatives who had emigrated as early as 1933 were unable to help us because they themselves were still struggling to build up a new existence. We were depressed and downcast. Then one day there came a ray of hope. We heard that the Chief Rabbi's [Religious] Emergency Council in London was issuing permits for teachers and rabbis and their families, on condition that some kind persons would provide the money for their support in England. We later learned that Dr. Schonfeld was the main person on that committee. One of my father's students, Raphael Posen, who had already emigrated to London and was living with his uncle and aunt—the very well-known, kind and generous Rabbi David and Mrs. Sassoon—appealed to the Sassoons to sponsor our permit and to place our family of five persons on the Chief Rabbi's list.

Had it not been for the kindness of the Chief Rabbi's Council, which was headed by Rabbi Dr. Schonfeld, and the great generosity of the Sassoon family, we would have gone with the other six million Jews.

We will always be grateful to Rabbi Schonfeld and the Sassoon family.

WE NEED MORE CHILDREN!
by Thea Fingerhut, nee Ginsburg
New York

1938 was a year of fear and terror for all the Jews of Vienna. I was seventeen at the time. Through the intervention of people I knew only slightly, I received a permit to go to London. I was safe in England, but my heart was full of pain and anxiety. I had left my family behind in Vienna. How would I find a way to help them?

"Go to Dr. Schonfeld," I was told. "He will help." With trepidation I went to him and told him about my three sisters and my one brother who were still in Vienna. "What? Four children?" Dr. Schonfeld exclaimed. "This is not enough for a transport. We need more children! Get me more names of children in Vienna!" I wrote home. My father promptly sent me a list of twenty-five more names. Eventually all these children arrived in England. I myself saw Dr. Schonfeld send drivers to Oxford Street with handwritten instructions; they returned with truckloads of cots, beds, towels, blankets and pillows. The young lady who worked in Dr. Schonfeld's office called me to help her.

We took over the elegant parlor in his mother's house at 35 Lordship Park. After storing the beautiful antique china and silver in a safe place, we set up two rows of beds—around fourteen of them— In front of the mantelpiece, and a row of cots on the opposite side for the younger children. Soon Mrs. Schonfeld's beautiful parlor looked like the dormitory of a camp.

What a joy it was when my sister arrived in London on December 22, 1938! (Today she is the mother and grandmother of a large family.) On January 12, 1939 my two younger sisters, along with our only brother, who was then ten years old, arrived. (Today he is a rabbi in the U.S.A.)

Dr. Schonfeld gave us care and attention. I remember how we all received new clothes for the first *Yomim Tovim* after our arrival in England. We were cared for at the hostel in Stamford Hill, 250 girls in all. We lacked nothing.

Life, with its tasks and problems, has obliterated many memories. But the comfort and the guidance that Dr. Schonfeld, this cheerful, energetic man, gave us will stand out in my mind forever.

THE GIANT
by Frieda Stolzberg Korobkin
Los Angeles, CA, U.S.A

The train is having a hard time getting through the snow. It labors forward a few yards, then churns back. Forward and then back again. The snow flies off the wheels and hisses softly against the train's windows, a myriad of tiny, whispering serpents. There are no men to clear the tracks. They are all in the army, the army of the Third Reich. Through the windows the landscape rolls away in one vast downy blanket for as far as the eye can see. A benign winter sun glistens playfully on the glacial surface. The Fatherland is pure and white and peaceful, entirely without menace. My sister hugs me against her for warmth in the unheated compartment.

Someone, one of the volunteers, comes around carrying mugs containing a steaming, foul-smelling liquid. This is tea, we are told: English tea made with milk. Drink it, the volunteer urges, it is nourishing and will warm your insides. We examine the strange mixture with suspicion. Tentatively, we take a sip, then shudder and grimace with disgust. Are they trying to poison us? The volunteer has gone on to the next compartment. Quickly, the boy nearest the window slides it open a crack and slops the alien brew out on to the snow where a brown stain immediately appears and spreads on the white surface, then recedes. It has taken only a moment, but in that short time a gust of arctic air had entered our compartment, making the atmosphere even more frigid than before. We stamp our feet and flap our arms around our bodies. Then we start to sing.

Steam rises from our mouths to the swaying ceiling as we sing songs with Hebrew words that everybody knows. We sing *Artza Alinu*. Someone attempts a song in German about a hat that has three corners. He is quickly hushed. We don't want to hear any more

German. We are going to a new country where we will learn a new language.

In this painfully slow fashion our *kindertransport* crosses from Austria into Germany and then into Holland. A journey that normally takes no more than a day has taken three. What has started as an outing, an exciting adventure, no longer seems quite so appealing. As soon as we cross the Dutch border everyone breathes deeply as if we have been saving our breath until this moment. Now we are safe. Safe to complain that we are cold, that we are tired and hungry. Safe to cry for our mothers.

"Why are you sending us away?" we asked our parents. "Where are we going? When will we see you again?"

"It is just for a little while," they reassured us, my father sighing, my mother's eyes filling with tears as she turned away wringing her hands in anguish. This time, they told us, this time only the children were allowed to go. The mothers and fathers and grandparents would follow in another train.

"When?" We wanted to know.

"We don't know exactly when," they replied. "Perhaps in a few weeks, a few months. But we will see you soon. Everything will be all right. Do you understand, children? Everything will be all right."

"We understand," we said, not understanding.

"Don't worry, children. You will be well taken care of. There is a man, a wonderful man, who has arranged this trip for you. He will meet your train. His name is Rabbi Dr. Schonfeld and he will take good care of you until we arrive. So you must listen to him and do as he says and be good children and make us very proud and we will all be together again soon, you will see."

In Holland we were taken to a building near the docks, where motherly volunteers hovered over us and catered to our needs. While we waited to board the ship that would carry us to England they fed us. It was nice to be on firm land for a little while without the constant shaking from side to side, backward and forward; it was nice to be warm and fussed over. Perhaps the trip would turn out well, after all. But where was the man our parents told us about?

Where was this Pied Piper a foreigner who nevertheless has such a comforting, *Umlaut*-sounding name? Where was this Rabbi Dr. Schonfeld? There was a commotion near the door. Everyone's eyes were drawn in that direction. The volunteers stopped their ministrations to turn, with adoring looks in their eyes. A man has entered. But no, he is not really a man; he is more like a giant.

Like the giants in the Bible stories our father used to tell us on Friday nights, he is big and tall and broad-shouldered, with a firm, strong stride and a ruddy beard and an undulating voice that is craggy like mountain ridges. He is quite old, like our father, 40 at least. But no, on the other hand he seems quite young, in fact ageless. That voice of his booms across the enormous hall and immediately captures everyone's attention. I do not listen to what he is saying, but peer out at him fearfully from behind my sister's skirt where I have taken refuge.

He has begun to move around the room, pausing here and there to chat with some of the children. His mountainous laugh reverberates through the room, making me quiver with apprehension.

"What is that behind your back?" the giant asks my sister, and at the same time shoots out his arm and pulls me from my hiding place. "What have we here?" he thunders, as I look fearfully up into his eyes that are a disturbing shade of blue. But no, perhaps they are green. It is impossible to tell. He bends down, impaling me with his gaze like a helpless butterfly, and in a voice very grim and serious inquires, "Can a little girl like you speak Yiddish?"

Ah, I think to myself, you believe you have found me out, but I will show you! "Yes," I answer defiantly, no longer afraid, "I can speak Yiddish."

"Then say something!" he commands, his eyes flashing, amused.

I realize I must say something that will make this big giant go away. But what? Ah, yes, I have it! My voice is steady and bold as I say to him, "Take your feet over your shoulders, and run!" And I only just manage not to stick out my tongue for good measure.

The giant straightens up and throws back his head, and his beard begins to wobble up and down and then he lets out a gust of laughter that sends me back behind my sister, not so much in fear now as in consternation, for this is not the reaction I expected. Once more he puts out his arm, but this time it is to draw me gently to his side.

"Very good!" he says, holding me close to him, still laughing. "Very good, my *Yiddishe maidele*."

Many, many years later, I arrived in London on a visit from my home in Los Angeles, a married woman with children older than I was when I first landed in England before the war. I hesitated about telephoning Dr. Schonfeld, feeling quite certain that he would not remember me out of all the hundreds of children he rescued both before the war and after. But, of course, he did. His voice had not changed from what I remembered. It was still firm, vigorous and authoritative with that distinctive, charismatic timbre, the voice of a giant.

He inquired after my sisters and my brother, recalling their names with ease, and spoke of many other children in my group as if he had only seen them yesterday. As I was about to hang up, he asked, "Do you still speak Yiddish?" "Yes, of course I do," I innocently replied, puzzled by the question. "In that case," he said, his voice alive with mischief and memory, "in that case, throw your feet over your shoulders, and run!"

His laughter still echoes in my ears.

HE SACRIFICED HIS OWN COMFORT
by Leo Schick
New York, NY

I was born in Vienna. Our family consisted of my father, Joseph Schick, my mother, three sisters, my brother, me and a nine-year-old orphan girl—a distant relative my parents had taken in. My father was a *gabbai* (sexton) in the *Schiffschul*. In 1938, when Hitler came to Austria, my father was at first in no hurry to leave. He figured that this Hitler thing would only be temporary. But he did get affidavits for my oldest sister and for the distant relative who was still living with us then. So, half a year or so later, both girls went to America.

One of them was employed for a time as a governess at the home of Irving Bunim (the well-known American Jewish philanthropist) in

Brooklyn. My brother, a second sister, the other sister who now has a restaurant in Brooklyn, and I, went to England. We got there with the help of Rabbi Dr. Solomon Schonfeld.

Dr. Schonfeld had been a *talmid* (student) at the Yeshiva of Nitra for a year. He studied under Rabbi Michoel Ber Weissmandl. For a time, both Dr. Schonfeld and Rabbi Weissmandl boarded, in Tirnau (Trnava) with an uncle of mine, whose name was also Schick.

In 1938 Rabbi Weissmandl visited London, where he established a close relationship with Dr. Schonfeld. At that time, just before the outbreak of World War II, Dr. Schonfeld had a "paper yeshiva." This meant that there was a rabbi in Poland who wanted to come over to England, and so Rabbi Schonfeld wrote to the Home Office and told them he was setting up a yeshiva in London, a rabbinical college, and needed the man as a teacher there. Then Rabbi Schonfeld heard about a rabbi from a Lithuanian yeshiva who also wanted to come out.

So again, he engaged a second *rosh yeshiva.* But Schonfeld's yeshiva had no students. Therefore, Rabbi Michoel Ber Weissmandl submitted thirteen names of boys still in Vienna who would be the students. I was one of them. Again, Rabbi Schonfeld wrote to the Home Office, saying that thirteen boys from Vienna had applied for admission to the new rabbinical college in London, and that he, Dr. Schonfeld, would take personal responsibility for their maintenance.

The visas were granted immediately. However, we had trouble getting an exit permit from Austria. We had to have an income tax clearance from the Austrian government. My father owed taxes and did not have the money to pay them. My parents had to scrape together a couple of hundred marks before I could get a passport to leave Vienna. As a result, I was one of the last of the thirteen boys to come out. Perhaps I was even the very last one.

Meanwhile, in England, Dr. Schonfeld went to the Home Office and asked for visas for another three hundred children. When he got them, the *Kultusgemeinde* in Vienna refused to pay the travel expenses for the trip to England because they claimed other organizations were already taking care of such children.

Eventually, the first transport of three hundred children left Austria for England. In addition, Rabbi Schonfeld brought out fifty older boys, yeshiva students, and another fifty *baaleh batim*, married family men. He also brought out a number of outstanding rabbis from Austria, including Rabbi Shlomo Baumgarten and Rabbi Isaiah Fuerst, both connected with the *Schiffschul*. He brought out Jews from Germany as well, but not many children. There was no need for that at the time. The German Jews, by and large, had more money than the Jewish community in Vienna, and they generally left together with their children.

Following my arrival in London, I lived at Dr. Schonfeld's school. The other boys and I had our meals with various families—one week at this home, one week at that home. Dr. Schonfeld had made the arrangements. I *davened* (prayed) at his synagogue. By that time, he had organized a yeshiva where he taught a *shiur* (Talmud class) at the Adas Yisroel at Green Lanes.

Rabbi Schonfeld was not my rebbe in the personal sense of the word. But I saw him and spoke to him several times each week. I acted as the spokesman for the boys. When we needed something, or they wanted to ask Rabbi Schonfeld something, I spoke on their behalf. Dr. Schonfeld was then twenty-eight or twenty-nine years old. He was absorbed in his work day and night, for there were plenty of problems.

For one thing, he had a lot of opposition in his own *kehillah*. His community had organized a committee to raise, I think, £10,000—a large amount, because at that time one pound was $5 U.S.—to bring five or ten children over to England and provide for them. But he wanted to bring out more than five children; he had taken upon himself the responsibility of bringing out three hundred. When he received the three hundred visas he did not have even one meal ready for the children. But by the time they arrived in England he managed to provide decent meals for them and they slept in the rooms of his school building.

He had, at that time, two schools in which he emptied out the classrooms. That was where the children slept. But it turned out that even this did not give him enough room. So, he emptied out his own house. Several rabbis who came out from Germany took care of the children and eventually certain families in London took them into their homes.

Dr. Schonfeld had plenty of trouble with the boys, especially those who were from ten to fifteen years old. Actually, they came from the best families, and eventually they became big assets to the Jewish communities in which they settled. But at the time, they were very wild; some were beaten by the Nazis in the streets of Vienna, and they had been uprooted from their homes. They did not know English.

Rabbi Schonfeld had one counselor for the boys, but he could not stand it for long. The second counselor was a Rabbi Babad, a very fine man who lived with his wife and little baby in an apartment consisting of one room and a kitchen. He had *tzorres* from the boys. They laughed at him and took food from his kitchen. Every night they were up late.

Next door to us resided an English gentleman, who lived alone with his butler. He got up in the middle of the night and complained that the boys were making noise and that he could not sleep. But Rabbi Schonfeld could take it. He was a very understanding man. He was so busy; he did not always have time to devote to individual children.

I remember that when I once came up to him in his office with a problem, I found him speaking on the telephone to one person while writing a letter to somebody else. That's how busy he was.

Yet I remember a touching incident when he first brought the children to his house. The youngest children, mostly girls, were placed in his own house. I remember there was one girl of six or seven crying for her parents in the night. Dr. Schonfeld told her, "If you promise me to stop crying, I will take you for a ride in my car." And he took this one little girl for a ride in his car. Rabbi Schonfeld also ran the two schools his father had organized. In addition to that, of course, he was in charge of the *kehillah* his father had established. I think he must have worked at least twenty hours each day.

After the outbreak of the war, the British set up tribunals to examine all Austrian and Germans and decide who was a true "enemy alien" and who was a "refugee from Nazi oppression." Initially, only "suspicious" individuals were interned. But after the German invasion of Belgium, the Netherlands and France, the British became so panicky that they did not take the time to distinguish between refugees and enemy aliens.

They took everyone and put us into internment camps. I was taken to Berry and housed in an abandoned textile factory together with two thousand other internees. I was there for a couple of weeks. Then I was transferred. By that time I already had an application pending for a visa to the United States, so they moved me to an internment camp just south of London. From there they took me to the American Consulate to pick up my visa.

I remember that Rabbi Schonfeld once came to the internment camp to see about the kosher food. In all the camps about 90 percent of the Jews ate *treyfe,* and they had plenty to eat. The 10 percent that observed *kashrus* had a less generous diet. They got a lot of cereal, a lot of coffee, but fish only once in a blue moon. I remember that Rabbi Schonfeld brought up some salami. Most of us Orthodox Jews took the hardship in stride. I was young then, only twenty-two years old, and I was able to take everything. Rabbi Schonfeld himself did not shy away from personal hardship. He sacrificed his own comfort for the children he brought out of Nazi Europe. His house was no longer his own. He slept on a couch in his attic.

His mother was then out of the country. When she came home in the late spring of 1939, she found, much to her surprise, that her whole house was full of children. In the end, mother and son divided the house in two. Rabbi Schonfeld and his refugee children occupied one half of the house and his mother lived in the other half.

I WAS DR. SCHONFELD KIND
by Tovia (Theodor) Preschel
Brooklyn, NY

1. I was a "Rabbi Schonfeld Kind."

I was in the first transport of children brought to England from Vienna by Rabbi Schonfeld. Most of the children were members of the *Jugendgruppe,* the youth group of the Agudath Israel in Vienna. I did not belong to that group, but my late father had arranged with Julius Steinfeld, the prominent Viennese Agudist and rescue worker, for my inclusion in the transport.

We traveled by way of Holland. After two days' journey by train and boat, we arrived in London. This was toward the end of December 1938. From the Liverpool Street railroad station we were taken to North London, which was Rabbi Schonfeld's "home base." Here was the Adas Yisroel, of which he was the spiritual leader. Here, too, was the Jewish Secondary School, of which he was the principal. Here were also the offices of the Chief Rabbi's Religious Emergency Council and the rabbi's private residence.

Before long, we met the Rav, as Rabbi Schonfeld was respectfully called throughout North London and as we, too, would call him forever after. He was a tall, broad-shouldered man with friendly blue eyes and a red-blondish beard. He walked erect, his step was brisk and his every movement exuded resoluteness. He was always dressed in black; black trousers and a black rabbinic coat. His headgear varied with the occasion—sometimes he wore a large black yarmulke, a Homburg or a top hat.

We children looked upon him with a mixture of awe and admiration and exchanged stories we heard about his rescue activities and the devoted care that he gave the refugees. Once, after he received an urgent call for help, he drove to the Home Office in Westminster late one Friday afternoon to urge the immediate issuance of visas for certain refugees. By the time he had finished his business at the Home Office, the Sabbath had already begun. So Rabbi Schonfeld made his way back to North London on foot, a walk of three hours.

He cleared his house to make room for the refugee children. Once it happened that a little refugee girl could not fall asleep. The Rav took her and another little girl into his big black car and drove them around the city until both of them had dozed off.

We were told that there was not much love lost between the Rav and the refugee committees of the establishment. They called him "irresponsible" for bringing refugees to England without having the means for their maintenance prepared in advance. He in turn criticized them for not caring enough for the Jewish education of their wards.

It is true that often he did not have accommodation and board ready for the children until after they had arrived in England. But the Rav knew then what others still did not understand—that the command of the hour was to save lives, no matter how or by what means.

It was not long after our arrival that I must have come to his special attention. Most of the children from Vienna were of East European descent. We had been accustomed to waiting six hours between meat and dairy foods.

When a group of the children was given *milchig* (dairy) after only three hours or so, as is the custom among West European Jews, they "revolted." I happened to become a *Redelsfiehrer* in that "revolt," which was soon settled. Probably because of some oratorical talents I must have displayed during the "revolt," I was chosen to say a few words at an Agudah conference that took place at Woburn House in January 1939. I spoke about the tragedy of the refugee children who had been brought to England by other committees and had been denied a Jewish education. Sometime later, on Purim, I "starred" in a play performed by the refugees at the Stoke Newington Town Hall.

Whenever I met the Rav thereafter, he greeted me with a broad smile and a drawn-out "The-o-dor!" This is my German name, which appeared on the collective passport of our group.

I admired, indeed adored the Rav. Could one do otherwise if one considered his prodigious achievements in so many spheres—and he was only twenty-seven years old?

As time passed, I learned more about the wide scope of the Rav's rescue activities. Almost every day, refugees arrived who had received their entry visas with the aid of the Rav: young people, yeshiva students and entire families. They came from Germany, Austria, Czechoslovakia, and even from Italy.

Some of the refugees settled in various parts of London, and in other cities, too, but most of them established themselves in North London, which became "Rabbi Schonfeld territory." Jews who had either been brought to England by the Rav, or were affiliated with one of the organizations he headed, settled entire streets in the neighborhood.

I was a student at the Jewish Secondary School for only a short time. Among my less pleasant memories from that period is the "caning" I received from the headmaster one day, a typically British punishment. Eventually I enrolled at the Etz Chaim Yeshiva.

2. In the early summer of 1940, after the fall of France, when the Germans stood at the gates of Britain, the British authorities interned all enemy aliens. The great majority of the internees were refugees from Nazi oppression, but there was the fear that German spies might have entered the country in the guise of refugees. Large numbers of the internees were deported to Australia and Canada, but most of them were held in camps on the Isle of Man.

I, too, was interned. I was actually not an enemy alien because I had never been an Austrian citizen, even though I had been born and raised in Vienna. My parents had been Polish citizens. But when I arrived in England, the police registered me as an Austrian. When I protested, the officer said, "You were born in Austria, so this makes you an Austrian." Thus, I unwillingly became an Austrian, and after the war broke out, I was classed as an "enemy alien" and eventually interned. I was held in several camps on the Isle of Man.

The first Jewish communal leader to visit the internees was the Rav. He took a special interest in our spiritual and religious needs. I still vividly remember his visit to the Onchan Camp on the Isle of Man. When the news spread that Rabbi Schonfeld had arrived at the camp, we all turned out to greet him. His imposing stature and dignified bearing inspired respect in everyone. The British soldiers who served as camp guards stood at attention as he passed them. As for us, the mere sight of the Rav gave us new hope and courage. We knew that we had not been forgotten.

3. After my release from internment, I returned to the Etz Chaim Yeshiva, where I had great teachers, among them the late Rabbis Eliyahu Lopian and Nahman Shlomo Greenspan and Rabbi Arye Ze'ev Gurwicz. It was through this yeshiva that I came to know the late Dayan Yeheskel Abramsky. He and his wife Reizel were more than kind to me. For several years I was a steady guest at their home on *Shabbossim* and holidays.

The yeshiva was located in London's East End, but I continued to live in North London, "in Rabbi Schonfeld territory." Thus, I was able to follow the work of the Rav and to observe the growth of his institutions.

Even those who did not know the full extent of his activities could get some idea of them from reading the announcement of his *Shabbos HaGadol drashot* (speeches) in the Jewish Chronicle. The announcement listed synagogues affiliated with the Union of Orthodox Hebrew Congregations and the hour at which Rabbi Schonfeld would appear at each of them on that day. Since these synagogues were scattered throughout London, this meant that Rabbi Schonfeld had to traverse large parts of the city on foot.

4. Soon after the war, the Rav again threw himself into new rescue activities. Once again children's transports were brought to England. The Rav visited the ravaged Jewish communities of Eastern Europe and gathered Jewish children who had survived the war in the camps and in the woods, or who had been hiding in convents and in non-Jewish homes. In the spring of 1948 I was on my way back to London from a visit to the Scandinavian countries. The Copenhagen-Brussels train stopped for a while at the Belgian-German border. Not far from us stood a train that had just arrived from Prague. This train was filled with children—Jewish children. They stood at the windows, looking out with curiosity at the bustle of the border station.

I got off my train, walked over to the rav and asked him whether I could be of any help. No, he said, there was no need for help. And then he added, with a friendly smile spreading over his face, "Ah! The-o-dor! Do you remember how you were on a transport just like this one, ten years ago?"

5. Jerusalem in the fall of 1954. I was on the staffs of the Agudist daily newspaper *HaModia* and also the now defunct *Herut.* One day I learned that the Rav was in Jerusalem. I was seized by a desire to write about him. I had written for both papers on a variety of subjects, but never about the Rav.

After the establishment of the State of Israel I left England and joined the Israel Defense Forces. I didn't know whether the Rav had had a lot of *naches* (pleasure) from me during my last years in

London. In the fall of 1945, the Betar (Revisionist Zionist) group I headed wanted to hold a mass meeting in London's Hyde Park to protest against Britain's Palestine policy. In order to make sure that the meeting would be well attended, the group sent telegrams to the major synagogues to which the signature of Chief Rabbi Joseph H. Hertz, the Rav's father-in-law, had been appended without his knowledge. Moreover, I had been active in London on behalf of the Irgun. But I also did not know whether the Rav knew how much I loved him.

So now, in Jerusalem, I wanted to interview him, to write about his achievements in the past and his plans for the future. I made telephone calls to find him. I had some clues about where he might be, but wherever I phoned, I was told that he had just left. In the end, I gave up. But then, did I really have to interview the Rav in order to write about him? Didn't I know him well enough?

So I went ahead and wrote my *HaModia* article without him. It carried the headline "The Savior of Tens of Thousands."

CHAPTER 9

SHEFFORD

EXCERPT FROM **SHEFFORD:**
THE STORY OF A JEWISH SCHOOL
by Dr. Judith Grunfeld
London, England

COMMUNITY IN EVACUATION

Rabbi Dr. Solomon Schonfeld, Principal of the Jewish Secondary School, had brought the first of two transports of three hundred children each from Austria in November 1938. He made himself responsible for the welfare of these children. The transport was to arrive on Saturday night. Members of our school staff and some voluntary assistants worked feverishly all Friday to prepare for this arrival. The Home Office had issued a special permit to each child, and we had to sort out a huge heap of photographs that came from the Committee in Vienna.

Furniture and school utensils, benches and blackboards were moved out into the yard, and the two school buildings were hurriedly equipped with beds, bedding and bare necessities to shelter these youngsters for the first nights, and perhaps weeks, until they could all be satisfactorily dispersed to families or hostels.

They arrived late at night, bewildered young boys and girls, with all kinds of warm clothing dangling around them, dragging little brothers and sisters along. There were tiny ones and big ones, some with tears in their eyes, some with glances of curiosity, some with gestures of proud independence and some with manners of gratitude. A hustling and bustling, a curiosity and anticipation governed the atmosphere. They were, and there was no doubt about it, an eager, intelligent crowd, alive to the challenge of this unusual departure from home and this arrival at a strange harbor. It seemed that each youngster carried the imprint of his own past, of his childhood days at home with him and each one seemed to represent the program of his own family with its heritage and special hallmark. They carried all this to the shores of a free world, there to plant new seeds.

Dr. Schonfeld brought various children's transports in like manner from other parts of the Continent. He had, with considerable risk to his own safety, traveled time and again to Europe to bring the children over. With the keenness of an adventurer he had taken all kinds of steps that at times seemed daring or even crazy, but in the end proved successful. He had coaxed the hesitant youngsters into leaving their parental homes and into following him. His spirits were high and a gust of fresh hope and promise radiated from him. Inspiring confidence, he conquered and gathered and brought back to London group after group of children, "one of a town, two of a family."

The mystery of their survival hung over them; they seemed to be in a strange state of detachment, appearing to accept everything as if it did not concern them. This young rabbi's forceful persuasion, punctuated by laughter, comfort and assurance, seemed to banish the fearful memories and anticipations of these youngsters. He was their conquering hero, the Pied Piper, a fatherly youngster, and at the same time, a gifted organizer. He seemed to them a messenger from that corner of the heavens whence our salvation cometh.

Our school now had a historic task to fulfill. Its very precincts became the first firm ground under these refugees' feet. Our welcome loosened their tensions. The intensely Jewish atmosphere we provided evoked the first echo of their home melodies. It was as if a message from home had actually reached them. They soon became aware that we were guiding their lives in harmony with their own familiar pattern.

Separate courses were arranged in the school curriculum to introduce these newcomers to the first stage of coming to grips with the spoken English language, while in other subjects like French, Hebrew and sports, they participated in the general school program. They were at first reticent and tended to cling together. But later on, one could see how they emerged out of the chrysalis stage as intelligent bright youngsters with a store of strength, moral fiber and integrity.

Until now our school had been fairly English in character. It aimed at providing an intensive Jewish education along with secular subjects in preparation for the General School Certificate at ordinary and/or higher level. After a decade, our school was still fighting for recognition and acceptance.

A Jewish Grammar School was something new in Anglo-Jewry and both its leaders and the general public needed time to recognize its worth. Up to now, parents who wished their children to receive a Jewish education had only one way of achieving it. They had no choice but to send their children to *cheder*, to Hebrew classes, as they were called, which were held in different communal centers after school hours, and on Sunday mornings. Pupils at these classes were often not happy to attend them, as they arrived there having already done a full day's work at school.

The Sunday classes were in danger of being considered an outright nuisance by the youngsters on a day otherwise free. Jewish education given in such Hebrew classes lacked the proper prestige, and, coming as it did at the end of a day, it was bound to appear in the eyes of the children as something of an imposition and of second-rate importance. It would often clash with the homework that was essential for examinations at school. It would also interfere with music lessons and other after-school activities. Teachers who taught at such classes were already fatigued and usually accepted such an evening job to supplement their income. In such circumstances Hebrew education failed to receive a place of honor in the child's mind. How could they look at it as their privilege and their foremost task? How could the Jewish subjects ever touch their resources of enthusiasm and pride if the "heritage" of which the rabbi spoke was only presented by tired teachers at a late hour of the day without the same backing of authority as their day school had?

The idea of founding a Jewish Secondary School had been to give Jewish teaching pride of place and a status of priority. This was done by putting Jewish teaching into the early-morning hours and by presenting it through teachers who had an honored status in a general academic way as well as in the field of Jewish learning. The artificial border between Jewish teaching and secular teaching was to be eliminated by allowing a Jewish atmosphere to permeate the entire school, the assembly, and all subjects. This was to be achieved through the influence of an orthodox, qualified staff in whose hands the entire education and tuition of the pupils should be entrusted.

This was at the time a new idea and an enterprise that could only gradually gain ground. The public had to be won over against the general argument that attendance at a Jewish Grammar School would alienate children from the general society and would place them at a disadvantage later on in life. This groundless fear was a powerful factor in the minds of many against the new venture, and only slowly did parents take to the idea of sending their children to a school where they would be taught secular subjects against a harmonious and predominantly Jewish background.

Today when we have many Jewish Day Schools and Grammar Schools, and the number of applications even exceeds the number of available places, we do well to remember the pioneering efforts of the late Rabbi Dr. Avigdor Schonfeld and his son, Rabbi Dr. Solomon Schonfeld, who introduced the Jewish Grammar School to this country, in the face of a wave of prejudice and ill-founded fear, and against a host of negative arguments. They established the school on the pattern of the English School System with prefects, house competitions, matches, sports competitions and sports days, prizes, uniform, academic gowns and speech days.

The school grew in size and popularity. With the influx of refugee children from the Continent between the years 1933–1939, many of the children who had already attended a Jewish Grammar School proved to be valuable pupil material. They were intellectually on a high level and at the same time they made a positive contribution to the Orthodox climate of the school.

As well as pupils, Jewish teachers came over to this country, men and women with first-class academic qualifications and with a sound and extensive Jewish knowledge. Although their knowledge of the English language was not without fault, nevertheless they became important pillars in the ever-spreading structure of Jewish education in this country.

Those were days of austerity, blackouts, rationing and emergency conditions. It was a time of hardship, which was nevertheless rewarding and creative from the educational aspect. High demands were then made on the single-mindedness and ingenuity of the teachers and it was here that outstanding and experienced teachers who came from the Continent made their special contribution to the further positive development of the school.

From Judith Grunfeld, Shefford: The Story of a Jewish School Community in Evacuation, London, *1980, pp. 8–12*

WHOEVER SAVES ONE LIFE
by Prof. Eleazar Birnbaum
Toronto, Canada

I. The German-Jewish Children Arrive

The scene is the school hall at "Northfield," the building in Stamford Hill, which houses the junior boys of the Jewish Secondary Schools. The time is one day in 1938 (or was it 1939?), and I am one of the "older" boys—already eight or nine years old.

We have been told that some more children from Germany will be brought to the school by our principal, Rabbi Dr. Solomon Schonfeld. He soon comes in, a very tall man followed by a lot of children. Dr. Schonfeld talks with our headmistress, Dr. Judith Grunfeld. The white cloth of her broad headband, crossing her head at an angle, contrasts strikingly with his dark square beard and black suit and his tall black skullcap. Then they give instructions to the teachers and lady helpers assembled in the hall. Chairs and tables are pushed around and rearranged, perhaps for serving a meal.

We Northfield boys look at the new arrivals with curiosity. We are a fairly scruffy lot. How different from us are these new boys in their outlandish little Shabbos suits, and how odd those girls look in their neat dresses, many of them with their hair in braids! These boys and girls seem unnaturally clean! Dr. Grunfeld had told us earlier to make our "new brothers and sisters" feel welcome. When we finally pluck up the courage to go and speak to them, they don't understand a single word of English. It is very disheartening at the beginning. . . . In a day or two, however, a pidgin English develops between us, made up of two-thirds broken English and one-third broken German, which allows us to play together.

Dr. Schonfeld appears and disappears at school somewhat erratically. We do not understand exactly what he is doing. We know only that he is "doing a big mitzvah"—one far greater than we could understand at the time. We had not yet learnt *"Kol ha-mekayem nefesh achas mi-Yisroel . . ."* (Whosoever saves one life . . .)

II. Evacuation

September 1, 1939. We children were told that the Germans might start a war and that we would be sent "to the country" for safety, because it would be dangerous to stay in London. My two brothers and my sister and I are among the hundreds from the "big boys'" school and from Northfield who assemble in the main school playground of the boys' school, at the corner of Amhurst Park and Bethune Road. Each of us has a rucksack stuffed with clothes and a *siddur*, and the boys are all wearing school caps with the JSS (Jewish Secondary School) badge. Like all the other children I wear a beige baggage tag around my neck, marked with my name and address. It makes me feel a bit foolish when I look at it. We stand lined up by classes, waiting expectantly.

Dr. Schonfeld steps forward and makes a little speech, telling us how to behave in the country, where all the people will be non-Jews. He says we should make sure to tell the country people that we are "fish-eating vegetarians." (I did not understand this expression, but later that day dutifully repeated it to my new "landlady." She did not understand it either, and she was a grown-up!).

Soon we are marched out of the playground, past sad-looking parents, to waiting buses. Some of the mothers are in tears. I have resolved to be brave and feel a little indignant at a few sissies who run

to their parents and refuse to come with us, and am even more
shocked at several mothers who grab their children out of the line in
a last effort to prevent them from going.

The buses take us to a station where we board a train. It is all quite
mysterious and exciting. No one knows where we are going. After a
while the train stops and we get out. I cannot see a sign on the station, but am told by another boy that we are at "Biggleswade." There
we stop briefly at a "rest center" where ladies gave each child a present in a brown shopping bag. Mine is very disappointing: it contains
a packet of *treyfe* biscuits, a tin of *treyfe* meat, and I believe, some
soap. These ladies clearly do not understand what Jewish boys like or
need!

Soon we are loaded onto cream-and-green buses, which move
along narrow country roads to a village, where we get off. We are told
that this village is called Shefford. The teachers line us up in twos and
we form long "crocodiles," each headed by one teacher and one gentleman from the village. My group walks along Ampthill Road, stopping at almost every house. Each time, one or two of our children are
taken from the head of the line and disappear into a house, and the
procession, grown smaller, moves on.

The kind-looking lady at 95 Ampthill Road takes two children, a
boy of eleven and myself (aged 9). She tells us that she is Mrs.
Handscombe and that she loves children. She says she has six in the
house already (five of her own and a niece), so we will have lots of
nice company. She is right. Within the hour I am with her children,
climbing up trees on the farm, falling into beds of green nettles and
generally having a wonderful time. What a lovely family, and what a
fine introduction to country life!

Later on we are summoned to a church hall. What? A church hall?
Yes, but it is not to be tried by some Holy Inquisition. The church hall
will become the kitchen and canteen of our school, and we are to be
fed the most kosher of kosher foods! Dr. Schonfeld has just arrived
from London in his car, and brought us a full carload of Vienna
sausages from "Kedassia."

THE SPIRIT OF SHEFFORD
by Ruth Simons, nee Hochdorf
New York, NY

I was born in Frankfurt. In 1934, after Hitler came to power, my father lost his job. After a while it became clear to him that we would have to leave Germany. He tried everything possible to obtain affidavits from the United States, but he did not succeed.

My parents were anxious that I, at least, should be brought to safety. They contacted a very distant relative of ours in England, who agreed to act as my sponsor and I arrived in London in February 1939, with a children's transport sponsored by The Refugee Children's Committee.

When we arrived someone called out my name, and an elderly gentleman came over and in a mixture of English, broken German and Yiddish explained to me that he was my relative. It was a Friday, just before *Shabbos* and I was taken to the Bloom family with whom I was to live. My relative could not take me in because he and his family did not have a kosher home. Dr. Bloom was a mathematics teacher at the Jewish Secondary School and after the weekend, introduced me to Dr. Judith Grunfeld.

Dr. Grunfeld talked to me in German. She asked me a number of questions about my schoolwork, what I had learned at school in Germany and how much English I knew. Dr. Grunfeld said that since I spoke some English I did not have to go to the special classes, and was placed in a regular class where I did not do too badly. The first English book I read was *Little Lord Fauntleroy*. Because I was able to read it and understand it in English, it meant something to me.

Dr. Bloom was British-born, and his wife was of German origin. Both Blooms spoke German, but were very insistent that we not speak German in public. It was considered very important for Jewish refugees from Germany not to stand out as the enemies of England. Notices had even been put up all over the Jewish Secondary School, instructing refugee children not to speak German in public. If you were caught speaking German, you had to write one hundred times,

"I must not speak German." If you were caught a second time, you wrote it two hundred times. If you were caught the third time, I think you had to write it five hundred or a thousand times. This was not nastiness on the part of the school. It was for our own best interest, because there were incidents in which Jewish refugees who spoke German in the street were molested by British citizens who could not have known the difference between them and ordinary Germans.

My interest in Judaism really started after my family arrived in Cologne. My parents, went to introduce themselves to a rabbi, whose name was Simons (and unrelated to the man I was eventually to marry). He was the rabbi of an Orthodox synagogue and asked my father if I had any Jewish education. I didn't.

I was nine years old, but I could not read a word of Hebrew. I went to the rabbi, and before long I was able to read Hebrew. He was a very perceptive man who did a lot of work with young people. On *Shabbos* he would arrange an *Oneg Shabbat* for the twenty children in the congregation, which was a very small community. We would sit around the table; there would be *kiddush*, and a little wine and a small piece of cake for each one of us. This was my first experience with real Jewish life and I was fascinated by it. I made friends with children from an, Orthodox family who lived nearby, and my parents understood that this friendship made me very happy. Since I was an only child it was very important for me to have other children to play with.

I became very much interested in Orthodox Judaism, and before long I transferred to Yavneh, the Orthodox Jewish high school in Cologne.

I studied at Yavneh from 1935 until 1939, when I left Germany. My parents were terribly upset when the letter came, specifying the date of my departure with the children's transport. My mother was grief-stricken, but I was a young girl and probably not very considerate of her. But the prospect of leaving home was not such a terrible thing for a child. It was a new life. Of course, I was a little afraid, but my parents kept telling me that I was going to leave Germany for a better country. Things would be different in England; there, I would not have to be afraid of anything. But on the morning I left Cologne, of course, everything was pretty awful. It was naturally very hard for my parents, and I realized, for the first time, that it was going to be very hard for me also.

I distinctly remember looking out the window of the streetcar on our way to the railroad station and thinking about the adventure I was about to begin. It was exciting, too, because I had a lot of new clothes and other things for my new life in England. At the station the parents of the children in the transport were not allowed to accompany their children to the train platform. At German railroad stations, if you wanted to see someone off and stay with him until the train came, you had to have a platform pass. But for some reason my parents were unable to get one.

My father said to me, "When the train goes out of Cologne and crosses the bridge over the River Rhine, come to the window of your car; we will be standing on the bridge, and we will wave to each other." But just as our train got to the bridge we were told to move into another car. Apparently, the Germans had decided that our particular group was in the wrong railroad car. I stayed at the window, but then another child came and said, "Come on! Let's get a move on!" I said, "I just want to look out of the window!" But then some grown-up shouted, "Go ahead! Everybody move!" So, just as our train crossed the bridge over the River Rhine I was caught between two cars, in a place where there were no windows. So I never got to wave to my parents and my parents never got to see me.

After the war broke out I got letters from them, from time to time, through Holland, and later through relatives in Sweden, which had remained neutral. Eventually, my parents were taken to a place called Litzmannstadt (Lodz). I never saw them again.

During that summer of 1939 the children of the school were sent on a summer vacation. All of us went to a summer camp in a place on the English seaside. It was very nice there; we had a wonderful time. We lived in a boarding house that wasn't very elegant, but it was a little better than the regular summer camps in Great Britain, where the campers lived in tents without sanitary facilities. We at least had bathrooms, after a fashion, and regular beds to sleep in.

During the last few days of the camp season it seemed that the political situation had deteriorated very much. Dr. Jacobsen, who was in charge, did not permit any newspapers. Since no one had radios none of us knew anything except for rumors about the big crisis that was going on in the outside world. When we returned to London the last Sunday in August, there was bedlam at the railroad station.

No one seemed to know what was going on. There was a huge crowd, including many men in uniform. Everyone felt the tension in the air. The two other girls and I who lived at Dr. Bloom's house went back to the Blooms. Mrs. Bloom explained to us that war could break out any minute and that we children would all be evacuated. She said that we would have to report to the Jewish Secondary School the next day for instructions about what to do.

On Monday, Tuesday, Wednesday and Thursday of that week we went to the school each morning with sandwiches, a change of clothes and some toilet articles in order to be prepared for evacuation at a moment's notice. No one really knew what was going to happen. We were divided into groups. I found myself in a group headed by Dr. and Mrs. Jacobsen from the summer camp. On Thursday we were told that in all probability we would be evacuated the next day, Friday, September 1.

On Friday morning we came to school very early and assembled in the playground, which was quite large. Dr. Schonfeld was there, and so was Dr. Grunfeld, along with all the teachers and leaders of the various groups. Dr. Schonfeld got up on a chair and made a speech in three languages—English, German and Yiddish—saying that we were going to be evacuated and that we would have to live with non-Jewish people. He wanted all of us to remember that we must not eat any meat at the homes of non-Jews. For the time being we would have to eat everything else they would serve us, but we should not eat any meat or meat products. Each child was given a package like the K-rations in the American army: crackers, a box of Schmerling cheese, and a chocolate bar. We still had with us the sandwiches and that little bag with a change of clothing, sweater, raincoat and so forth that we had brought to school each morning all that week.

After Rabbi Schonfeld's speech everyone lined up in groups and we marched out of the schoolyard behind our leaders. I remember that the parents of some of the children were there. They were carrying on very badly, hugging their children and crying. Some of the children were crying, too. For me, who had left my parents behind in Germany, it was a kind of repeat performance.

From the school we marched to the Underground station. On that day all the Underground trains were reserved exclusively for the transportation of evacuees. No other passengers were allowed aboard the trains. There were crowds and crowds of children, all very orderly. Walking two abreast, we filed into the Underground train that took us to the railroad station—I don't remember whether it was King's Cross, Victoria or Paddington.

At the station we were escorted on to the trains. After a journey of about an hour and a half—it was all very jolly; we were singing and having a lot of fun—we stopped at a place whose name I no longer recall. All I remember is that we got off the train and boarded a fleet of buses that were lined up at the station waiting for us. I am afraid it was not very well organized. We all just ran, the buses were filled up in no time, and off we went. There were hundreds of children in this group. Most of them were from the Jewish Secondary School, but there were also a number of children who did not attend that school but wanted to be evacuated along with us because they wanted to be in a Jewish environment. It must have been quite an experience for Dr. Grunfeld; imagine all this disorder on Friday, on *Erev Shabbos*. We were only children and so we did not worry about it that much, but I can imagine that Dr. Grunfeld had her hands full.

I spent six months, from September 1939 until Passover 1940, in a place called Stotfold. A very beautiful charming young lady took charge of the children from the Jewish Secondary School; she was Dr. Schonfeld's sister Asenath Petrie. She was married to Dr. Ernest Petrie, who was already in the army. Stotfold, like every other village in the area, had a billeting officer who was responsible for placing the evacuated children into the homes of local families who had room for them. The billeting officer would take several children and lead them from house to house, from door to door, ringing doorbells. If someone opened the door, the billeting officer would ask, "I have some evacuees here. How many could you take into your home?" Some people would say, "I can take one." Others would say, "I could take two." A few said, "I have room for three." Some of them had very definite ideas about what the children they wanted should look like or be like. Some said they wanted only blonde girls, or only boys.

My friend Clara Jeidel and I were taken to the same house. Since we only stayed there for three days, I don't remember the people very well. They had never heard of Jews before. They did not understand what we meant when we said we were not supposed to eat any meat at their place. I am certain that we ate plenty of food that we should not have eaten, but then we were not as educated about kosher and *treyfe* ingredients as present-generation Americans. When we first arrived at Stotfold, before being turned over to the billeting officer, we were instructed to report the next morning, *Shabbos,* at a certain hall in the village at such and such a time.

That Friday night we evacuees had no real *Shabbos.* I can imagine that some of the children were very much upset about this. But I don't recall that Clara or I were all that upset, other than by the strangeness of the whole situation. We were looking forward excitedly to meeting all our classmates at the hall the next morning. The people with whom Clara and I had been billeted made up their minds right away that they were not interested in keeping us.

On Sunday we were moved to another home, where we stayed for the next six months. Our new foster parents were very nice people, and they were very kind to us. They were a couple with only one son and told me that they had always wanted a daughter. When they heard that I had left my parents behind in Germany, they even wanted to adopt me. But I explained to them that I was not up for adoption because I really had parents, even though they were not available just then. I remember that during the next few months Clara and I had a very happy-go-lucky life, because the school was still in the process of getting organized. I think that the main organizing effort of the Jewish Secondary School was concentrated in Shefford, because Dr. Grunfeld was there, as were many more children and teachers than in Stotfold.

Stotfold was a very nice little village, somewhat prettier than Shefford. It had a movie theater, and a fish-and-chips store around the corner. Our landlady bought some of that stuff every week and that is what we ate. I'm afraid that during those days in Stotfold we ate quite a lot of food that we should not have eaten. simply because our land-lady did not know any better. The laws of *kashrus* were too difficult for her to understand.

Our schooling continued after a fashion, but it wasn't very well organized, and as a consequence most of us lost six months of class work. I eventually ended up in a class lower than the rest of my age group.

One time we arranged an evening's entertainment in honor of our landladies, our non-Jewish foster parents. We put on a play, sang some choral music and performed gymnastics. We invited Dr. Grunfeld, who rode over from Shefford on her bicycle; there was no public transportation between Stotfold and Shefford then. When Dr. Grunfeld arrived in the auditorium she got quite a shock. Her girls on stage were dressed in pants, standing on their heads, making hand-stands and cartwheels that the landladies enjoyed, but Dr. Grunfeld did not consider very modest.

I think it was then that she decided that we must be moved from Stotfold to Shefford because Stotfold was not a good influence on us. I do not remember too much about the first Rosh HaShannah and Yom Kippur of the war, but I'm certain that there was no real Rosh HaShannah dinner, because at that time we still had no communal kitchen and dining hall for the evacuees. I can imagine that many of the children must have found this very difficult.

At Passover in 1940 many of the children who had parents in London went home for the holidays. I went to my distant relatives in London, who were not at all observant. I should not have gone there, but I did not realize this at the time. After Pesach I did not return to Stotfold but went to Shefford, where the rest of my classmates had already moved.

During the first months of the war we knew only what we heard second-hand. At the movies, we saw some newsreels and they came as quite a shock. But beyond that we really did not notice too much about the war except that we all were given gas masks, which we had to lug around with us wherever we went. If you did not bring your gas mask to school you got into trouble. It was in a kind of cardboard case, and every once in a while the air raid warden would come and say, "Everyone put on your gas masks," just to see how it fitted. Thank God, we never had to use them.

The change from Stotfold to Shefford was difficult for me. First of all, I had made some friends in Stotfold. By that time I was no longer living with Clara Jeidel but with another girl. This girl and I decided that when we moved to Shefford we would live together. We were placed in Clifton, a village about a mile or a mile and a quarter away from Shefford.

I really don't recall too much about my first impressions of Shefford. Some of the girls there had been my classmates in London, so I was not a stranger to them. All of us were put into regular classes and our formal schooling began. We had pretty good teachers and all the most important subjects. There was English, English history, mathematics (consisting of arithmetic, algebra, and geometry), French and *Ivrit* (modern Hebrew), *Chumash* and Jewish history. There also were many lessons on the Bible, the Prophets and topics of general Jewish interest. Dr. Grunfeld gave these classes in her tiny crowded office. There was one table and a few chairs or benches. Usually two people shared one chair. It wasn't very fancy, but Dr. Grunfeld was most inspiring, particularly just before the High Holy Days, when she would talk to us about the *Viddui* (Confession of Sins).

Most of her talks had to do with *mussar* (ethics). Dr. Grunfeld told us the story of Soroh Schenirer, who founded the Beth Jacob schools in Poland. We got to hear that story many times, but it never failed to fascinate us. Recently, when she was here in the United States, I went to one of Dr. Grunfeld's lectures in Borough Park and I heard it all over again, and I was just as fascinated as I had been years ago, when she first told it to us in Shefford.

M'orle Grunfeld, Dr. Grunfeld's brother-in-law, taught us Hebrew subjects and was a very popular teacher. He came to Shefford some time after we did because he had been interned in 1940 as an enemy alien on the Isle of Man. He was released only after it had been established that he was a refugee from Nazi oppression.

M'orle Grunfeld was then still single and had his bachelor quarters in a building that we called the White House. This was the main building of our school in Shefford. It was a very simple place. There was an entrance hall, then a room on the one side where you came in and Dr. Grunfeld's office. The kitchens were behind the dining room and upstairs there was a study hall and the room where M'orle Grunfeld lived. There was also a "welfare room," where lady volunteers took care of our personal needs, such as mending clothing, or giving us first aid if we were hurt.

One lady in Shefford negotiated with various refugee committees for new clothes. There was also an old clothes center to which English people sent used clothing for us. Other women sorted out and repaired them, and then gave them out to children who were in need of this and that, a coat, a sweater or a dress. There was also a boys' room, which had a few beds, for those few boys who could not be placed in any of the homes in the village because they were bed wetters. They had psychological problems; most of them were younger boys who had been badly upset by the separation from their parents.

Halfway along our time in Shefford—I think it was 1942—we got what was known as the "hut," a prefabricated building set up on the grounds that surrounded the White House. The hut was quite big. It contained a kitchen, with lots of room for tables, chairs and benches. Once we had the hut we no longer had to eat any meals with our non-Jewish foster parents.

Our foster parents then gave the school part of the money for our meals that they had received from the government. They kept only a certain percentage for the expenses that they had in connection with our lodgings. One of the highlights of our years in Shefford was the wedding of M'orle Grunfeld to Lotte Eiseman in 1942. The wedding took place in London on a Sunday and many of us went into the city to attend. I do not remember whether the school got special buses for us, or whether we took regularly scheduled transportation. It was a daytime wedding, and we came back to Shefford the same day.

I seem to remember that we spent much more time on secular subjects than we did on Jewish studies. But a lot of emphasis was put on Jewish attitudes and on *Hashkafah* (Jewish outlook) in general, and this made up for any lack of textbook knowledge. So, perhaps I could not read Rashi that well, or translate as many passages from the Prophets and so forth, the way my own children were able to do after they graduated from a yeshiva high school in the United States. But because of our general Jewish outlook on life and the moral example set for us by our teachers, I believe we got far more than any child has here in the United States today even if he or she has graduated from the best of *yeshivos*. I have many more meaningful recollections of my school than they.

Of course one might argue that in retrospect everything looks rosier to me now than it appeared in those days during the 1940s. But I know that although I had to grow up without parental guidance, the school, teachers, and the friends whom I made at the school gave me values which I developed in my subsequent life and which I have pre-served to this day. The teachers in Shefford, I think, were much clos-er to their students than the teachers in American *yeshivos* are to their pupils.

Oh, we did have our complaints. For instance, I remember the cook in Shefford. She is now living in Australia. We didn't like her very much because she made us do what she called "kitchen duty." The kitchen was awful. There was no hot water, and because there was no scouring powder you had to scrub the pots with sand. Imagine having to remove all that greasy stuff with ice-cold water! It was just terrible! But we were told that in order to be loyal members of our school community, with the proper community spirit, we had to do things for others and not mind getting our hands dirty. After all, everybody had to eat, so somebody had to wash the dishes. Paper dishes were not known in those days. We did not even have china dishes, but only tin plates. We could not wash them very well; most of the time they were sticky.

I did not stay in Shefford until the end of the war. I left in 1943, after I finished my studies and took the exam at the University of London. I was then eighteen years old and went to a place called Letchworth, near Shefford. There were many religious Jews in Letchworth at the time and I found a room with a very nice family. I worked in Letchworth for about a year, in a factory, which produced instruments for testing the gas pressure for various scientific installations.

I could have gone to the University of London, but there would have been a tuition fee, so I went to work instead. But I returned to Shefford many times for visits. The teachers and the other students were always glad to see me. They would invite me to spend the night and talk about "old times."

I remember one of our escapades in Shefford. One day the entire class simply took off and ran away from school. The teacher came to the classroom and there was no one there for her to teach. We had taken a bus to a nearby village and gone to some kind of cafeteria. I think we had some tea and muffins. When we came back to Shefford the teacher was horrified. "You ate muffins!" she said. "That means you actually ate *treyfe*! I don't know what to say to you girls." We were punished by being expelled from the White House. This meant that we were allowed to come in only for meals. We were not permitted to do our homework in the study hall, where we used to do our lessons together before going home to our non-Jewish foster parents for the night.

This was quite a severe punishment and we were very much upset. But we also played other tricks on our teachers. We had one teacher who taught us German and who was very nearsighted. We rigged up a window that was high up in such a way that it kept going bang, bang, bang, all the time the lessons were going on. I remember the time a girl called one of the teachers a pig. For this Dr. Grunfeld herself publicly caned her. The girl had to hold out her hand and Dr. Grunfeld slapped her on the palm with a very thin cane, a very severe punishment given only on very rare occasions. This was done in front of all of us. We could hardly bear to look.

I think that my experience at Shefford meant more to me, who had left my parents in Germany, than it did to some of the girls who had families in London to fall back upon. For me my school was everything. This is one of the reasons why today I never say "No" to anyone who asks me to do anything at all on behalf of Dr. Schonfeld or Dr. Grunfeld, because I owe both of them a never-ending debt of gratitude.

After Purim at Shefford, Purim anywhere else was a disappointment to me. Usually there was a play making fun of this or that personality, mostly the teachers. We even made fun of Dr. Grunfeld, whom the children used to call "The Queen." She took it very well. We also had what was called the "Purim paper," which contained humorous verses and favorite sayings of some of the teachers.

Simchas Torah was marvelous. I don't know how many Torah scrolls we actually had in Shefford. We must have had at least two, but probably no more than that. Some of the teachers would dance with the *Sefer Torah*; it was a wonderful sight to behold. We would all sing and we were very good at it. We knew some lovely songs, very loud and rhythmic. We would sing, clap and dance. On *Simchas Torah* we sneaked past the *mechitza* dividing the men and the women in the synagogue. We would stand together watching the procession and the dancing with the Scrolls.

Tisha B'Av was a very solemn day. We would sit on the floor. No lights were on, only candlelight. That was the only time I remember Dr. Grunfeld's husband, Dayan Grunfeld, being present and participating in a school function. He sat on the floor with us and read with us the Book of Lamentations. On *Tisha B'Av* itself we would always read *Kinos* (Lamentations) until at least 12 o'clock noon. We were all expected to stay in the synagogue until that time. Dayan Grunfeld also would come to Shefford for Shabbos. Every Shabbos afternoon there would be an *Oneg Shabbat*, just an hour before the Sabbath closed, and we would sit there in the dark room singing sentimental Hebrew songs, most of the time.

It was in Shefford, too, that I made my first acquaintance with classical music. One of the teachers knew Sir Adrian Boult, a well-known British conductor, who gave a concert in a small town nearby. Our school received about forty or fifty tickets. I had never heard classical music before. There were no record players or records at Shefford because there was no money for such things. I remember one of the numbers on Sir Adrian's program. It was *Eine Kline Nachtmusik*; it has been one of my favorite pieces ever since.

Attendance at these concerts was in keeping with the education that Dr. Schonfeld, Dr. Grunfeld and our other teachers sought to give us. They trained us in the spirit of *Torah im Derekh Eretz,* which was to enable us to live as Torah-true Jews and productive citizens in a modern world. If I, who came from a non-Orthodox home, have remained observant and have developed a religious attitude based on deep Jewish conviction, this is due largely to the training I received at Shefford and at the Jewish Secondary School under the guidance of Dr. Grunfeld and Rabbi Dr. Solomon Schonfeld.

I never had any personal contact with Dr. Schonfeld, but I have every reason to be thankful to him.

After the war I visited the United States on a "stateless" travel document. While I was in New York I met a very nice young man, who in due time became my husband.

But at a crucial stage in our acquaintance, my time in the U.S. ran out. In those days it was very difficult for an alien to obtain permission from the British authorities to extend her stay in a foreign country. However, I was most fortunate, for Dr. Schonfeld came to my rescue. One of my friends in London approached him and within a couple of days he obtained the necessary extension from the Home Office. During that extended stay I became engaged, and my dear husband and I have been blessed with thirty-two years together and with children and grandchildren. But for Dr. Schonfeld, this might never have come about, and I have always been very grateful.

FISH-EATING VEGETARIANS
by Miriam (Eiseman) Elias

I was eight years old when my family came to England from Germany in May 1937. Hitler had passed a law forbidding Jewish doctors and lawyers and other professionals to practice their vocation in Germany. My father was a dealer in antique books and prints and rare manuscripts. This was one of the professions affected by the Nazi order. Since my family still had some means, we were able to take a lift van and most of our things with us.

We settled in North London in a nice house in Bethune Road and I was enrolled at the Jewish Secondary School in London. The principal was Rabbi Dr. Solomon Schonfeld, son of the late Rabbi Dr.

Victor Schonfeld. Dr. Schonfeld was also the rabbi of the Adas Yisroel Congregation. Before long, more and more refugees from Germany and other places such as Vienna had entered the school. There must have been between five and six hundred children, ranging from kindergarten age to the age of sixteen and matriculation.

The overall headmistress of the girls' school was Dr. Judith Grunfeld; the boys' headmaster was Dr. Abraham Levene. The school was run in the English manner, complete with school uniforms and English-style sports. We studied what they called classical Hebrew one hour each day, and modern Hebrew twice a week.

In 1939, when I was eleven years old, toward the end of August, our parents were told that if there would be a war all children would be evacuated into the countryside to get them out of danger from air raids. Each parent was asked to prepare a knapsack with one change of underwear, an extra blouse for the "tunic" of our school uniform, some chocolate and barley sugar, and a few other miscellaneous items, which each child was to take with him or her to the country. My mother proceeded to do all this very calmly. None of us was really afraid. We thought we were going to have a great time, like at a summer camp or some such place.

On Friday morning, September 1, 1939, hundreds of us children were lined up in the school playground. Among these children there were a great many who had arrived from Europe in children's transports only that week and who had not yet learned a word of English. They had been sleeping in the school gymnasium and in various makeshift classrooms. I remember that we had gone out to collect coat hangers and canned foods for them. At any rate, here we were all lined up, ready to board the evacuation buses. Not one of us had any idea where we were going.

I remember seeing my father standing at the window of a room inside the school building where a group of adult men had gathered for daily morning services. He stood there, wearing his *talis* and *tefillin*, looking out into the schoolyard, watching us lining up to leave. None of the parents had been told where we were going or how long we would be gone.

Finally we all got on the buses. After we had traveled for two hours, our bus stopped and we were told to get off. We found ourselves in a square in a little village, with lots of non-Jewish people from the village milling around and looking us over, trying to decide which of the little evacuees to take into their homes. This village was called Shefford, and it was in the county of Bedfordshire. Not all the busloads of children who had been evacuated from the Jewish Secondary Schools were taken to Shefford. Some of them went to other villages—Campton, Stotfold and Clifton are those that I remember. No one village would have been able to absorb all the children from this one school.

Among the villagers in Shefford who had come to meet the evacuees was the proprietor of the village laundry, who owned three cars. He was the one man in town who was really well to do.

I remember he had a little white beard. He said, "I don't want to have to take charge of these children all by myself, but I'd like to have five children, along with a counselor, an older child who will take care of the others." Now, all of us Eisemans, my four cousins and I, were standing together in a little cluster. So we were selected to go with him, as a ready-made faculty group of five. A girl named Jenny Wexner (she is now living in *Eretz Yisroel*) came along as our counselor. The Taylors—that was the name of our foster father and his wife—had a beautiful house set in a park-like estate.

When we arrived there we were taken to a self-contained part of the mansion, almost like a separate little flat. We were told that this would be our home and that Jenny would be in charge of us. In accordance with Dr. Schonfeld's instructions, we informed the Taylors that we were "fish-eating vegetarians" and that therefore we could not eat any meat. After unpacking our things in our little flat we came down to the dining room where the table had been set for lunch. And there, to our great shock, we saw prepared on each of our plates a huge red lobster! Jenny, who was no more than sixteen or seventeeh at the most, had to explain to the Taylors that there were also certain fish that we couldn't eat. Our foster parents accepted her explanation.

Later we went outdoors and played on the grounds of the Taylor estate. After a while, one or two older boys from our school came by. They had been going from house to house, checking to see where the children from our school had been placed, and informing the children that Friday night services would be held that evening in a place called Ashby Hall, on the main street of the village. I think this was a simply terrific organization, our having a real *minyan* already that very first night. It was really a wonderful reunion.

Before the service began, Dr. Judith Grunfeld got up and said, "I don't want those of you who were separated from your brothers and sisters to worry. If they left London on another bus and you have not yet found them here, it is because we have been distributed in four or five other villages. I've been to all these places, and I've seen all your brothers and sisters. Shefford is the main village, and the largest number of children are here. But don't worry. We'll all be together in due time." After the services we were told that there would be services again the next morning, on Shabbos.

When we returned to the Taylors, there was a knock at our door. It was the Taylor's chauffeur. He said he had to speak to us. Two little boys from Vienna had been assigned to his little house, which was also located on the Taylor estate. These little boys, who were perhaps six or seven years old, couldn't speak one word of English. He, the chauffeur, had prepared a nice hot bath for them before bedtime. Well, when these two boys, who wore *payes* (sidecurls), were faced with a bathtub and soap on Shabbos they screamed and screamed. They couldn't say a word in English, and the chauffeur's wife did not know what was wrong. So we had to explain to the chauffeur that our religion forbade us to have a bath on our Sabbath day.

After a while we settled down to life with the Taylors. Gradually, they became accustomed to our religious observances. For instance, I remember our fast days. The Taylors didn't want to believe that a girl of twelve could go for an evening and an entire day thereafter without eating a bite of food or drinking a drop of water. Mrs. Taylor said to me, "I simply can't believe that you don't take a drink or a cookie when no one is looking." But when the Taylors saw that we were really serious about our religion, they came to admire us tremendously. One day Mrs. Taylor said to me, "Without ever having met your parents, I can tell that you come from a house where you were taught manners, because I see that you wash your hands every time you come out of the bathroom."

We had our meals with our non-Jewish foster parents until the school was able to set up a canteen for us. From then on we ate our meals in a big building, which had been donated to the school for this purpose. Our classes were held at various locations. The staff, I think, was composed of refugee teachers who were already able to speak English and could teach us the language. Not all the English staff from the school had come along with us from London. Dr. Grunfeld shuttled back and forth between all these villages, making sure that all was well with us.

The holidays were outstanding highlights of our years in Shefford. We had Passover *sedarim*, Chanukah and Purim. At other times we had concerts, plays and other cultural activities. Of course, we had duties, too. There were lunch duties, which we hated because we had to peel mountains of potatoes. There were no modern labor-saving devices. After a while the government requisitioned the Taylor's estate for army officers. So the five of us had to leave. We were split up. I was assigned to the home of a retired school principal, a nice lady who took her duties very seriously and made me feel very much at home. It was a much simpler life than the flat on the Taylor estate, but it was comfortable.

We had our chores to do wherever we lived, but mostly we helped in the school. I think that living this way for three years proved to be a most interesting and formative phase in our lives. My mother always said we would have turned out entirely different if we hadn't spent these few years away from home. Our mother and father did not want to have us stay with them in London for even one night, for by that time the London blitz had begun. When I went to London for my bas mitzvah, I stayed in London for perhaps about four hours and returned to Shefford that same evening.

Living away from our parents during our formative years really made us very independent. I remember we were touched by our *shiurim* with Dr. Judith Grunfeld, who especially had a great influence on me. We were inspired to do much more for each other and for *Yiddishkeit* in general than we might have been if we had lived a normal, sheltered life at home.

For example, I remember two of us going into Dr. Grunfeld's office, her "inner sanctum," and saying to her, "Dr. Grunfeld, could you suggest something we could do for *Yiddishkeit*?" We were only thirteen or fourteen years old at the time but we were dead serious. Dr. Grunfeld took us seriously, too. She said she'd think about it. She'd let us know.

Later, she called us back and said, "Yes, I thought of something you could do. Why don't you organize a 'big-sister' system? There are all these little six and seven year olds far away from home. If each one of the older girls would take charge of one or two little ones as 'big sisters,' that would be a wonderful mitzvah and a great thing for *Yiddishkeit*." So we made lists and paired off the older girls with little boys and girls. The "big sister" would teach her charges about the weekly Biblical portion, take walks with them, tell them stories and see to it that they wore their gloves and boots when the weather was bad.

There were times when we were placed completely on our honor. In the evening, after our teachers had gone to their homes for the night, we children were completely unsupervised. We could have roamed the streets and done whatever we wanted, but we were put on our honor not to do anything improper, for instance, not to hang around the pub, from which people came out late at night dead drunk. This was really a challenge to the character of the children.

Our years in Shefford were not all fun and laughter by any means. Many of the children received letters from the Red Cross that their parents whom they had left behind in Europe had been deported or had died. And so those fortunate others who had families in London or elsewhere to lean upon, adopted their orphaned friends, in a manner of speaking. Many children from irreligious homes became Orthodox through the influence of Shefford. One of my best friends today, for instance, came from a home where the family had a Christmas tree, but she now covers her hair and her sons study at *yeshivos*.

Another case in point is the lady who is widely known today as *Morah* (teacher) Blanka and whose Jewish children's records are selling all over America and elsewhere, too. Blanka had come to London as a refugee from Vienna, had enrolled at a non-Jewish public school in London and had been evacuated with her school to a village not far from Shefford. There she was billeted at the home of a non-Jewish butcher. When Dr. Grunfeld heard about the little Jewish girl billeted with a non-Jewish butcher, she was determined to get her out of there. She chose two girls, of whom I was one, to go to that place and get the little girl to leave the butcher and join our school. At first Blanka didn't want to come with us. The butcher only said, "If she wants to come with you, I'll let her go. I'm not going to hold on to her."

And here was little Blanka crying in the corner, refusing to come with us. But Dr. Grunfeld did not give up. She herself went to see her, and this time Blanka came to us. She was, I think, twelve years old at the time, but she could barely read Hebrew. However, before long she was studying Rashi with the rest of us. It is impossible to count the children who were saved for Judaism through this memorable experience of ours in Shefford.

After a while, some parents took their children back to London because they just could not bear to be separated from them for so long. They were willing to take the risk. But others, including my own parents, refused to take us home. Eventually we were all concentrated at Shefford and Clifton. Those few who were left in Stotfold and Campton came to us. Our classes were held in Clifton, which was only a mile away from Shefford. We older children ate our meals and lived in Shefford. We made the one-mile trip back and forth twice each day. Some of us hitched rides. Of course, we shouldn't have done that, and we must be grateful to God that nothing untoward ever happened to any of us.

After a while it became necessary for the children to participate more actively in cleaning chores. There simply wasn't enough help. One of the teachers devised an "army system" whereby we were all either privates or corporals or lieutenants and so forth. We scored points for various cleaning and tidying jobs. It was all very well organized and taken very seriously.

There was much stress on athletic activities. We had a lady
teacher, a refugee from Berlin, who coached us in handball and bas-
ketball. There was Sports Day, a typical English custom. There was
always a game of table tennis going on. You had to put down your
name seventeen games ahead, and wait your turn. There were dra-
matics, artwork and sewing classes.

We were kept very busy and occupied. The older girls were group
leaders. I was a group leader when I was thirteen. Every Shabbos
afternoon, after the group meetings, we had a beautiful *Oneg
Shabbos*. This was all co-ed—boys and girls together. We sang
together beautifully. One of our music teachers was Dr. Jacobsen
from Hamburg, who composed several very well known songs, such
as *Yehuda L'Olam Taishev*.

There was Dr. Hugo Mandelbaum, and, of course, Dr. Judith
Grunfeld. These people all had a very great impact on our lives—
each one in his or her way. They would call you in for private talks.
It might be nothing more than to tell you that you were going to be
in charge of clearing the tables after lunch, but it was put to you in
such a way that you felt truly honored. There were very close friendships among the students—I think more so than would have been the
case if we had lived with our parents, because when you are away
from home you depend more on one another.

Naturally, we were not always little angels. I remember one time
when my whole class, which, I think, consisted of nine girls, ran
away from school. We had a teacher who couldn't control us, and so
we simply walked out. We hitchhiked, the nine of us together, to
another village. We spent the afternoon there. We went to a movie,
and goodness knows what else. When we came back to Shefford, of
course, we were in plenty of trouble. By way of punishment, we were
not permitted in the community hall. But the worst of all our punish-
ments was that for three weeks we girls were not allowed to attend
the *shiur* of Dr. Grunfeld, which I think we had about three or four
times a week. To me this was what really hurt the most. That's how
much we enjoyed Dr. Grunfeld's class.

After I had been in Shefford three years, my parents rented a home
outside London so that they could take us children back with them.

So we left Shefford while the war was still going on.

But the influence of Shefford on our lives continued. I was then 15 years old and my parents enrolled me at a very high-class English non-Jewish school. At this school I met a few Jewish girls who were completely irreligious. This was our last year in high school. I took it upon myself to sit down at home and write letters to the parents of these girls, mostly wealthy, prominent people. I wrote to them that I had been at a Jewish school with refugee children who had lost their parents in the death camps. Would they care to "adopt" one of these orphans by undertaking to support him or her financially? Or would they make a one-time contribution for the upkeep of such an orphan? To my own surprise, I got a very good response. Four children, I think, were "adopted financially" by individuals to whom I had written.

One Purim some friends and I arranged a traveling Purim show to raise money. I sent the money to Dr. Grunfeld in Shefford to be used for buying a heater for the dining room.

So you see that Shefford created in me, at least, a strong feeling of responsibility for those who had lived in such close proximity with me for three years. And I believe this is a wonderful thing. I wish that the children today would feel as much as we did that *Kol Yisroel Areivim Ze LoZeh* (All Jews are responsible for one another).

SHEFFORD HEALED US
by Betty Rosenblat Retter

Berlin, 1937. We knew that our days in Germany were numbered, but where would we go? Who would have us?

And then one day Papa said to us, "There is a young English rabbi here who says he can help us. He's talking about children's transports; affidavits and visas to England . . . *Halevei* . . . Let's have *bitachon* (faith). We had caught a glimpse of that handsome stranger closeted with my father in our library. When he came out, my father introduced us to him. We curtsied as all good German children did when meeting grown-ups. Dr. Schonfeld just smiled and murmured something like, "*Sheine Kinderlech.*" As he left our house, I heard him say, "Mr. Rosenblat, you have a beautiful home here . . . but London is not so bad either."

In 1939 we escaped across the border into Belgium and there we waited for our papers. Week after week, the British consul said, "No visas."

"Have *bitachon*," Papa said to Mama, "See Rivaleh, I told you Rabbi Schonfeld is a man of his word."

When we arrived in England, the immigration officer told us to register at our school the next morning, "if you wish to stay in this country."

And so on Friday, September 1, 1939, my three younger sisters and I were taken to the schoolyard of the Jewish Secondary School. Hundreds of boys and girls were assembled there when we arrived. I felt my little sister Lea's hand tremble in mine. Millie and Margot drew closer. And then we saw him. Towering above all on a raised platform stood Dr. Schonfeld, this unbelievably tall, blond, blue-eyed man. He stood with his arms stretched out as if to embrace us all, and in his booming voice, he announced: "*Kinderlech meine*, boys and girls, all schoolchildren are going to be evacuated by order of the British government." He spoke in English and in Yiddish, and we stood there, frightened.

There were buses waiting for us. We were given a box of sandwiches and a funny looking canvas bag—gas masks. I understood that. I had had a year of French in school in Berlin, but we had picked up a few words in English on our own, such as "Thank you ever so much," "jolly fellow," "good show," "my bonnie lies over the ocean," and of course, "yes" and "no," "good-bye," and "terribly sorry, sir."

"Don't talk to anyone," I whispered to my sisters. "Don't say anything. We mustn't speak German, or people will think we are German spies."

We traveled for hours on buses and trains until we arrived in a village called Shefford. We piled out of the bus as villagers milled around, looking at us curiously. One of the teachers asked us, in Yiddish and English, to line up against a wall of the market square.

My sisters and I huddled closely together. We wore red and white summer dresses with puffed sleeves and matching white socks and shoes. We stood out conspicuously against the sea of children wearing school uniforms around us. Little Lea's eyes filled with tears, but she never uttered a sound; Milly, Margot and I just stood there. We were 14, 12, 11, and 5 years old, and we were terrified. This was a strange country and the people were strange to us, too. Where were Mama and Papa?

Then a little old lady approached us. She pulled at the billeting officer's arm and said something to him. He motioned for us to come forward, and we stepped forth, clutching each other's hands. The little old lady took my hand, and, with my sisters in tow, we crossed the square. She stopped, smiled at us and pointed to a big, black car. It was a hearse!

My heart stopped, but smiled bravely. Pulling my sisters along, we climbed into the back of the hearse. The door closed on us, and we sat there in petrified silence. Later we learned the little old lady was the village undertakers' wife.

After 10 long, unbearable minutes the hearse came to a stop and the lady opened the door. We climbed out and entered a typical English village home. She spoke to us and motioned for us to sit down. We sat. She talked some more. We stared at her in uncomprehending silence. Suddenly she rushed out of the house and returned a few moments later with a tall, imposing woman who peered at us curiously. She nodded in greeting; we nodded in return. Then she smiled, raised her hands and began signing—using the language of mute and deaf people. I was mortified, confused and angry.

"*Madame*," I stammered at last, '*Parlez-vous Francais, peut-etre?*'"

The woman looked at us hard, and then turned to the mistress of the house and burst out laughing. "These children aren't deaf and dumb! They are French!"

The other villagers in Shefford were just as confused. Who were these evacuees, these children from London who spoke hardly a word of English? They are Jewish children. Oh, but what are Jews?

The light shone brightly through the stained glass windows of the Abbey Hall when Dr. Schonfeld walked in. The hall was packed. I think all the people of Shefford turned out to see and greet the children of the Jewish school and their principal, with whom they were to share their homes—by order of the British government. We were not British children, and we were also not gentiles. What then were we?

Dr. Schonfeld approached the platform and a hush fell over the hall. Someone sang out *"Heyveynu Shalom Aleichem,"* and all of us joined in the singing. Our voices rose as we continued with *"David Melech Yisroel."*

Dr. Schonfeld looked out over us and smiled. "My children," he told the people of Shefford, "are Jewish children, and being Jewish means..." and then he spoke for a long time, his voice rising and falling with such heart and fervor, I could taste my tears on my lips. My foster mother was crying, too, and when we got back to her home, she said, "Would you believe it, my dear? Your Dr. Schonfeld looks just like Our Savior! He must be a Godly man!"

It amazed us to learn English as quickly as we did. We spent only our nights in our foster homes. Our daytime hours were spent in the "White House," which Dr. Schonfeld rented for our use, and which we all helped paint a shade of off-white. It is where we ate our meals, had our lessons, prayed, studied, danced and sang. The White House was where we celebrated the holidays, too. When some of us took geography exams for the County Council, one of the questions asked for the location of The White House. Our students answered: "Shefford, Beds."

Shefford was where Dr. Hugo Mandlebaum taught us how to repair and resole shoes and Miss Thea Dym, one of the volunteers who worked with us, put us on kitchen duty. "Betty," she would say, "you peel the skin too thick. Didn't your mother ever teach you...." Then she would stop herself, and say quietly, "No, I guess not. Just do the best you can." I caught on quickly, and to this day my potato peelings are paper-thin.

Where did Dr. Schonfeld find the money to feed us, to supply us with books and *seforim* and to hire his teachers for us? We had teachers like Dr. Levene, who made me learn Silas Marner by heart, so that, as he put it, "I would master the English language." Dr. Bloom was our mathematics teacher, Mr. Genser our French teacher. Dr. Jacobsen was the finest music teacher ever, and our beloved and revered headmistress was Dr. Judith Grunfeld. I don't think anyone in our group paid tuition fees. We were all so poor and helplessly dependent, yet rich in love and care. How did Dr. Schonfeld do it all? How did he travel 60 miles from London under wartime conditions to talk to us and guide us, while at the same time continuing his duties as the rabbi of the Adath Yisroel in London?

The White House in Shefford was our world. It shut out the horrors of our pasts. There we wrote and put on shows for our foster parents. There, we fasted together and celebrated each other's birthdays. We encouraged and cheered each other in the White House. "Don't worry, your parents will be all right," or "Look how well you are doing! Your mother would be so proud of you!"

I remember Lottie Jacobovits, a lovely human being, letting me know, "Your skirt is getting a little short, Betty. Do you want me to release the hem?" What a wonderful group we were—pure, decent, brave and supportive of one another.

Friday night was "our night," a night for singing, talking and philosophizing to our hearts' content. Shabbos was ours. No homework, no getting up at 5 a.m. to pick potatoes and peas in the field for a few pence to replace an outgrown blouse or pair of torn shoes. We loved Shabbos and we loved one another. We were a big, beautiful family. We were a wonderful people. Dr. Schonfeld told us that over and over again. Hearing him, we lifted our heads and stood tall. With him as our principal, how could we be the ugly race, the *verdammte Juden* of the vicious caricatures staring out from the pages of *Der Sturmer* and other German newspapers? Shefford healed us. I know it healed me. The Shefford experience restored our belief in dignity as Jews and as human beings.

After the war, Dr. Schonfeld rescued the sick, the orphans, the skeletons, the little boys and girls with their memories of Dachau, of the chimneys. Thousands of children—and grown-ups, too—from all the corners of Europe were given a chance to live again, to aspire to the heights of human morality, to give, to achieve, and by their own worthy acts, offer praise to God.

Dr. Solomon Schonfeld made that chance possible. He brought them to London, and families there responded to his call for help, opening their homes, and his own home, as well. We knocked on doors, we cajoled, and if necessary, shamed people into taking our Holocaust survivors into their homes.

"What do you mean they do not want to take a little boy?" Dr. Schonfeld would shout in anger. "Go back and tell them that they must." And they did.

We volunteered to help him wherever and whenever we could. How else could we have faced him, this man who knew no night and day, who risked his life, his health, his marriage, his family for the sake of the children, for his people?

Did anyone of us ever say, "Thank you, Dr. Schonfeld for having saved our lives, for single-handedly getting out of Germany, Austria, Czechoslovakia or Poland?" Did anyone of us ever go up to him and say, "Without you, we would have perished."

I often thought of doing so, of writing it, of saying it, but somehow, until now, I never did. How can you thank a man who never stopped to pick up thank yous, to collect the gratitude and the blessings that were justly his, because he had no time for nonsense?

How do we thank you, Dr. Schonfeld? By telling your deeds to our children and our children's children, from generation to generation, so that they may know the story of a man who set an example to us all by fearlessly badgering his way through Heaven and Earth to save us—the children of Israel.

CHAPTER 10

INTERNMENT

A WEDDING ON THE ISLE OF MAN
by Meir Eiseman
Netanya, Israel

I was born in Frankfurt and came to England in May 1937. Three months later I was a bar mitzvah in the Adas. Dr. Schonfeld was then a tall, dashing, handsome, red-bearded young leader who inspired all the young people in the community. Before the Agudah youth groups arose in the England of the 1930's he strengthened Ben Zakkai, a co-ed youth club that had been organized by his late father, Rabbi Dr. Victor Schonfeld, for Orthodox young people. I very vividly remember Dr. Schonfeld leading the *Simchas Torah* parade down Lordship Park, a main traffic artery, with hundreds of the young people marching and singing.

The Jewish Secondary School had an excellent name and some fine students. I still remember how it came about that Rabbi Schonfeld got started on his rescue work. It was in London, the day after *Kristallnacht*. I remember my family and I were sitting at lunch; I can still see it before my eyes. A close friend of my father's, Mr. Herbert Kruskal, who was in the wine business in Frankfurt but held a Dutch passport, came in with his father. Mr. Kruskal had just arrived in London from Germany on an important mission. He called my father away from the dinner table and they went into another room. When they returned they told us that something very serious was happening in Germany. Then they said they had to leave immediately on an important errand. They went out and took a taxi to the home of Mr. Jacob Rosenheim, president of the World Agudath Israel, who at that time lived in Clissold Court in London.

Mr. Rosenheim suggested that my father and Mr. Kruskal meet
with Rabbi Dr. Solomon Schonfeld, to whose synagogue Mr.
Rosenheim belonged. Rabbi Schonfeld, though a close sympathizer,
was himself not a leader in the Agudah, but he already had a reputation as a big activist who had a knack for dealing with problems in
the most direct manner possible. This was probably the greatest gift
that Rabbi Schonfeld had, a gift given by the *Ribbono Shel Olam* (the
Creator): He could assess a situation in a cool, calm manner and
straighten it out with seemingly little effort, and only the aid of his
charm, wit and dedication.

At that time Rabbi Schonfeld still had no official connections. But
I know that Rabbi Schonfeld immediately contacted the Home Office
and that he obtained entry permits, I believe, for two hundred people,
or more accurately put, two hundred rabbis, to come to England. He
chose rabbis because there seemed to be a better chance to get religious leaders out of Austria and Germany. But, of course, he put on
his list also names of people who were not rabbis at all, but who had
connections outside Nazi-occupied Central Europe and who, Rabbi
Schonfeld thought, would therefore be able to help with some sort of
hatzalah work. So he went ahead and wrote out rabbinical ordination
certificates for these people in order to bring them out of Austria and
Germany. Herbert Kruskal took these documents and went back with
them to Frankfurt. [Kruskal was himself active in relief work during
World War I in Nazi-occupied Holland and did not return to England
until after the war.]

I think that this was the beginning of Rabbi Solomon Schonfeld's
relationship with the Home Office. These associations made it possible, among other things, for him to intercede with the Home Office
on behalf of refugees who had already arrived in England and needed to have their legal status changed from that of temporary residents
to permanent residents. I remember that my own father and mother
and my older sister (I was still too young) were notified to appear
before a "tribunal" to receive their permanent resident status. Two
weeks after we left Germany we learned from German newspapers
that we (and probably all Jewish emigrants) had been declared "state-

less." As a result, we had a certificate of "statelessness," meaning that we were not legally considered citizens of any one country.

At any rate, the case of Mr. and Mrs. Eiseman and their daughter came up for a hearing at the Home Office "tribunal" on a Shabbos. My mother could not walk so far, but my father and sister decided to make the journey to the Home Office, which involved a walk of two or three hours from our home. Dr. Schonfeld insisted on accompanying them on this long hike. I know that he did such things for my parents and many others as well. And of course, he also interceded on behalf of temporary residents when it was not Shabbos. Here was a man willing and able to turn the world upside down. No individual was too young or too insignificant to be taken care of—rich or poor, child or adult, student or teacher, every individual counted.

Rabbi Schonfeld has always been particularly concerned about *shidduchim*, that young people should find the proper marriage partners and should be married at as early an age as possible. When the war broke out, Sir John Anderson, England's Home Secretary decided that every male enemy alien between the ages of sixteen and sixty should be interned in order to protect England from Nazi spies. These internees included mostly, of course, Nazis and Nazi sympathizers, but a great many innocent Jewish refugees were interned also. Many of the refugees were released a few months later, but some of them remained interned for much longer than that. Some of them were even deported to Australia or Canada. In some instances internment caused terrible hardships. I note the case of one young engaged couple, where the future bridegroom was interned on the Isle of Man.

However, he already had a visa for Cuba. This meant that he would be released earlier than the others because the British did not really suspect Jewish refugees and were willing to let them leave England if they had visas to another country. But the young man's fiancee did not have a visa for Cuba, so that if he went to Cuba she would have to stay behind. The only way in which she could go to Cuba with him would be if he and she were legally married. But he was in the internment camp on the Isle of Man and she was in London.

Dr. Schonfeld came to her rescue. He got permission from the Home Office and from the camp commander on the Isle of Man to arrange for the young lady to be flown from London to the Isle of Man to be married, and a local newspaper ran this amazing little story. Five thousand internees witnessed the ceremony. The commander of the Isle of Man was there and so was the camp doctor; they brought roses for the young couple. The bride was allowed to remain on the Isle of Man for two or three hours; after that she went back to London. Eventually the young husband was escorted from the camp directly to the boat; at the dock he met his bride and together they set sail for Cuba.

Such ideas, and the unique way of carrying them through were typical of Rabbi Schonfeld. Do it yourself and do it right—that was Rabbi Schonfeld.

Let me tell a little about Rabbi Schonfeld's work as an educator and rescuer of Jewish children. During the late 1930s I lived on the same street as the Jewish Secondary School, Bethune Road. In December 1938, the week of Chanukah, the first transport of three hundred refugee children arrived from Vienna. Rabbi Schonfeld went to Vienna himself to pick them up.

Meanwhile, a group of volunteers, including me—young people from the Ben Zakkai youth group—were asked to help clear out the whole school building. All the desks and classroom furniture were thrown into the backyard, and the schools—the one in Northfield, the one in Stamford Hill, and the one in Amhurst Park—were emptied and converted into hostels for the refugee children. I remember that it was a pretty cold winter, with lots of snow. I believe that these children landed in England on a Shabbos.

Dr. Schonfeld attempted to convince the mayor of Harwich to allow the children to stay there over Shabbos so that they would not have to violate the Shabbos by traveling. Unfortunately, he was not successful. So the children boarded the train on Shabbos and arrived in London just as the Shabbos ended. Rabbi Borenstein, the rav of the *beis medrash* at the Jewish Secondary School and I waited with the staff at the school until the first of the refugee children walked in with their knapsacks. This happened about an hour after nightfall. Since it was Chanukah I lit the candles for them. Many of these children afterwards became my very good friends.

The Jewish Secondary School served as a hostel for the refugee children for several weeks. Since it was the winter vacation anyway, classes were suspended until the middle of January 1940. At the school/hostel several refugee rabbis whom Dr. Schonfeld had helped—directly or indirectly, to come over to England—supervised the young refugees.

But of course the children could not live at the school forever. They therefore had to be permanently placed, and this was also the work of Dr. Schonfeld. I remember that we young people walked the streets of N. 16 [London], going from house to house asking the people whether they would be willing to take a refugee boy or girl into their homes. These houses were mostly one-family homes, not small apartments. So, the people did have room, but it was hard work to persuade them to take in refugees. The British Jews in those days didn't quite believe what was going to happen. Had they known, I am sure they would have opened their doors wide. But they did not know. Some of them said to us, "Now what do you think? I have no room," when in fact they had five, six, seven and even eight rooms in their houses. So they missed their chance to perform an act of *chesed*.

Perhaps they weren't ready for such things yet. In those early days the old neighborhood was composed largely of plain folk who somehow were not able to grasp the seriousness of the situation. We children probably didn't grasp it either, but we had a lot of fun doing the things we were doing for the refugee children. It did not occur to us that we were doing something great; we simply enjoyed ourselves.

Of course, we all loved Rabbi Schonfeld. The man dazzled me. I would say that everything I have done as an organizer and administrator has been inspired by the example set by Rabbi Solomon Schonfeld. There is no question about that.

During the war, I came to Shefford. I went because my sisters were students at the Jewish Secondary School and our parents did not want us to be separated. I, however, had never been a student at the Jewish Secondary School, although I certainly should have been. So, although I was with the Jewish Secondary School community at

Shefford, I attended a school that was evacuated from London to Bedford, about 10 miles away from Shefford. I traveled to that school by bus every morning. At Shefford I was put to work in the office. I did the typing, and ran errands for Dr. Judith Grunfeld. I had a motorcycle, so I was the messenger for organizing things in Shefford.

I remember certain incidents involving refugee children who were evacuated to Shefford with the Jewish Secondary School. One particular incident stands out very much in my mind. Rabbi Lipa Honig was one of the active Agudah members who arrived from Vienna and subsequently was very much involved in the Agudah in London. He arrived in England with his two sons, Chezkel and Nuta, who were very young children at the time. I myself heard Rabbi Schonfeld tell Rabbi Honig that he, Rabbi Schonfeld, would not be able to take the little boys with him to Shefford with long *payes*. Dr. Schonfeld was never a man ashamed of *Yiddishkeit*. But he told Rabbi Honig that he did not know how the non-Jewish youths in the countryside, some of whom had never seen a Jew before, would react to children who spoke no English and looked "funny."

Rabbi Honig trimmed the *payes* of his boys, so that traces of them were left, but the children no longer had rolled up sidecurls. That night the two little boys were sent to a non-Jewish landlady. They sat in her house and did not stop crying. Since Dr. Grunfeld and the other teachers and leaders were busy trying to settle the other children in the headquarters we had established for the school, the non-Jewish woman was going out of her mind. The children would not answer her questions; they would not even take a glass of water from her. Finally I was sent to that house to straighten things out. I was perhaps fifteen or sixteen years old at the time. When I came to the house I saw these two little boys sitting there, with their hands covering their *payes* and their fingertips holding down their caps. They were afraid that someone would take away their caps, and that they might also be forced to cut off what remained of their *payes*. It took us hours to get these children to sleep. That was my first night's work in Shefford. But, *Baruch HaShem*, a miracle came to pass.

The non-Jews who took in the evacuees had the patience to go through with all this and did not rebel against the idea of Jewish children living in their homes, Jewish children who could not speak English and who looked and behaved differently from anyone they had ever seen before. Although Dr. Schonfeld himself never lived in Shefford, he was naturally the moving force behind it all.

Two or three years later I became involved in an effort to see to the needs of religious German and Austrian refugees who had joined the English Pioneer Corps. The British at the time did not take refugees from Nazi Europe into the army, but there were many young people who wanted to perform some patriotic service for England, and they volunteered for the Pioneer Corps, which performed auxiliary tasks such as repairing highways and transporting munitions.

That year, as Pesach approached, I was working in a little town called Biggleswade, where I taught Hebrew classes for children, much like the Talmud Torah here in the United States. I was also in charge of the little synagogue there. When Pesach came and we had all these Pioneer Corps men and Jewish soldiers around us, I tried to persuade the community—mostly Jews who had been evacuated there from the larger cities—to permit us to organize a Pesach canteen. It would not be just for the *Sedorim*, but a canteen where Passover food would be served for the entire Passover week. How we managed to convince the Jews to allow us to do this is a story in itself. It was not as easy as it sounds today. Most of the local Jews were not observant and they felt that this was not all that important. So my friends and I organized the women and went behind the backs of the men. By the time we finished getting the women involved, everyone had promised to contribute some food; one a pound of butter (which meant a great deal then), another half-a-dozen eggs.

Of course, I also had to get new knives and forks and matzoth and wine. I estimated that about 150 people were involved. My friends and I did the organizing, but it was Rabbi Schonfeld who told me how to go about it. It was he who sent me to the office of the local quartermaster corps to requisition the new utensils we needed. Here was young Meir Eiseman, still wet behind the ears, walking into a huge air force camp and demanding to speak to the commanding officer. I learned these tactics from Rabbi Schonfeld; I alone would never have done it. I was successful. I got all the equipment I could possibly have wanted. We then went to the church hall where we had been given permission to set up our Pesach kitchen for that week.

We made arrangements with the local gas company for new ovens and we koshered the sink. But we still did not have enough Pesach food. So I said to Dr. Schonfeld, "We need food." He said, "Very well, I will supply you with all the meat, all the *matzohs* and all the wine you need." And that is precisely what Rabbi Schonfeld did, through the Chief Rabbi's Religious Emergency Council. We had about 160 or 170 people at our *Sedorim*. During the rest of the week there were only about thirty people who came and made use of the Pesach canteen, but those were the thirty for whom we had really done the whole thing, because they were the ones who needed the kosher food.

And through it all, Dr. Schonfeld was never far away. If he thought that we had done something wrong, he criticized us mercilessly. He was not the man to mince words. On more than one occasion he called me a "blithering idiot," but I considered that a compliment because I knew he loved me; otherwise he would not have cared. I once heard him yell at Ruth Lunzer in a way that should have sent her through the floor, but it was only Dr. Schonfeld's way of showing that he really cared. He was really happy to have around him people like himself who wanted to help others.

I remember what happened the year after the war. Shortly before Passover he had gone to Czechoslovakia on a rescue mission. On the Friday night before Passover we did not as yet expect him back in London, so the Friday night services at the Adas started without him. Everyone thought that he was still in Czechoslovakia and that there would be no *Shabbos HaGadol drosho* (sermon). Suddenly, as the congregation finished *L'chu N'rannenoh*, Dr. Schonfeld walked in. He was in full military uniform. He went straight to his seat and began to *daven*. The next day he delivered his *Shabbos HaGadol drosho*. During the *mincha* (afternoon) service I stood near his seat. He called me over. "Meir," he said, "I want you to come to my office tonight, immediately after *maariv* (evening service)."

After *maariv*, Ruth Lunzer and I met Rabbi Schonfeld in his office. He turned to me and said, "Very well, you get the telephone numbers on one line from the directory assistance. Ruth, you make the connections, and we will start calling every Jewish hotel in England." And so we dialed the numbers of all sorts of fancy hotels including the Majestic, the Green Park and the Cumberland in Bournemouth. Dr. Schonfeld would then get on the line. "Hello, Dr. Schonfeld here. How are you this evening? Surely your hotel must be full up for Pesach.

"Well, this is the season to be full up. But I will tell you a secret. I will give you a surprise; you will have five additional guests. Oh, don't tell me you have no room to put them up. You will put them up. Who? It's five girls. Yes, five girls. Would you really like me to leave those girls in Czechoslovakia? Now don't give me no for an answer. Now you will take them." In this way he got his girls into every hotel. By midnight Rabbi Schonfeld had found places for sixty or seventy girls whom he had planned to bring over just before Pesach.

I don't know where the hotels found rooms for the girls, but they did. And the hotel people thanked Dr. Schonfeld in the end. Here, I think, was Dr. Schonfeld at his greatest. There was no audience. He wasn't trying to impress anybody. Meir Eiseman and Ruth Lunzer were just little shnooks working in his office. Nobody else heard us. But this is exactly how Rabbi Schonfeld always got things done. In this he was an absolute master.

There are many, many more things I am sure that people more closely associated with Rabbi Schonfeld, people who worked with him for many years, could tell. Rabbi Schonfeld was a man filled with enthusiasm for everything he did. On Sports Day, when children from the Hasmonean Schools, from the Avigdor School and even from [Rabbi Baumgarten's] Yesodei HaTorah assembled, he took an interest in every 100-yard dash or hurdle or high-jump performed by a boy or girl, and at the end of the evening gave out the prizes and shook hands with every one of the young athletes, whether they were nine years old or whether they were already thirteen or fiftenn.

The same enthusiasm that Rabbi Schonfeld showed on a Sports Day or in a personal encounter with a family, he showed in *hatzalah*, in communal polities and in his work with his *kehillah*. He is no doubt a very unusual man, and I think all of us have become richer by having sat at his table and by having him been brought up to emulate him.

NO LONGER A REFUGEE
by Trude Wiener, nee Farntrog
New York, NY

My parents, my two sisters and I came to England from Nuremberg. We three sisters arrived first, in April 1939. We had been brought to England by relatives of my mother's—the family of her sister—who lived in Green Lanes and belonged to Rabbi Schonfeld's congregation. My parents joined us two months later, in June. My aunt's family got Rabbi Schonfeld to sponsor our parents and bring them over to England through the Chief Rabbi's Religious Emergency Council.

I did not attend Rabbi Schonfeld's school because I was already seventeen years old, but I attended the private *shiurim* he gave for older girls. Rabbi Schonfeld was always interested in how we were getting along. I remember asking him once to give me some information about a certain family with whom I had planned to spend the summer as a mother's helper. He looked into that. I felt he was someone to whom you could always go for help, advice and guidance. Rabbi Schonfeld never patronized us. He treated us as equals. So many of the English Jews in those days looked down upon us refugees, but Dr. Schonfeld made us feel worthwhile.

Some time during the war we were interned on the Isle of Man and Rabbi Schonfeld came to visit us there. He wanted to know whether there was anything he could do to help us, and to find out whether we had kosher meat. He sent us *seforim* and kosher packages.

After we were released from internment on the Isle of Man we came back to Green Lanes. Soon after our return, my parents made an arrangement with Dr. Schonfeld whereby he rented his home at 35 Lordship Park to them. In fact, I think that initially we lived there rent-free. He himself moved to another place.

We remained members of Rabbi Schonfeld's congregation until we left for the United States. I arrived in New York in 1947. During the postwar years in England I interceded with Rabbi Schonfeld on a number of occasions on behalf of other people. I remember that when my mother taught at a Talmud Torah in Edgerton Road, a non-religious girl who had become Orthodox wanted to study at that Talmud Torah.

However, her parents did not want to pay the tuition for her. My mother turned to Rabbi Schonfeld, who said that of course he would take the girl into the school, regardless of whether or not she would be able to pay. This was an example of how Rabbi Schonfeld endeavored to bring non-religious young people closer to traditional Judaism. It was Dr. Schonfeld's way to open doors for other people, to enable them to develop all their potentialities and to make their own contribution to Jewish life and to mankind.

INTERNMENT BECAME BEARABLE
by Hugo Mandelbaum
Jerusalem, Israel

As one of the rescued, when I attended the services at the Adas Yisroel Synagogue on my first *Shabbos* in London, I experienced a blending of Jewish tradition that I had not known before. After a sermon of penetrating thought in connection with the biblical portion of the week, Rabbi Schonfeld suddenly changed the tone of his voice and, in the singsong of *maggidim* (old-time preachers) began to talk *mussar* to the assembled congregation. Coming from Hamburg in Germany, I had never heard this kind of *niggun* before, nor had I ever experienced so natural a combination of West European culture and East European Jewish warmth, such soul-searching closeness, such profound Jewish feeling. I was startled and deeply stirred by the naturalness with which the rhythm of the singing words followed the clear logic and profundity of the Rabbi's English sermon.

I was fortunate to have been able to assist in a small manner in the evacuation of the Jewish Secondary School from London at the outbreak of the war. The children who experienced the building up of an entirely new Jewish community on completely alien ground will be forever indebted to Dr. Schonfeld, through whose effort and initiative the school was founded and through whose sustained assistance the new plant could produce outstanding fruits and an indelible influence on the lives of all who came in contact with it.

After we were interned as "enemy aliens" in Preath-Heath in Middle England we had no official contact with the outside Jewish community for over a month. We had established, for those interested, a self-made kosher kitchen, but we were deprived of essential ingredients with which to make food palatable, for instance kosher fat. Dr. Schonfeld was the first and only representative of the Jewish community who cared enough to come to visit and inspect our internment camp, to give us encouragement in a very discouraging environment. He took note of urgent requirements to make life in internment bearable for those who did not want to give up the essentials of Judaism in an enforced alien environment.

I express my admiration for his constant efforts for the welfare of others and for his great achievement in helping create a center of genuine Jewish life in an alien surrounding. When I was in England with my family, waiting for permission to immigrate to the U.S.A., Dr. Schonfeld was not yet thirty years old, but already he had accomplished what others could hardly have achieved in a lifetime.

CHAPTER 11

SURVIVORS

A VISITOR CAME TO CRACOW
by Henya Mintz

I was born in a small Polish town near Lemberg. My father was a Belzer Hasid. When World War II broke out, I was only eleven years old. When the Nazis first came to my hometown in the fall of 1939 they stayed for only about two weeks. Then the Russians took over and were there for about a year and a half, but they didn't bother the Jews. I went to a Russian school and everything was all right. But in 1941 the Germans came back. We were six children, three girls and three boys. Two were already married when the war broke out. One brother escaped into Russia. The Gestapo took my sister and her small children to Bielice. They died in the gas chambers. But the younger, unmarried ones, one sister and two brothers and myself—I was then twelve years old—were taken to work in the fields, on an estate a few kilometers from our town.

The Ukrainian police guarded us so that we should not run away, but it was not too bad. We would pick potatoes and other vegetables for ourselves from the fields. We met young non-Jews who were also working there. They told us we had better run away. They had heard that we were going to be taken to a camp that would be much worse than that place. My brother said that the four of us should not stick together because we should not all be killed; at least one of us should survive to tell the story. As it happened, I was the only one fated to survive. My brother was shot just two weeks before the war ended.

I became a fugitive moving from one non-Jewish family to the other. One non-Jewish woman brought me food. I hid out at her house for about two weeks. But she was afraid that her children or her husband might discover me and give me away to the Germans. Another woman told me to come right before Christmas when there would be lots of food. So I came to that family on Christmas Eve right before dark. Her sons were students and had come home for the Christmas holidays. When they spotted me they began to yell, "Jew! Jew! There's a Jew here!"

So I ran away. I ran and ran until I lost my skirt and I couldn't go on anymore. The two boys caught up with me. I said to them, "Please don't touch me! If I have to die, I want to die a natural death. I don't want you to kill me." I said, "You must know you are celebrating the birthday of a Jew."

I don't know what made me talk. The words simply poured out of my mouth. I noticed that the boys really didn't have any weapons on them, any guns or knives. After a while I started walking and they no longer followed me. I walked and walked until I came to another place where a man was milking cows. It turned out that he had known my father. He saw the way I looked, in rags and tatters. He asked me why I was breathing so heavily. Had anyone seen me? I said, no, I was just tired and the weather had been very cold. No one had seen me coming.

He gave me a blanket and told me to climb up a ladder to his hayloft and stay there for two weeks. I could not come down because his sons were home from school for Christmas. He said he would bring me food once each day. He said that his signal would be a cough. If he coughed I would know that he had come with the food. If I heard footsteps without a cough I should not move. I remained in the hayloft for two weeks, and then one day the man said to me, "Well, you will have to leave, because sooner or later somebody may spot you."

During the summer I slept in the fields. It was warm. Food during the summertime was no problem because there were always apples on the ground to pick up. Only the winter was bad. Then it was cold and there was no food around.

The Russians liberated me. I remember lying on the straw roof of the place where I was hiding, and seeing the Russian patrols coming. There was another Jewish girl hidden in that village. Together, we two girls followed the Russian army back to our hometown, which was about 20 or 25 miles away. When we came to the town we found only a few Jews left there. Some of them had been partisans. These survivors rented a house for us, in which we could recuperate. We received clothes and bedding, and a Polish woman came in to cook for us. We rested at this house until we regained our strength, just as if we had been in a convalescent home. Eventually I went to live with a family from Belz, a fine Jewish family. They were fairly well to do; they owned a flourmill and plenty of flour so there was enough for me to eat.

I stayed in our hometown for about a year. Then the Russian occupation announced that all people who wanted to go to Poland had better do so now because after a certain date they would not be permitted to leave the Russian occupied area. So the Jews from Poland began to leave. The family with whom I had been staying set out for Cracow. I went with them but I did not intend to stay in Poland. I knew I had an uncle in the United States, my father's brother. I remembered only his name, but not his address. I had always dreamed of going to the United States. The Belz family wanted to immigrate to Israel. But in either case, wherever you wanted to go, to *Eretz Yisroel* or the United States, you had to get out of Poland and into Germany.

When we arrived in Cracow, I no longer wanted to be a burden to the family because they themselves were destitute. I figured that in Poland there must be many groups of young Jewish people, organized by Mizrachi and other Jewish political parties planning to move into Germany and from there into *Eretz Israel*. Naturally, I wanted to join a religious group. After all, my father had been a Belzer Hasid, and my mother had had all her hair shaved off beneath her wig. So I looked for an Agudath Israel group. I found one that I liked, a fine, young group of Jewish girls. They were making arrangements to go to Germany on the way to *Eretz Israel*. But then a visitor came to Cracow and changed the course of my life.

One morning, in the dormitory, I heard the girls say that a rabbi had arrived from London. His name was Rabbi Schonfeld. He was looking for war orphans to take with him to London where he would give them a home. When I heard this I got very excited. I wanted to get out of Poland as quickly as possible, because the night before rocks had been thrown at the building where we lived. I was frightened. I had gone through so much and now it seemed that the Poles were going to kill us. I was afraid to walk in the streets. We were afraid to talk Yiddish in public. I said I would be glad to go any place, as long as I could get out of Poland.

I jumped off my bed and said to the girls, "Let's go see where this Rabbi Schonfeld is." I was told that he was staying in a hotel in Cracow. At first the girls did not want to go. I did not want to go by myself. I had a friend name Chana, who had come from Belz, like me, and I said to her, "Chana, let's go. Don't you want to go to London too?"

At the hotel we found many people already there waiting for Dr. Schonfeld. I asked one man, "Is Dr. Schonfeld supposed to be here?" He replied, "Yes, we are waiting for him also. He is supposed to come, but we don't know when. So we'll just wait for him." So Chana and I waited for Dr. Schonfeld all day long, from morning till night, but Dr. Schonfeld did not show up. In the end, we said we would go home to our Agudah group and come back to the hotel the next morning.

Just as we were ready to go down the steps of the hotel, Rabbi Schonfeld arrived. He was wearing an army uniform. I think he wore it because he thought this would help him in Poland. He said to us in Yiddish, "Are you girls waiting for me?" I said, "Yes, we've been waiting for you ever since this morning." He pinched our cheeks and said, "Well, come back with me to the hotel, girls. I want to talk to you."

There were a lot of people who wanted to pay him, so that he would take them out of Poland to London on one of his visas. He was not supposed to take people older than eighteen. Since I was over eighteen, I had to make myself younger.

I told Rabbi Schonfeld that I had heard he was taking orphans to London, and that Chana and I would love to go to London with him just to get out of Poland. We are orphans, we said, who have survived the war. So he took down our names and our ages. He told us to make ourselves one year younger. My friend Chana was even older than I. Then he said to us, "We'll let you know. I'll send you a telegram to report to the British Consulate in Warsaw as soon as your visa is ready. We'll give you a sponsor." Our sponsor was a Rabbi Dr. Spitzer.

Two weeks later, Chana and I received a telegram to report to the British Consulate in Warsaw. When we arrived at the consulate we found that everything had been taken care of. We only had to mention the name of Rabbi Schonfeld and all doors were opened for us because of his personal reputation. The British knew very well that we had not told the truth about our ages, but they turned a blind eye to this because they thought so highly of Dr. Schonfeld.

From Cracow we were to taken to Gdansk by small planes, which could only take twenty passengers at a time. Our transport consisted of 110 to 120.

When we arrived at Gdansk, Rabbi Schonfeld was waiting for us there. I remember it was a Friday. He shepherded us aboard the boat, which was to take us to England. We boarded the boat just before Shabbos. The journey took about four days. Rabbi Schonfeld was the only adult with us on the boat. He personally took care of every child in the transport. Some of us got quite sick on the boat, so Rabbi Schonfeld had his hands full. However, he remained cheerful all throughout the crossing. He tried to cheer us up and taught us English songs such as "Daisy, Daisy." He kept talking to us, trying to teach us English. He told us about the beautiful place to which we were going. He tried to talk to us in Yiddish, but the trouble was that some of the girls in the transport did not understand Yiddish because they had come from very assimilated Polish homes. But here was Rabbi Schonfeld telling us stories, cheering us up and trying his best to make everyone comfortable.

I remember that we landed in England on March 27, 1946. In London we were taken to a beautiful house where dinner was waiting for us. We were given towels and toothbrushes and we found nurses waiting to take care of all our needs. We were given clothes and boxes of sweaters. After we had settled in at this house, we were asked where we wanted to go.

Whoever wanted to be with an Agudah group could transfer to an Agudah hospital. Some had relatives with whom they went to live. Rabbi Schonfeld interviewed each one of us to find out about his or her background, about relatives who he or she might have in England, and then allowed the newcomers the choice of where they wanted to go. I went to the Beth Jacob hostel because I wanted to live with a group of religious girls. I remember that we had a separate building in Stamford Hill, N.16, in the Orthodox section of London. We were about thirty girls. There was a cook who prepared the food for us, and a woman came in to clean the house every day.

We started to explore the city of London. We had heard that a great many areas had been hit quite severely in the German bombings. Yet, somehow, we did not feel that we were going through a city that had been devastated by the war. There still was some food rationing. We did not get very much meat or candy, and the food was not too good. Yet, after the war years in Poland, we considered the food we received in England quite abundant.

The younger refugee children started school right away. It was considered very important that we learn the basics of English as early as possible. Dr. Schonfeld took care of everything. He made sure that everyone was eventually placed in a proper family environment. I was placed with the family of Rabbi Jacob Twersky. Rabbi Twersky came to the hostel every day for an hour to teach the older girls English. The younger girls who were still of school age went to school to learn English. I could have gone to school, too, but I already wanted to work and earn my own living. I enrolled in an art school to study costume design and sewing.

Meanwhile, I picked up English very fast. At the same time I learned Hebrew. I had known, of course, how to read the Hebrew of the prayer book, but I had never really known the Hebrew language, because in the old country, girls were not taught Hebrew. Only the boys were taught such things. In Poland there was no yeshiva in that sense of the word for girls. There did exist a Beis Yaakov movement, which had 38,000 students by the late thirties, ed.*

I lived in London for three and a half years. I was in constant touch with Rabbi Schonfeld. He made sure that the girls had everything they needed. After I started working I gave the hostel about a pound from my salary. If I made four pounds I would give them one pound. Rabbi Schonfeld made arrangements for us girls in the hostel to go on vacations, to spend a week with a family on the beach.

I remember one year I liked the place on the beach so much that I called Rabbi Schonfeld and asked whether I could stay longer. He said, "Yes, if you want to stay another week, stay another week." He made all the necessary arrangements. Everybody I met, whether in London or in the countryside, had only the greatest respect for Dr. Schonfeld. All you needed to do was mention the name of Dr. Schonfeld and you would get all kinds of favors done for you on account of his fine reputation. All the Jewish families I met seemed to know what he had done.

In the three and a half years I spent in London, I saved about a hundred pounds. When I had saved up the money, I went to Rabbi Schonfeld and told him I would like to visit Israel. I also told him that I had an uncle in the United States, but that I did not have his address. All I knew was his name. Dr. Schonfeld said he would put an advertisement into the Jewish papers so that I might be able to find my uncle. He immediately placed the advertisement.

One day very soon thereafter, while we girls at the hostel were having dinner, I received a cable from the U.S. that said, "Please contact me immediately. Your uncle, Isidor Thaler." My uncle tried to send me papers to come to the United States, but he could not get special priority for me. I had to wait until my number came up under the Polish quota, which is why I remained in England so long.

I wanted to utilize the waiting period by going to see Israel, so I made arrangements with the American Consulate that if my quota number should come up while I was away they should notify me at the place where I would be staying in Israel and I would return to London at once to claim my visa.

When I told Rabbi Schonfeld that I wanted to make a trip to Israel he had no objections, although he seemed a little surprised. He asked me where I expected to stay and whether I had enough money to find the proper accommodations in Israel. He gave me a very nice letter of introduction to a rabbi in Israel, Rabbi Jacobson.

The boat on which I made the trip to Israel was full of refugees who planned to make Israel their home. This was in 1949, the first year after the establishment of the Jewish State. When I got off the boat, I saw Israeli officials all over the pier waiting for the refugees. Each official was trying to grab immigrants for his own political party or for his own kibbutz. Everyone seemed to say, "Come to our kibbutz! We are looking for young people." Our boat landed in Haifa. Rabbi Jacobson, to whom Rabbi Schonfeld had addressed his letter of introduction, was also in Haifa. I immediately went to the address written on the envelope, which turned out to be a hostel for young girls. They gave me a bed right away with free meals. Nobody asked me any questions. Rabbi Schonfeld's word was enough.

So I had a home in Israel immediately. The day after my arrival in Haifa, I went out at once to look for a job. I wanted to be independent even during my visit to Israel, to have my own money. But I could have stayed at this hostel free of charge if had wanted to do so. All I would have to do in return for food and lodging was to wash the dishes. I remember there were about 60 girls at the hostel. It was beautiful, especially on Shabbos. I think that most of the girls had jobs outside and paid some money for their room and board. The hostel had a cook who prepared the meals for the girls. The food on Shabbos was plentiful. Eggs and potatoes were scarce, but I, as a visitor, was given a special tourist ration book and was therefore able to buy canned chicken, meat and candy.

After I had been in Israel for six months, I received a letter from the American Consulate in London, informing me that my quota number had come up and that my American visa was waiting for me. So I left Israel and went back to London, to the hostel where I had been staying before. I remember I was so excited at the prospect of leaving for America that one day while I was boiling some water— there was no hot water at the hostel—I poured some of the water on my head and needed a doctor's care.

Luckily, medical treatment in London was free. Still, I asked the doctor whether I owed him anything. I told him that once I arrived in the United States I would get in touch with him and I would send some money to pay for my treatments once I would have a job in

America. Then I boarded the Queen Mary for the trip to the United States.

GENERATIONS
by Daniela Grunfeld
Riverdale, N.Y.
January 2002

It was Thursday, blustery and gray. In the bleak confines of Hendon, the rain would not relent. Huddled in the barely heated assembly hall, the girls whispered and giggled, restless with waiting. Thursdays were his day and he was, as always, delayed. He appeared in a swoosh, striding up the steps of the rickety stage, raindrops glistening on his red beard. Primly, the headmistress shrank into the protective folds of her academic cloak and the gaunt, ramrod figure of the biology mistress shifted and stiffened in her corner.

Chodesh Tov, he rasped and he cupped his ear with his hand, leaning forward to catch the required response.

Chodesh Kislev Tov came the chorus of girlish voices.

"Toldos," he roared. "Generations." *"Ve eile toldos Yitzchak*—And these are the generations of Yitzchak. . . . Abraham begat Yitzchak." Anyone know what "begat" means?

The embarrassed silence was palpable in the damp, overcrowded hall.

He asked, but not because he did not know. He knew all about "begat." He knew when the begetting ceased and the burning began. He knew, this mighty, broad-shouldered man with sea captain's eyes.

It was on one of his chartered boats from war-ravaged Poland to London, crammed with hordes of children he had scooped off the streets, collected from orphanages and ransomed from their gentile keepers, that my sister, Cecilia/Cesia Maas, made her way into my life.

Blonde and breathtakingly beautiful, with haunted, green eyes and a tiny pointed chin, her father, her mother and her only sister had perished in Lvov. She was the smallest child in the group.

He lost no time in finding her a foster home. In July 1946, a year before I was born, my father took her out of Woodbury Down Hostel and brought her home.

Eight years older than me, she was my idol, I was her shadow. We shared a room and whispers in the dark and when it rained and there was thunder, she sought refuge in my bed.

Gifted with extraordinary compassion, she became a nurse and when she later married, she would have none other than he, her savior, to be her rabbi and officiate at the ceremony.

Four children were born, Amanda, Howard and the blonde twins, Jeremy and Angela. She left London for the United States, where she raised them on her meager nurse's salary, working night shifts to make ends meet. As they grew, she began to take patients into her home and before long, hers became known as the most sought after group home for geriatric Alzheimer patients. Old and ailing, unable to communicate their basic needs and thoughts, these aged outcasts are placed by their families in Cecilia's Maryland home, where she nurses them devotedly, day and night, until the end.

And her four children had children. Amanda had Crystal, Benjamin and Jessica. Howard and his wife, Janice, had Sarah and Jason. Jeremy had Elizabeth and Angela had Samantha.

Toldot—Generations. Lives that came to be because of the courage and compassion of a legendary man with bright, blue eyes and a singular vision.

Ve eile Toldot Yitzchak. And these are the generations of Yitzchak. These are the generations of Yitzchak Maas who begat Cecilia Maas.

HE MADE ME FEEL PROUD
by Joshua Olshin
Queens, NY

I come from Bialystok. My father, at one time, was president of the Jewish community of the town of Sokoly. We were five brothers and two sisters. I was the youngest, but when the war came I was already married, with a family of my own. I had a position as manager of the cooperative bank of the town.

When the war broke out, the Nazis marched in, but then the Russians came and occupied our town. In 1940, however, the Russians left, and the Germans came back. In November 1941, we heard that the Germans were going to clear all the Jews out of the town. So we took to the woods. I left my father, my wife and my two children—a girl of four and a boy of two—in a bunker in the woods. At one point, as I later learned, my father walked out from the bunker and hid under a tree. When the Germans searched the woods, they found him and the bunker and they took my entire family to an assembly point in Bialystok, from where they were deported. I never saw them again.

I survived partly because I worked with the partisans and partly thanks to the help of a priest and a Franciscan nun. When the Russians came back to Bialystok in the summer of 1944, we Jewish survivors organized a Jewish Committee of sixty persons, of which I became president. We searched the surrounding villages for Jewish children who had survived the war. By 1945, thanks to my contacts with the priest of our locality, we had gathered a total of forty-eight Jewish children. Eventually we organized an orphanage for these children somewhere in Lower Silesia. I chose two doctors—a mother and a daughter—to run this orphanage.

Then I myself went to Warsaw and looked for ways to leave Poland because I felt it was dangerous for me to remain there. The Polish underground was after me. Thinking that I was an influential person, they had asked me to secure the release of some Polish people who were in prison. But I did not feel that these people should be out of jail. This made the underground very angry and I began to receive letters threatening that I would be killed. Somehow I managed to get a visa for Cuba, but the visa was waiting for me in France. In order to pick it up I would have to go to the Cuban consulate in Paris. But I had no permission to enter France, nor was I able to get an exit permit from Poland.

Just then, in Warsaw, I heard that a Rabbi Schonfeld had come to town from London. I was told that he was an army chaplain looking for young war survivors from Poland who would come to England to study at a yeshiva in London. Since I had an Orthodox background, I started looking for ways of contacting Dr. Schonfeld. A Jewish chaplain in the American army—a lieutenant—gave me an introduction. I wanted to tell Rabbi Schonfeld my problems and ask him to use his influence with the French consulate in Warsaw so that I could receive permission to leave Poland and go to France to pick up my Cuban visa. I wanted to tell him that my life was in danger, that the Polish underground was out to kill me.

I met Dr. Schonfeld at the headquarters of the Jewish Committee of Warsaw, where he was interviewing boys for his yeshiva. When I saw Dr. Schonfeld in his resplendent army uniform and with that radiant look on his face I already felt that my troubles were over. Merely to walk and talk with him made me feel proud to be a Jew. It gave me a new sense of dignity as a Jew, as a human being and as a citizen of the world. We spoke in Yiddish. He showed a great interest in my private life; I felt he personally cared about me as an individual. He made an appointment to go with me to the French embassy in Warsaw for advice on how to go about getting a French visa, but they could not give him any satisfaction.

But Rabbi Schonfeld did not give up. He made an appointment to go with me to the Belgian consulate in Warsaw. There, he managed to get me a Belgian visa for one day, which would make it possible for me to cross from Belgium into France. The French consul, knowing that I had the Belgian document, gave me a transit visa for ten days. This, I thought, would allow me sufficient time to arrange for a flight from France to the United States. My plan had been to fly to Florida and take a boat to Cuba from there.

I never got to Cuba. I was able to remain in France long enough to apply for, and to receive, an immigration visa for the United States. Eventually I settled in the New York area. I never saw Dr. Schonfeld again. I heard that he stayed in Poland for a while, until he gathered, I believe, some 60 students for his yeshiva in London. But all these years I had hoped that someday I would be able to find this man and express my appreciation to him.

HE NEVER FORGOT MY NAME
by Judith Alter Kallman, nee Mannheimer
New York, NY

When the war broke out; I was a little girl in Slovakia, the youngest of six children. My parents were Orthodox Jews. My father was a businessman; he owned some real estate. My mother was at home. She had a governess to help her take care of us. We had a comfortable, happy home.

And then, all of a sudden, one day in 1942, the Nazis came and forced us out of our home. We were sent to some sort of camp. I was too young at the time to remember what kind of a camp it was, but I think it was an "experimental" camp from where many people were sent to Auschwitz.

Luckily, my parents had some money, so they were able to buy our way to freedom with fake Aryan passports. We went to live in the town of Z. We lived as non-Jews. But, of course, that's a very hard thing for Orthodox Jews to do. My father had no beard, but my mother covered her hair, and naturally we observed the Sabbath very strictly. The older children went to school, but otherwise we led very withdrawn lives. Perhaps this was what made the non-Jews around us suspicious. One morning there was a knock on our door.

It was the Gestapo—two big strong men in Nazi uniform. I was at home alone with my parents; my older sisters and brothers were at school. The Gestapo men spoke in German to my parents, who answered in German. It seemed the Gestapo wanted to see our passports. Something was wrong with our papers, they said. The Gestapo took the passports and left. Later my other brother and sister came home from school. That afternoon the Nazis came back and took away my parents, my brother and my sister. When my other brother and sister came home from school, all the others, except myself, were gone. We had nowhere to go. The Jewish community got together and hid us along with a number of other children.

In the meantime, word got around that if we wanted to see our parents, we should go to the railroad station the next morning; they would be on trains leaving for Auschwitz.

The next morning my brother and I really went to the railroad station and there we saw our parents, and our other brother and sister aboard a cattle car. Of course I became hysterical; I screamed for my mother. But someone told us that if I kept up my screaming and yelling I, too, would end up on the train. I suppose that my instinct for survival took over at that point, and I stopped crying. I saw the train pull away. I never saw my father and mother again.

We had an aunt who lived near Nitra. Her name was Kacser. Her family had been friendly with Rabbi Schonfeld's family for years. (Later, this aunt settled in the United States and became a mainstay of the Nitra Yeshiva in Mount Kisco.)

My aunt was a landowner, who had practically all the peasants in her little village working for her. When she heard what had happened to our parents she made arrangements for some peasants to pick up my brother and me and to take us to their home. We were to stay with those peasants until we could cross from Czechoslovakia into Hungary, which at that time was still neutral. In Budapest we had another uncle and aunt, who my aunt assumed would take us into their home.

I remember how my brother and I crossed the border of Czechoslovakia into Hungary. We were dressed like peasant children. We stopped at a farmstead; the peasants who owned it were supposed to guide us across the border the next morning. But during the night I overheard the peasants talking. They said that they would take only my brother across the border. They wanted to keep me with them at their home. When I heard this I was petrified. I couldn't sleep. The next day I would not let go of my brother for even one moment. But at the end, the peasants took both of us across the border. In fact, they escorted us by train all the way to Budapest and brought us to the house of our aunt and uncle.

But when my brother and I, accompanied by the peasants, arrived at my uncle's house, we were rudely disillusioned. My uncle refused to take us in. He said that anyone caught hiding illegal immigrants was subject to the death penalty. We children spoke no Hungarian; we only spoke Czech and German. So the neighbors would find us out soon enough, and that would be the end of my uncle and aunt. The peasants said, "All we know is that we were paid to bring these children to your house in Budapest. Good-bye." With that, the peasants left us out in the street, alone. The police picked us up and took us to a prison; later, I learned that this was the prison where Hannah Szenes was hanged. I remember that our heads were shaved and that we were thrown into a prison cell. It was a terrible experience.

But it turned out that there were in Budapest still some Jews who were not afraid of helping Jewish children. There was a man named Tenenbaum, a watchmaker. He was very much involved in the Jewish underground. When word got to him that two Jewish orphans from Czechoslovakia were being kept in prison, he was determined to get us out.

Mr. Tenenbaum took my brother and me into his home. I remember it was Chanukah, and that we lit the candles. We spent a few days with the Tenenbaums. Then Mr. Tenenbaum introduced us to a man whom he called Stern-*bacsi* (Uncle Stern). Stern-*bacsi* had a very famous kosher restaurant in Budapest. Everyone knew Stern-*bacsi*'s *cholent* (Shabbos stew). Stern-*bacsi* had very good connections in some high circles; he was said to be on very friendly terms with Admiral Horthy, the Regent of Hungary. Mr. Tenenbaum told Stern-*bacsi* to try and do something for us.

The result was that Stern-*bacsi* and his wife adopted me. They had no children. Their only child had died many years before. So they took me into their home and I immediately called them Mother and Father. But I never got to know their first names. I asked them whether my brother and sister could also come and live with us.

Meanwhile, we heard that Budapest's largest synagogue, the Dohany Ucca Synagogue, had been turned into an emergency shelter for refugees. There, by a miracle, I found my other brother. The brother with whom I had crossed the border into Hungary had been with me all the time. I would never let go of him. He was my security blanket; I would go with him even into the bathroom. Then my other sister appeared. All the four of us—she and my two brothers—came to live with Stern-*bacsi* and his wife. I remember that until the war came to Hungary I lived like a princess. I was driven to school by car and had a maid to take care of me.

I remember that the Belzer Rav came to Stern-*bacsi*'s house; he, too, had taken refuge in Budapest. I remember that people were standing in line on the street in front of Stern-*bacsi*'s house, waiting to see the Belzer Rav. But the Belzer Rav did not stay all that long; he was with us only one or two nights. I remember that Stern-*bacsi* and his wife gave a big dinner for him at their house; I was allowed to stay up because I wanted to drink from the Rav's *kiddush* cup. The Belzer Rav told Stern-*bacsi* that my brother—the older one, who was then about nine or ten years old—should go to *Eretz Israel* before the war came to Hungary. And he indeed made arrangements to send my brother to Palestine by way of Romania. Eventually both my brothers ended up in Israel.

My sister was sent to live with another aunt who lived in a place called B., in Hungary. That aunt's name was Itzkowitz. They were wealthy car dealers. When the Germans occupied Hungary, Stern-*bacsi*, his wife and I moved into one of the "protected houses." The house into which we moved was under the official protection of neutral Sweden. As long as we stayed there we could come to no harm. This is how we managed to survive the war.

Unfortunately, right after the war, Stern-*bacsi*'s wife passed away. Not long thereafter Stern-*bacsi* remarried. His new wife said that she did not want any children around. So I went back to Czechoslovakia. I had to go to the Tatra Mountains because I was not well. I stayed there for one year. While I was there I learned that my aunt, Mrs. Kacser, and my cousins had returned to Nitra. They had survived the war. I got in touch with them. Eventually I went back to Nitra and entered a convent school. In those days all the Jewish children in that area went to convent schools because there was no other place for them to get an education.

The nuns at the convent tried to persuade the Jewish children to become Christians, but if a Jewish child refused to give up his or her religion, the nuns respected that decision. It was at that point that Rabbi Dr. Schonfeld entered my life.

It seems that my cousins, the Kacsers, learned that Dr. Schonfeld had come to Czechoslovakia and that he was organizing a transport of war orphans to take back to England with him. My cousins informed him that I had been left without my parents, that I was attending a convent school, and that they would be happy if he were to take me to England. I don't know exactly what arrangements my cousins made to have me placed in Dr. Schonfeld's transport. All I know is that Dr. Schonfeld personally assumed the responsibility of taking care of me. However, I was not to meet him personally until after our arrival in England.

When I got to London I was sent to a hostel in Stamford Hill. My cousins, who were also in the transport, were sent to Ireland with a group of children who still had parents. The orphans were not sent to Ireland but were kept at the hostel in Stamford Hill. I was enrolled at the Avigdor High School. My headmistress was Dr. Judith Grunfeld. That was the first time I met Dr. Schonfeld.

I was fascinated with him immediately. He reminded me a little of Stern-*bacsi*, who also had that indefinable something we call charisma. But Stern-*bacsi* had been a much older man, and his beard had been white. Dr. Schonfeld had a little red Van Dyke; his eyes sparkled, he had a warm smile. He would reach out and put his hand on my shoulder, and somehow I felt as if there were some invisible tie between us.

There was something very good about it. He said, "What is your name?" I said, "Judith Mannheimer." He said, "Judith, from now on you will be very well taken care of." From that time on he never forgot my name. I felt as if I had become one of his favorite little girls. He had a way of picking me out from a whole group of children in the auditorium at roll call when the attendance was taken before school began. I remember that whenever he entered the room we would rise out of respect for him. As he passed he would wink at me, and say, "How are you this morning, Judith?" He made me feel as if I were one of the most important children in the group. I remember that there was some sort of special occasion in London, a reception for some important person. I was chosen to go to Covent Garden, ascend the platform and to present flowers to the guest of honor.

Eventually—I think it was 1948—I was transferred from the hostel to a family named Warhaftig, who lived in the Golder's Green section of London. I went to the Hasmonean Grammar School. My headmistress was a Mrs. Herman, a very kindly woman whom I liked very much. Dr. Schonfeld frequently came to visit the school and see how the students were doing. And every time he came, he would say, "Ah, Judith Mannheimer, how are you today? Any problems?" He always took an interest in me. I was so impressed by this. To me, he was the most beautiful person. I was a child, sensitive, insecure. My world had collapsed, but Dr. Schonfeld made me feel ten feet tall. I felt that in his eyes I was something very special, and I think it was thanks to him that I grew up feeling good about myself. He gave me confidence.

Years later, I went back to London from America on a visit. One of my Kacser cousins took me to a place where Dr. Schonfeld happened to be. My cousin took me over to Dr. Schonfeld and said, "Would you remember this young lady?" And Dr. Schonfeld said, "How could I ever forget? It's Judith Mannheimer!" Just like that. I was by then a married woman with children of my own. Three years ago, on a visit to Israel, I met him again in the street. I figured that he would hardly be likely to recognize me, but I stopped and said, "Dr. Schonfeld, how are you?" And Dr. Schonfeld stopped and said, "Well, let me see who that is. I know that face. Of course, it's Judith Mannheimer!"

I owe more than just my physical survival to Dr. Solomon Schonfeld. Had I stayed on in Czechoslovakia I do not know whether I would have been able to hold on to my Judaism, or even to life itself. I was in desperate need for someone to uphold me and to show me the way. It was then that Dr. Schonfeld came into my life. He gave me that kindness, that love which no one else could have given me at that point, because all the people who had meant most to me were gone. I was totally alone. I think Dr. Schonfeld sensed it. He actually gave me the feeling that he was glad to know me. Whenever he said, "Why, Judith Mannheimer!" I felt as if the sun had begun to shine again for me, that, after all, God had been very good. If today I am a mature woman, a proud Jewess, the mother of three beautiful children who love their Judaism, then I owe it all to Rabbi Dr. Solomon Schonfeld.

CHAPTER 12

HARVEST

THE ONE-MAN VAAD HATZALAH
by Rabbi Fabian Schonfeld
Kew Garden Hills, NY

I was born in a small town in Russian Poland, not far from Katowice. My parents moved to Vienna when I was still a very young child. My father had been in Vienna before, because he had run away from the Polish army. But when my mother was about to give birth to me, she went back to her own mother. This is how I came to be born in Poland. Anyway, I was brought to Vienna as a very young child, when I was just about a year old.

My father, Shabse Schonfeld, was the secretary general of the Agudath Israel World Organization, which then had its headquarters in Vienna. He was the editor of *HaDerekh*, the first Hebrew weekly newspaper to be published in Vienna by the Agudah. My father was also the secretary of the *Moetzes Gedolei Hatorah* (World Council of Torah Sages). So his involvement in Jewish communal affairs was very well known. The Gestapo had him on their list, and in March, 1938, when Hitler marched into Austria, they came to look for him.

My father was able to escape to Czechoslovakia alone. Then he went to Antwerp, Belgium and from there to England. My mother, my brother and I left Vienna in June or July 1938. Our first stop was Luxembourg. From there we went illegally across the French border to Paris, where we had relatives. We bribed a guard; that is how we were able to cross the border into France. In Paris, we went to a Jewish school, the Ecole Maimonides.

It was in Paris that my brother and I received a visa to go to England. We got this visa through Rabbi Dr. Solomon Schonfeld, to whom, by the way, our family is not related. My father was in England by this time, and he knew Dr. Schonfeld through his contacts with the Agudah. My brother and I were too young for the yeshiva transport, which was for boys of fifteen and above. We therefore came to London with the children's transport.

From the moment we arrived in London, Dr. Schonfeld acted toward us like a substitute father. He took an interest in us. He took us into his school. When World War II broke out we were evacuated with the school to Shefford. The Shefford story, of course, has become very well known, especially through the book recently published by Dr. Judith Grunfeld. Shefford was something of a Boys' Town situation, except that it included both boys and girls. Dr. Schonfeld would come from London to Shefford, I would say, about two or three times each month. He cared for us and about us.

Most of the children at Shefford, of course, had no parents. They had left their parents behind in Germany. My brother and I were fortunate in that both our parents had managed to come to England before the outbreak of the war.

I think Dr. Schonfeld's greatest achievement in Shefford during the years of World War II was to save this group of children physically and spiritually. With the exception of a very few British children, most of the children at Shefford were refugees from Germany. A few came from Vienna and some from Poland. I think the preponderant majority came from Germany. This is how I first became involved with German Jewry.

In fact, it was in Shefford that I met my first wife, Lottie. She was the daughter of Rabbi Julius Jakobovits and a sister of the present Chief Rabbi. Dr. Schonfeld took an interest even in this *shidduch*. After we got married in 1946 he gave me a job in London at the office of the Chief Rabbi's Religious Emergency Council. My wife was teaching, and that is how we managed. Meanwhile, I went to the University of London, from which I got my degree.

All this time Dr. Schonfeld took a personal interest in me. Perhaps it was because he had a special liking for me. Or perhaps it was because of my father's friendship with him. But I think he really was this way with everyone, basically because he cared. Whenever I think of Dr. Schonfeld there occurs to me a special verse in the Torah: "Do not stand idly by while your neighbor's blood is shed."

I always wondered why this precept is expressed in the singular. After all, it is a mitzvah given to the entire Jewish people. I think the answer is that only individuals are in a position to do true justice to this commandment. Groups and organizations cannot really do it. If you get bogged down with organizations, meetings and conferences, not much gets done. But when one individual puts all his energy into the cause, there is a chance that he will succeed. Dr. Solomon Schonfeld was such an individual. For him there was no day, no night, no lunch, breakfast or supper. This man gave up all his personal life, first for the rescue of children from Nazi Europe, then for the education of these children in the evacuation center during the war years, and finally for the cloak-and-dagger operation in which he spirited Jewish children out of Poland after the war.

When I came back to London after the war I saw Dr. Schonfeld every day. After I graduated from college he gave me a position as a teacher in the grammar school, which he had founded. Actually, his father, the late Rabbi Dr. Victor Schonfeld, had established the Jewish Secondary School but it was Solomon who developed it into a whole network of Jewish day schools. Since I had graduated from the University of London in languages, I taught French and Latin at Dr. Schonfeld's school. I also taught what was called Religious Knowledge—Chumash and Rashi. So you see, Rabbi Schonfeld first brought me out of Vienna, then to safety in Shefford. Next, he gave me an opportunity to work my way through college, and finally, after my graduation, he employed me as a teacher at his school. So, I would say without any reservations that whatever I was able to accomplish in my younger years was due to Rabbi Dr. Solomon Schonfeld.

I taught at Rabbi Schonfeld's school for almost ten years. Rabbi Schonfeld was a man with very definite ideas of his own. Some people called him dictatorial. But he had a sound philosophy of education. He spelled it out in his book, *Jewish Religious Education*, of which I still have several copies. It is a textbook on curricula for Jewish day schools. Not all educators might agree with it in every detail, but it was a serious plan, and he followed it through at his school. It was a program of *"Torah im Derekh Eretz."* He wanted his students to be very learned in Yiddishkeit; he wanted them to be what was called *frum*, but at the same time he wanted them to be good Englishmen. Dr. Schonfeld himself was thoroughly at home in British society and had important contacts with highly placed individuals in the British government.

The British authorities with whom he came in contact were impressed with his powerful personality. They respected his sincerity. He was not one of those British Jews of his day who would kowtow to the big shots, and if nothing got done simply went back home to their books. He was persistent, and so he was able to get through to the highest quarters in the British government. I myself once watched him negotiate with the Minister of Education. It was a matter of obtaining recognition for his Jewish day schools from the British authorities. In order to gain official recognition in England, a school must satisfy a long list of requirements. Now the British are not antisemites, but they are very British and they did not like the idea of these "foreign" intruders becoming part of their school system.

At this meeting with the Minister of Education—I cannot remember the man's name—Dr. Schonfeld would lay it on the line. He was not embarrassed to say, "We are Jews first and foremost; we provide the best education for our children, superior to anything you provide for yours; so why shouldn't we be recognized as a school?" Dr. Schonfeld was able to say things to *goyim* (gentiles) that few other Jews were ever able to say. And he got away with it, because he was not a sycophant and he was not afraid of anybody. He spoke with respect, with courtesy, but also with firmness. And he let the non-Jewish world know that he was a Jew who would not yield one inch when it came to *hatzalahs nefoshos* (the saving of lives).

It all came through—Dr. Schonfeld's sincerity, his iron determination and iron will. He would appeal to the British sense of fair play. He would arouse the conscience of the *goyim*. There were many gentiles with more than a little streak of antisemitism who found themselves helping Rabbi Schonfeld in his self-imposed task of rescuing children, because sincerity is a trait all Englishmen appreciate. Dr.

Schonfeld was a diplomat, but it was not the unctuous diplomacy of the *shmeer*. He put things straight, the way it was. As far as my brother and I are concerned, our debt to Dr. Schonfeld is one we will never be able to repay. When I go to England, which is not too often nowadays, I make it my business either to go to see Dr. Schonfeld or at least to telephone him. My conscience really bothers me that I do not have more contact with him these days.

To Dr. Schonfeld, Jewish education was part of *hatzalahs nefoshos*. This is something which a lot of educators in America are only beginning to realize now: that the Jewish day school movement is not merely an educational process, but that it is in fact an aspect of *hatzalah*. Dr. Schonfeld had a lot of trouble, and it came from within the Jewish community. The establishment does not like a maverick. The very *frum* Jews didn't like him because they considered him too modern. The modern Jews didn't like him because they thought he was too *frum*. I remember that he was a most outspoken fighter against Reform Judaism.

I remember one Chanukah he came to the school where I was teaching and addressed an assembly of students on the subject of Orthodox Judaism. There was at that time in England one Reform rabbi who had come from the United States to head the Reform movement in Great Britain. I remember Rabbi Schonfeld saying, "I have nothing against this man personally, but why does he call himself Rabbi Such-and-Such? He ought to call himself Father Such-and-Such." Rabbi Schonfeld really meant this. To him a rabbi was someone who believed in *Torah min hashamayim* (Divine revelation) and he stressed this at every turn, at every opportunity, even in interviews with the *Jewish Chronicle*.

No wonder the establishment did not care for him, and this is why he developed his father's Adath Yisroel Congregation, which was a kind of *Austrittgemeinde* (secessionist Orthodox congregation). Rabbi Schonfeld was not a "fanatic," not a person who would be a stickler for rigid observance when you didn't have to be, but he was a tremendous fighter for unadulterated, undiluted Orthodoxy. At the same time he was proud that his students went on to universities. He was proud of his own college education. He made sure that everyone knew him as Rabbi Dr. Solomon Schonfeld. He would never do without his Ph.D. In fact he created a yeshiva college for his students in which I was the first member of the faculty. Unfortunately, it did not last too long. There simply weren't enough students around. I think it was an idea whose time had not yet come.

Even after I left England and settled in the United States Dr. Schonfeld continued to take an interest in me. After the death of my first wife—she left me with four children—Dr. Schonfeld sent me a letter in which he quoted something his father had once said: "If God in his wisdom decides to send us an evil decree—there is nothing we can do about it. When we pray on Yom Kippur to *Avinu Malkeinu*, our Father, our King, not to afflict us, what we really pray for is that if misfortune comes, its consequences should not cause us to give way to despair." In that spirit, too, Dr. Schonfeld later urged me to consider remarrying. In fact, he lectured me on the subject, and when I married my present wife he sent me a note of congratulations.

Rabbi Schonfeld always said what he meant and meant what he said. As I have already said before, he was irrepressible. He could say things no one else could say and get away with it. He might upset the establishment, but his audiences ate it up. I remember one occasion in the middle 1950s. I'd been in America only a few years in my own *shul* and Dr. Schonfeld had come to the States for a visit. I invited him to spend Shabbos with me and he spoke at my *shul* that Friday night. He was trying to stress the importance of *yichus*, family background. When you get married, he said, be sure you know whom it is you are marrying. And this is what he said: "When people go to a race track, they bet on a horse. They know the whole *yichus* of the horse, the horse's father, the horse's mother, the horse's grandfather, and the horse's grandmother. But when it comes to a *shidduch*, they don't care who it is. Anyone will do." He said: "You want to know the *yichus* when it comes to horses; why, then, don't you want to know the *yichus* when it comes to people?"

In those days Rabbi Schonfeld was blessed with incredible physical stamina. He was used to walking for hours on Shabbos from his home to his synagogue. So he thought it would be just as easy to get from one part of metropolitan New York to another on Shabbos. On one of his weekend visits to New York, he agreed to speak at my *shul* in Kew Garden Hills on Friday night, and to speak at the Fifth Avenue Synagogue—where Sir Immanuel Jakobovits was then the rabbi—the next morning. Crossing the Queensboro Bridge from Long Island to the Upper East Side of Manhattan held no terrors for him.

When he got to the Queensboro Bridge he found that there was no room for pedestrian traffic, except for a precarious catwalk that had been built for emergencies. When the police saw him on the catwalk they thought that here was a madman bent on committing suicide. So they told him to get into their car. Dr. Schonfeld explained to them that he was the Presiding Rabbi of the Union of Orthodox Hebrew Congregations and that he did not ride on the Sabbath. The police car thereupon drove slowly ahead of him and cleared the whole bridge of traffic so that he could cross the bridge on foot without danger to life and limb, and then they escorted him all the way to his destination.

To get serious again, I consider the valiant, irrepressible Dr. Solomon Schonfeld the world's greatest one-man Vaad Hatzalah (Rescue Committee). I would not hesitate to call him the Mordechai of World War II, who championed the cause of his people before the highest authorities in Great Britain. After the war he risked his life to bring out Jewish children from Communist Poland. If there is an active, effective Orthodox Jewish movement in England today, the credit largely goes to him. The present Chief Rabbi of Great Britain, Sir Immanuel Jakobovits, was one of the children whom Dr. Schonfeld brought out from Nazi Germany.

When it comes to Ahavas Yisroel, I consider Rabbi Dr. Solomon Schonfeld the greatest Jew I know.

THE PRESIDING RABBI
by Meir Raphael Springer, Honorary General Secretary,
Jewish Rescue and Relief Committee
Agudath Israel World Organization
London, England

I have known Rabbi Dr. Solomon Schonfeld since his early student years in 1932, when he studied at the world-renowned Yeshiva of

Rabbi Shmuel Dovid Ungar in Tirnau (Trnava) and later in Nitra, Czechoslovakia. According to reports from his fellow students (Rabbi Shmuel Wosner of B'nei B'rak and others) and his direct mentor, Rabbi Michoel Ber Weissmandl, he already showed as a young student the outstanding qualities of leadership which he brought into play after succeeding his father, the late Rabbi Dr. Victor Schonfeld, as Presiding Rabbi of the Union of Orthodox Hebrew Congregations of the British Commonwealth.

Dr. Schonfeld's leadership abilities were demonstrated during the war years when, together with the late Dayan Dr. I. Grunfeld and the late Agudah leader Harry Goodman, he founded the Chief Rabbi's Religious Emergency Council under the presidency of his late father-in-law, Chief Rabbi Dr. J.H. Hertz, C.H. Thanks to this collaboration, hundreds of rabbis and lay leaders, together with thousands of Jewish families and children, were brought from Germany, Poland, Czechoslovakia, Hungary and other Nazi-occupied lands, to England, the U.S.A. and other democratic countries and received financial support until they became integrated into Orthodox economic and communal life.

Prior to the war and soon after assuming office as Presiding Rabbi of England's Orthodox Jewish community, the Adas Yisroel Synagogues, he founded, together with his friends, the Jewish Secondary School movement and pioneered in the establishment of Orthodox Jewish day schools. He carried out these endeavors successfully despite great opposition from the establishment, which saw in these Jewish schools a danger to relationships with the non-Jewish population.

I would like to express my profound thanks to Rabbi Dr. Schonfeld for permitting me to take a small part in these fruitful activities by serving as former chairman of the Avigdor Primary School and as vice-chairman of the Hasmonean Grammar School for Boys, and by cooperating in his outstanding activities in connection with rescuing the remnants of once-flourishing Jewish communities on the European Continent.

HEIR TO HIS FATHER
by Rabbi Jonah Indek
Rabbi Emeritus, Bournemouth Hebrew Congregation
Bournemouth, England

I write as a very old friend of Dr. Schonfeld's family, and my pre-
vailing thought at this time is one in connection with his dear parents.
For, to me, Rabbi Dr. Solomon Schonfeld is a true example of a son
who stepped into his father's place. From the moment he responded
to the call from the old Adas Yisroel Hebrew Congregation to assume
the position of his illustrious father he strove to emulate his faith and
goodness that was so wonderfully supported by his dear mother.

As a teacher at the Adas and later, from 1929, in the Jewish
Secondary School, I saw at first hand how ably and enthusiastically
he applied his talents as a religious leader and educator, and with
what amazing vitality he attended to his many duties. The synagogue
flourished under his leadership. As principal of the Jewish Secondary
School he succeeded in steering it through its most difficult years,
witnessed its achievements and saw it become the pioneer in a wider
Jewish Secondary School movement—the dream of its founder, his
father, realized by Dr. Solomon Schonfeld, his son.

But, above all, having worked with Dr. Schonfeld on the Jewish
Refugee Committee, I think of him as a man who took a deep and
loving personal interest in the welfare of his fellow Jews, so many of
whom he rescued from the Holocaust. In so doing, regardless of danger and risk to his health, he gained an outstanding share in preserv-
ing generations of our people. Such self-sacrifice is the highest qual-
ification that a man can possess.

So the time for praise and gratitude has come and Rav Shlomo
deserves it in full measure. I hope this will remain with him as a
source of satisfaction at this stage of his well-spent life. I pray that it
may afford him and his devoted wife much solace and cheer in the
years ahead, for he stands out as one man who gave so much of himself to so many.

RESCUER AND COUNSELOR
by Dov (Bernard) Levy
Ashkelon, Israel

We were a family of five when Hitler occupied Austria. I was fifteen years old; my two sisters were thirteen and twelve. When my parents realized the danger we were in, they tried to get us children, at least, out of the country. There was some talk about sending fifty boys to a yeshiva in England, but the committee which dealt with the matter seemed to take their time and nothing ever came of it. Then, on November 10, 1938, my father was arrested. A few weeks later he was released and given two weeks to leave the country.

It was only then that we first heard of the children's transport to England that Dr. Schonfeld was organizing. He cut "red tape" and didn't rest days and nights until he succeeded in obtaining permits for five hundred children. Our parents registered us at once and we left Vienna on December 12, 1938. Four days later, during Chanukah week, we arrived in England. Among the other children in the transport was the girl who eventually became my wife, her sister, and my little cousin. Had it not been for this wonderful man, Rabbi Dr. Schonfeld, what would have become of those five hundred children?

Since the Avigdor High School was then closed for Chanukah vacation, we were placed temporarily at the school until arrangements could be made to move us elsewhere. The youngest children were taken to Rabbi Dr. Schonfeld's private residence, where he and other volunteers looked after them. The refugee committees, which were supposed to be helping the refugees, refused to help us, claiming that Dr. Schonfeld, who had brought us over, should look after us himself. To this day, I can't understand why this man who saved our lives should have been refused cooperation from the "establishment." In the meantime several synagogue committees were formed; they put up some hostels to look after us. I was placed at first into a hostel on 65 Lordship Road. Later on I was assigned to a hostel on 44 Rectory Road until we were evacuated with the Jewish Secondary School at the outbreak of the war. My two sisters and my future wife and her sister were placed into a well-run hostel, financed by a joint committee of the Grove Lane and Egerton Road Synagogues. A family adopted my little five-year-old cousin. But after a few months that family sent her back to Rabbi Dr. Schonfeld. Dr. Schonfeld knew all the names of the children and kept contact with most of us for many years to come. He never refused us help or advice.

When we were evacuated to Shefford with the Jewish Secondary School, our hostel on Rectory Road was abandoned and all our belongings, which we had managed to bring from home, were stolen or destroyed. Rabbi Dr. Schonfeld took us back and arranged to get us clothing, pocket money and other needs.

When I started work as an apprentice after leaving the Jewish Secondary School in Shefford and I didn't earn enough to pay for lodgings, Rabbi Schonfeld supported me until I earned enough to pay my own way. When I returned to London toward the end of the war and started to work as a carpenter, he helped me again by employing me as a teacher at a small Talmud Torah at his premises at 86 Amhurst Park. When I left for Israel in 1951 he tried to encourage me to enter the teaching profession because I had made a success of my work at the Talmud Torah. Eventually I took his advice and to this day have never regretted it.

He even visited us a few years ago when we were on vacation in Jerusalem and when my wife mentioned to him what he had done for us, that he had actually saved our lives, he didn't want to hear about it. "Forget what has been," he said. But we have not forgotten. The six children whom he took out of the Nazi hell have now produced a total of forty children and grandchildren. We hope there will be many more to come. We will always remember this wonderful man, who sacrificed much to save thousands of children, to give them new homes and to make them an asset to *Am Yisroel*.

GIVE ME YOUR DAUGHTER
by Helen Olyech, nee Rosenberg
London, England

When we returned to London after the evacuation, my late mother was most anxious for me to attend a Jewish school. Since we happened to live almost opposite the school in Lordship Road, it seemed natural for me to attend it. Unfortunately, my father had just passed away and the expenses of his long illness had left us virtually penniless.

When we went to see Dr. Schonfeld the school charged a tuition fee. But all that he said to my mother was, "Give me your daughter." There was no mention of money at all! My mother was speechless; we just didn't know what to say. As long as I was at the school, no mention of fees was made to her, or to me. I am happy to have a chance now—as the mother of three fine sons—to say these long-cherished words of deep gratitude to him who has probably long forgotten the kindness he has done.

KIDDUSH IN CAEN (FRANCE 1944)
by Maurice Berenblut (a British Soldier)
London, England

A story told to me as a child ran like this. A *melamed* in a small *shtibel* used to say that if he had Rothschild's money, he would be richer than Rothschild. When someone had the audacity to question this claim, the reply was simple: "If I had Rothschild's money, I'd be richer than he because I'd take in a few students on the side."

Similarly, Dr. Schonfeld can claim to have kept *Shabbos* "on the side" for an extra four years, for while I was in the RAF during the war, I was always able to observe *Shabbos*, with the cooperation of my commanding officer. This was due to Dr. Schonfeld's willingness to back my efforts to remain observant.

During the Allied invasion of Europe in 1944 I was one of a small advance party, which landed in Normandy at dawn on a Friday, only to find that the enemy still occupied our intended destination. We were allocated to the only building in Caen that still had a roof after the devastating run of day and night air raids. Caen was a pile of rubble with roads bulldozed through, as if Moshe Rabbenu had returned to do on dry land that which he had done to the Red Sea.

Once we had settled in, everyone disappeared except for me. I started getting ready for *Shabbos*. Then someone rapped on the door.

"Come in," I said. It was our sergeant. He put his head round the door, saying, "Oh, sorry! I'm looking for people to put on guard duty tonight." I told him that all the others had gone into town, but that I was available. "Oh, no," said he. "Commanding Officer's orders before we left the United States stated that you are off duty till Sunday morning."

Obviously Dr. Schonfeld had quietly but effectively brought his powerful connections into play in order to help me observe my Sabbath.

I went off into the sea of brick dust and found a Pioneer Corps company of aliens, many of them Jewish refugees from Central Europe, who had volunteered for wartime service. We *davened mincha* and *maariv*, and made *Kiddush*.

Dr. Schonfeld's constant availability to me and I am sure also to others who were trying to maintain Jewish traditional standards was and is a true example of *Torah im Derekh Eretz.*

MY PHILOSOPHY OF LIFE
by Martin Eiseman, BA, Dipl. EW
Lucerne, Switzerland

Dr. Schonfeld was not often seen in Shefford. His duties kept him in London, where he was Acting Rabbi of the London Adas Yisroel. But as our indefatigable headmistress, Dr. Grunfeld, impressed upon us, he was constantly operating behind the scenes from his office in Amhurst Park and cared for all our needs. One Purim we expected his visit and we felt that we wanted to give him a gift as a sign of our affection. After long deliberation it was decided to present him with a potted plant. But there was no flower shop in our idyllic little village. How proud I was when Dr. Grunfeld charged me, a mere child, with the task of going by bus all the way to Bedford on Purim morning to purchase the plant! Full of trepidation, but without betraying my excitement, I set out on what seemed to me a global mission. I arrived back safely with the potted plant safe and sound in my arms. The presentation on that memorable Purim morning was a major event in our school community. Somehow this event serves as a diminutive illustration of the deeply felt admiration in which we held Dr. Schonfeld.

My second memory is one of the many spontaneous addresses Dr. Schonfeld delivered at our school assemblies in wartime Shefford. He told us that whenever he drove toward a red traffic light he felt pleased because he knew that by the time he reached the crossing, the light would have changed to green and he could safely pass. A green light, however, made him feel uncomfortable because he knew that by the time he got to the crossing, the light would have changed to red. The same thing, he told us, holds true also in life. Misfortune can suddenly be followed by good fortune; conversely, good fortune must be enjoyed with caution. How strange that after forty years this analogy still influences me and has indeed become part of my life's philosophy.

Years have passed. I have become a teacher myself, and I am the father of married children. The lessons of childhood, many of them derived in Shefford, have accompanied me all along. The personal example set by this active, cheerfully impressive personality helped weave the fabric of my mind during my formative years.

AN OPEN BOOK:
A Review of Solomon Schonfeld:
Message to Jewry, 1959

The picture that Rabbi Dr. Solomon Schonfeld has created of himself in the public mind is of a man of action. It seems a miracle that in the 25 years of his meteoric passage over the Anglo-Jewish scene he has found time to put pen to paper at all. Yet we remember his book on "Jewish Education," still a standard work on the subject, his occasional pamphlets such as the gallant "Child-Estranging Movement" and lately, his "Universal Bible." Now, to mark his semi-Jubilee, appears this volume of collected messages and miscellaneous writings: it conjures up the image of a man sitting at his desk high up in Highgate in the small hours of the morning, writing instead of sleeping and resting. While Dr. Schonfeld is, in the finest sense of the word, the *Macher Supreme*, he stands out in this category from the ordinary run by being a "believer" as well, in fact, a thinking and thoughtful believer.

This volume is a message to Anglo-Jewry, disregarded at its peril—it provides the *Rashi*, the running commentary to the life and activities of the most dynamic, the most colorful and, to those who are not blinded by prejudice and are above resentment against minor irritations, the "most lovable character that adorns an otherwise rather dim and dull contemporary Jewish scene." This message makes Shloime Schonfeld an open book for all to read; it provides the rationale of his work, it tells us what makes him tick. Although he may be the supreme tactician (with the occasional blunder) of communal politics—how else could he stand up to the tough operators of Anglo-Jewish affairs? What makes him and his ways so eminently bearable is his patent sincerity, the most total absence of pride and prestige in the personal sense. To this rare and inspiring aspect of his character, every line in this book bears witness.

But this volume is really more than just the mirror of mind and soul of a formidable contemporary. It is a record of a chapter, nay, several chapters, in the history of our community over the last quarter of a century, which must not be lost, however much some might wish to see it obliterated. Here we can see the Jewish Secondary Schools Movement rising slowly and laboriously with no help, to put it mildly, from those circles that today champion their Jewish schools. Here we watch the growing strength of the Union of Orthodox Hebrew Congregations as the unifier and spokesman of varied and difficult Orthodox elements, new but invaluable to Anglo-Jewry.

Here our memories are jolted and brought back to the somber and anxious days before and during the last war; the days of the rescue work of the Chief Rabbi's Emergency Council; of the help given to evacuees and the men and women in H.M. Forces, of the senseless turmoil of interned refugees, of the agonizing news of extermination of Hitler's Europe and the steps taken by Schonfeld to get something done, with "official" Jewry trying shamefully to throw some spanners into the works. Here is the record, both tragic and glorious, of his relief and rescue work after the war—lest we forget!

Many a reader will look in this volume for the system of ideology of Judaism, Orthodox Judaism, that is the writer's. This will not be easy to find. A rather wide mantle is protectively thrown over a multitude of virtues and a few weaknesses as well. Where does the Presiding Rabbi stand between the often-conflicting claims of West and East, of German or Hungarian or Galician ways, between Agudists and Mizrachists? Without wishing to minimize the difficulties of a task that would baffle an accomplished tightrope walker, Dr. Schonfeld, in his own non-stop subtle, slap-dash and extrovert manner manfully attempts to be many things to many men. And yet his work in the field of education should go to show that he is firmly set on a European, an enlightened form of Orthodoxy. . . .

This collection cannot be read straight through and to be appreciated is to be taken in small doses. Dr. Schonfeld is not the man of the polished phrase or the subtle argument. For that little shade, the sun shines all the brighter. This resounding Message is a fitting Finis written under a memorable and tremendous epoch just when the author has closed it with a bang: Dr. Schonfeld had just resigned from the rabbinate of the Adas Yisroel. While he turns, as yet inscrutable, to new fields of constructive adventure, he takes with him the admiring though bewildered blessings of uncounted friends and well-wishers.

Jewish Post 3, 4 1959; reprinted in *Men and Ideas* (1982), pp. 114–16.

EPILOGUE

(Ashrei Mascil El Dol) - Forward strides he who gives understanding care to him who has been brought low: [What is described [in verses 2,3 and 4] is not the reward of the Mascil El Dol but the importance and effect of his acts of mercy.
Samson Raphael Hirsch on Psalm 41:2.

The words Mascil El Dol as interpreted by Samson Raphael Hirsch epitomize the manifold activities and extraordinary personality of Rabbi Dr. Solomon Schonfeld. For close to a half a century he raised downtrodden individuals from the depths of despair, and was equally adept at resuscitating and uplifting the *Klal*, in the sense of a local community and, even beyond that, of *Klal Yisroel*.

My own life bears witness to this twofold talent with which Rabbi Schonfeld was so richly endowed. I was one of the thousands of human beings whom Dr. Schonfeld saved from joining Hitler's six million Jewish victims. Later, as an admiring participant in his life's work, I was to observe his endeavors for the Jewish community at large. Although he had known nothing about my family or me, Dr. Schonfeld took an active interest in my personal survival and future. For this alone I consider myself forever in his debt. But there is yet another blessing which, at least indirectly, I owe to Dr. Schonfeld.

Even as he rescued me from Austria and became my mentor and friend, so he brought out of Germany the Rosenblat family. One of the Rosenblat's daughters, Betty, who was educated at his school and is a "graduate" of Shefford, eventually became my wife. As secretary of the Union of Orthodox Hebrew Congregations, I was privileged to be Dr. Schonfeld's close helper and confidante as he worked on a broad array of issues. I watched him nurture his educational institutions at home and was actively involved in his many relief and rescue

schemes during and after World War II under the aegis of the Chief
Rabbi's Religious Emergency Council.

It is my great privilege to extend my deep-felt gratitude to Rabbi
Dr. Solomon Schonfeld for a lifetime of education, communal and
rescue work on behalf of Klal Yisroel. He is indeed a *Yachid B'doro*,
a unique personality in his generation.

Marcus Retter

GLOSSARY

Page	Term	Definition
	Aliya Bet	Illegal immigration to Ertetz Yisroel
	Anschluss	German annexation of Austria
	Arba Kanfos	Fringed four-cornered garment
	Arba Minim	Combination of Palm Fronds, Myrtle, Citron and Willow)
	Ashkenazim	Jews of central European origin
	Austritt	Separatist Orthodox community
	Auswanderungsamt	Emigration Office
	Baalei Koreh	Readers of the Torah portions
	Beis Din	Jewish Court
	Bitachon	Faith
	Boruch Hashem	Thank G-d
	Bricha	Postwar Illegal immigration to Palestine or Yishuv
	Bris	Circumcision
	CBF	Central British Fund
	Chacham	Sephardi equivalent title for rabbi
	Chalutzim	Zionist Pioneers
	Cheder	In Britain, after school Hebrew classes
	Chesed	Lovingkindness
	Chevrah Limud Hatorah	Association for the study of the Torah
	Chodesh Tov	Happy New Month
	Cholent	Shabbos Stew
	Chumash	Five Books of Moses
	Chutzpah	Gall
	CRREC	Chief Rabbis' Religious Emergency Council
	COSBRA see COBRA	Council of British Societies for Relief Abroad

Page	Term	Definition
	Davened	Prayed
	Die Kinder	The Children
	EAC	(Agudah's) Emigration Advisory Counciil
	Einheitsgemeinde/ Grossgeminde	Overall (all-inclusive) community
	Erev Shabbos	Sabbath Eve (Friday)
	Eretz Yisroel	Land of Israel or the Yishuv
	Erlichkeit	true honesty and sincerity in Judaism
	Es Muss so zein	It must be so
	Esrogim	Citrons for Sukkot ritual
	Gabbaim	Beadles
	Gozer	Religious Decree
	Hachnossas orchim (heb.)	hospitality
	Hachsharot	Preparatory farms (for settlement in the Yishuv)
	Haggadah	Printed Guide to the Seder
	Hakosoh Boruch Hu	The Al-mighty
	Halachic	Jewish legal aspect
	Halevei	Were it only so
	Hast du Taschengelt?	Do you have any pocket money?
	Hatzalah	Rescue
	Hatzolas Nefoshos	Rescue of lives
	Hashkafah	Jewish perspective
	HMG	His Majesty's Government
	Ish Chadash	the Zionist iodeological "New Man"
	Israelitische Volkschule	(German) Jewish elementary school
	JCRA	Jewish Committee for Relief Abroad
	Judenrein	Clear of Jews
	Jugendgruppe	Youth group
	Kehillah	Jewish community
	Kibbutznik	Member of a (kibbutz) collective in the Yishuv

Page	**Term**	**Definition**
	Kiddush	"Sanctification" of the Sabbath, usually preceding collation following morning prayers
	Kinderlach meine	My dear children
	Kindertransport	Children's transport
	Kinos	Elegies
	Knessiah Gedolah	World Conference of Agudath Israel
	Kol Hamekayem Nefesh Achas mi Yisroel	Whosoever saves one life – (is as if he saved an entire world)
	Kristallnacht	Massive Nazi Pogrom of the night of Nov. 9-10, 1938
	kultusgemeinde	Official overall Viennese Jewish Community
	Lecho Dodi	Friday evening hymn
	Lechu Nerannanu	Friday evening prayer
	Leining	Reading Torah portion
	Loshon Hakodesh	The Holy Tongue
	Lulavim	Palm Fronds utilized with esrogim
	Maariv	Evening Prayers
	Macher Supreme	"Big Shot"
	Machzorim	Holiday Prayer Book
	Magen David	Six-cornered Star of David
	Maggidim	Old-time preachers
	matura	(European) University entrance exam
	Mechitzah	Synagogue partition separating men and women in (Orthodox) synagogue
	Melamed	Hebrew Teacher
	Mezuzah	Parchment scroll with Biblical portions written on it placed on doorpost of rooms occupied by Jews
	Mikvos	Ritualaria
	Mincha	Afternoon Prayer
	Minhagim	Traditions
	Minyan	Quorum
	mitzvah	Divine commandment
	Moshe Rabbenu	Our Teacher Moses

Page	Term	Definition
	Mussar	Study of Ethics
	naches	pleasure
	Nansen Pass	"Stateless passport" issued by the League of Nations
	NCRE	(Agudah's) National Council for Religious Education
	Nes	Miracles
	Neolog	Hungarian Reform Judaism
	Neshamos	Jewish souls
	Niggun	Wordless song
	Oberlandisch Haredi	Strict Hungarian Orthodoxy
	Oneg Shabbos	Sabbath enjoyment (usually a snack of meal)
	Payes	Hassidic side curls
	pidyon shivuim	ransom of captives
	pikuach nefesh	Danger to life (command to rescue)
	Pram	Baby carriage (Brit.)
	Rav	Rabbi
	Redelsfiehrer	Head
	Reichsvertretung der Deutschen Juden	Reich representation of German Jews
	RELICO	Relief Organization for Polish Zionists
	Schechita	Jewish ritual slaughter of animals
	Seder	Passover evening meal and rituals
	Seforim	Hebrew books
	Sephardim	Jewish of Sephardi or Spanish origin
	Shabbos Hagodol Droshos	Sermons for the Sabbath Before Passover
	Sheine Kinder	Beautiful children
	Shidduchim	Helping youth meet for marriage
	Sheva Kehillos	The Seven (Jewish) communities (of Burgenland)
	Shiurim	Lectures on Jewish subjects
	Shmure Matzohs	Especially supervised Matzohs
	Shofar	Ram's Horn

Page	Term	Definition
	shtiebel	One-room synagogue
	Shomrei Shabbos	Sabbath Observers
	Siddurim	Prayer books
	Simchas Torah	Holiday celebrating conclusion the annual reading of the Torah
	Smicha	Rabbinic ordination
	Sochnut	Jewish Agency
	Status Quo	Hungarian version of Einheitsgeminde
	Sukkos	Holiday of Booths
	Taleisim	Prayer shawls
	Tefilin	Phylactories
	Toldos	Genealogy
	Torah min Hashomayim	Divine Revelation
	Torah im Derech Eretz	Hirsch's ideology of the primacy of the Torah while accepting secular studies
	Treyfe	non-kosher food
	Ungarisher Yid	Hungarian Jew
	UNRRA	United Nations Relief and Rehabilitation Administration
	Vaad Hatzalah	Orthodox Rabbis Rescue Committee (NY based)
	Ve eile Toldos Yitzchok	These are the descendents of Yitzchok
	Verdampte Juden	Damn Jews
	weltanschauung	ideological perspective
	Yachid B'doro	Unique in his generation
	Yarmulkes	Skull caps
	Yichus	Family background
	Yiddishkeit	Judaism (Orthodox)
	Yishuv	Modern Eretz Yisroel
	Yomim Tovim	Holidays
	Zemiros	Sabbath songs
	z"l	abbrev. *zochreinu livracha* – in loving memory

FOOTNOTES

I have utilized two primary sources for the Schonfeld documentation. When I first met Dr. Schonfeld, during the early 1970s, he granted me a taped interview. Of greater importance was his providing me with access to all his papers, which were lying in paper-wrapped packages in the attic of the Hasmonean School. I hired one of his former students, Mrs. Ilse Cohen, and a man from the Kodak Company in London to microfilm the papers of the Chief Rabbis' Religious Emergency Council. This organization was created and headed by Schonfeld (although technically the head was Chief Rabbi Joseph H. Hertz), through which he pursued his rescue and relief efforts during the decade of 1938–1948. When I paused for a while in the microfilming project, due to insufficient funds, the collection was transferred to the Archives of the University of Southampton. The microfilm reels in my personal collection were organized in a single alphabetic order for the entire decade. These reels will be designated, for example, Schonfeld Mss. Fa-Fy, and so on, or briefly as Fa-Fy. SP.

Since the university reorganized the entire collection, I have designated the documents derived from that collection according to its system: Schonfeld Mss. 183/

SETTING

1. Steinfeld's son-in-law, Charles Richter, worked with his father-in-law's efforts to secure visas and affidavits for potential refugees seeking a haven in the United States. He provided me with copies of the above-mentioned letterhead used in their correspondence with American Jewish organizations and personalities.

242

INTRODUCTION

1. Schonfeld. *Report. CRREC. 1940–41*, [*Report. 1940–41*] p. 2. Schonfeld Mss. 185/117/8
2. *Jewish Chronicle*, February 2, 1982.

CHAPTER 1
BACKGROUND

1. Unless noted otherwise, the primary source for Schonfeld's family and background are the biographical sketches compiled by the Chevra Ben Zakkai about Rabbi Dr. Victor [Avigdor] Schonfeld, shortly after his demise in 1929, entitlted, *In Memoriam—Rabbi Dr. V. Schonfeld* [*Memoriam*], edited by Naphtaly Lipschutz (London, 1930).
2. *Ibid.*, pp. 8–9.
3. *Ibid.*, p. 9.
4. *Ibid.*, pp. 9, 22–23.
5. Although there is no direct reference to Hirsch's concept of Torah im Derech Eretz [TIDE], it is quite evident from his words that this was his ideology. Similarly, in regard to the separatist or secessionist idea of *austritt*, his actions clearly denote this concept. For a few definitions of these concepts, see Eliyahu Meir Klugman, *Rabbi Samson Raphael Hirsch* (Mesorah, 1996), parts 4–5; Isidore Grunfeld, *Three Generations*, (Jewish Post Publications, 1958), chapter one; *Samson Raphael Hirsch: The Collected Writings*: Vol. VI, Part Two—Independent Orthodoxy.
6. *Memoriam, op.cit.*, p. 9.
7. For a comparison of the two societies, see Jacob Katz, *A House Divided: Orthodoxy and Schism in Nineteenth Century Central Europe.* (Brandeis University Press, 2000)
8. *Memoriam, op. cit.*, p. 9.
9. *Memoriam, op. cit.*, pp. 9–10. For the German youth groups, such as Esra and Zeirei Agudath Israel, see Mordechai Breuer, *Modernity Within Tradition* (Columbia University Press, 1992), in the index under Esra, Youth movements.

10. *Memoriam, op. cit.*, p. 10.
11. For the impact of the First World War on Orthodox Jewry, see the historical introduction to my forthcoming biography of Guta (Eisenzweig) Sternbuch.
12. *Memoriam, op. cit.*, pp. 11–12.
13. *Memoriam, op. cit.*, pp. 12–13.
14. Concerning Harry Goodman's change of ideology from Mizrachi to Agudah, see my interview of Bertha Arens, Harry Goodman's daughter.
15. *Memoriam, op. cit.*, p. 13.
16. *Memoriam, op. cit.*, p. 13.
17. *Memoriam, op. cit.*, pp. 13–14, 22.
18. *Memoriam, op. cit.*, p. 15.
19. One of a series of interviews with Mr. Marcus Retter.
20. *Memoriam, op. cit.*, pp. 15–16.
21. *Memoriam, op. cit.*, p. 16.
22. *Memoriam, op. cit.*, pp. 17–18.
23. *Memoriam, op. cit.*, pp. 27–28.
24. Retter interview.
25. Retter interview.
26. See Bermant, "Cossack."
27. Retter interview.
28. Retter interview.
29. Retter interview.
30. Retter interview.

WEISSMANDL INFLUENCE

31. See letters by Weissmandl to Schonfeld in the former's *Min Hametzar*, a posthumously published collection of Weissmandl's documents relating to the Holocaust (n.d., n.p.). Despite the fact that it was incomplete, his explanatory notes are few, and so many more of his documents are now available, it is undoubtedly the most profound book about the Holocaust. Another miscellaneous collection of letters and other writings appeared in a book called *Toras Chemed* (Yeshiva Press, 1958). A second edi-

tion appeared in 1994. Some of the letters to Schonfeld do not identify him by name, but I was able to determine his identity from the contents.

32. Retter interview. Retter got to know Weissmandl during his last visit to England in 1939 as well as through Schonfeld with whom he worked for years on relief and rescue.

33. For a biographical sketch, see Abraham Fuchs, *Unheeded Cry* (Mesorah, 1984), chapter 1.

34. A copy of this early talmudic commentary is in my possession, courtesy of Rabbi Sholom Moshe Ungar.

35. For example, although my father-in-law, Rabbi Yaakov Bein of Budapest, Hungary, owned five thousand Hebrew books, I purchased his first set of the *Mishne Berurah*, the classic halachic work by Rabbi Israel Meir Kagan (known as the Chofetz Chaim).

36. During the early thirties Weissmandl made the unusual trip through Poland to get to know personally East European Jewry and their rabbinic and lay leaders. Interview with Siegmund Forst, a lifelong friend of Weissmandl.

37. Retter interview.

38. Seen during a visit to the Bodleian Library at Oxford University during the Conference on the Holocaust of "Remembering for the Future 2000."

39. Retter interview.

40. Retter interview.

41. Interview with Dr. Jeremy Schonfeld, son of Rabbi Solomon Schonfeld.

42. For Weissmandl's "bewitching" personality, see my two taped interviews with Andre Steiner, a member of the "Working Group," who negotiated on behalf of Weissmandl with SS Dieter Wisliceny for the ransoming of Slovak Jewry. This secularist Jew, who knew virtually nothing about Judaism, told me that he first met Weissmandl when the former asked Steiner to arrange for kosher food at the Slovak labor camps, which he was designing. Ever after, he was totally under Weissmandl's spell.

    For some of Weissmandl's rescue schemes, see Fuchs, *Unheeded Cry*. For new details about Weissmandl's dispatching

to all Jewish factions in Switzerland, the two versions of the Auschwitz Report on May 16, 1944, a day after mass deportations started from Hungary to Auschwitz, see my *The Man Who Stopped the Trains to Auschwitz* (Syracuse University Press, 2000, pp. 68–72).
43. Fuchs, *Unheeded Cry*, p. 25.
44. Retter interview. See also Weissmandl letters to Schonfeld in *Toras Chemed* (first edition), pp. 138–44.
45. *Toras Chemed* (first edition), pp. 138–41. For the visas for the sixty rabbis on the Danube, see Fuchs, *Unheeded Cry*, p. 26.
46. Interviews with Retter, Richter and Siegmund Forst.
47. *Toras Chemed* (second edition), *op. cit.*, p. 259.
48. *Min Hametzar*, *op. cit.*, pp. 139–41.
49. Pamela Shatzkes, *Anglo-Jewish Rescue: 1938–1944* (unpublished Ph.D dissertation, London School of Economics and Political Science, University of London, 1999), p. 68.
50. Mr. Retter agreed that it was Weissmandl who originally conceived of the idea of a separate kindertransport. Interview.
51. Taped interview with Boruch Meshulem Leibowitz. Mr. Leibowitz also gave me a number of these documents.
52. *Toras Chemed* (first edition), *op. cit.*, p. 144.
53. See also, for example, Schonfeld to Home Office, October 29, 1939; November 28, 1939. Gi-H. SP. Among other things, these letters manifest Schonfeld's efforts to rescue Weissmandl and the entire yeshiva group even after the war began.
54. Retter interview.
55. Although various theories have been proposed for the name "Canada," I believe that Weissmandl's project fits best. See Rudolph Vrba, *I Cannot Forgive*, p. 287.
56. Retter interview.
57. Interview of Ernest "Brudi" Stern, one of Weissmandl's students who taught the method of escaping from the train. Although Weissmandl himself accomplished this feat, none of the students did.
58. Copy of this letter, part of the Harry Goodman Album on his Fiftieth Birthday, is in my possession, courtesy of Mrs. Bertha Arens, daughter of Harry Goodman.

59. Schonfeld tried frequently but unsuccessfully to rescue his former teacher. See for example, above, n. 53.
60. Bermant, *op. cit.*, "Cossack."
61. Retter interview.
62. Cf. P.D. Langdon, of the Movement for the Care of Children from Germany, to Schonfeld December 15, 1938; December 19, 1938 demanding that the transport of two hundred seventy children be halted until proper accommodations for them could be found. Schonfeld Mss. 183/658 Mov-Mz. See also below, piece by Leo Schick and Retter interview.
63. Schonfeld, *Interim [CRREC] Report* [ca/Jan. 1939] [*Interim Report*], p. 2.
64. Retter interview
65. Colonial Office to Schonfeld, December 7, 1942. Schonfeld Ms./290.
66. See below, note 67.
67. Schonfeld to Lord Cranborne of the Colonial Office, October 29, 1942.
68. *Ibid.*
69. Retter interview. Retter told me that he wrote this speech for the Chief Rabbi.
70. Cf. Shatzkes, *Anglo-Jewry, op. cit.*, pp. 38–39.
71. Cf. Shatzkes, *Anglo-Jewry*, pp. 38–39. Cf. also Schonfeld, *Message, op. cit.*, pp. 139–41.
72. Interview with Dr. Judith Grunfeld.

CHAPTER 2
PREWAR RESCUE

INTRODUCTION – REFUGEE SITUATION DURING THE THIRTIES

1. For example, Cecil Roth, *Jewish Contributions to Civilization* (Hebrew Union College, 1940); C. A. Stonehill, ed., *Jewish Contribution to Civilization* (Stonehill Ltd., 1940); Charles Lehrman, *Jewish Influence on European Thought* (English translation of much older German edition) (Fairleigh Dickinson

University Press, 1976); Ada Sterling, *The Jews and Civilization* (Aetco Publishing, 1934).

2. See Laura Fermi, *Illustrious Immigrants* (Chicago University Press, 1968).
3. See the pages of *Der Stürmer*, the vicious anti-Semitic paper edited by Julius Streicher.
4. See John M. Cuddahy, *The Ordeal of Civilization* (Beacon Press, 1974)
5. Jerry Muller, "Communism, Anti-Semitism and the Jews, " *Commentary* (August 1988), pp. 28–39.
6. Norman Cohn, *Warrant for Genocide: The Myth of the Jewish World Conspiracy and the Protocols of the Elders of Zion* (Harper, 1966).
7. Interview with Mr. Samuel Rosenheim, son of Jacob Rosenheim.
8. Rita Thelmann and Emanuel Finerman, *Crystal Night: 9–10 November 1938* (Coward-McCann, 1974).
9. For a fictitious, albeit highly accurate description of the Evian Conference, see Hans Habe, *The Mission* (Coward-McCann, 1966).
10. For the best overall picture of the refugee problem and the United States see David Wyman, *Paper Walls: America and the Refugee Crisis 1938–1941* (University of Massachusetts Press, 1968).
11. Bernard Wasserstein, *Britain and the Jews of Europe 1939–1945.* (Clarendon Press, 1979).
12. See Shatzkes, *Anglo-Jewry*, *op. cit.*, p. 338. Any German Jew with a visa to another country, or even a ship card to Shanghai, was not only free to leave until mid-1941, but was even taken out of the concentration camp. See my *Japanese, Nazis and Jews: The Jewish Refugee Community of Shanghai, 1938–1945 [Japanese, Nazis and Jews]* (Yeshiva University Press, 1976), chapter 1. The first 47 rabbis rescued by Schonfeld were all incarcerated following Kristallnacht.
13. Interviews with more than one hundred refugees who made it to Shanghai. For a detailed history of this haven for close to 18,000 German-Austrian and Polish refugees, see my *Japanese, Nazis and Jews, op. cit.*
14. See *Agudah Report*, July 4, 1939. Schonfeld Mss. [S-Mss] Ag-Az.

15. R.W. Oppenheimer (Secretary of the Agudah's Emigration Advisory Council)—Schonfeld, July 4, 27, 1939. S-Mss. Ag-A.

16. See correspondence between R. W. Oppenheimer and Chief Rabbi Hertz, May 15, 19, 1939, also to the Council for German Jewry, May 22, 1939. S-Mss. Ag-Az. The Agudah established a special committee to look into the location of Shomer Shabbos homes.

17. One need but look at the hundreds of German Orthodox Jewish youth (Mizrachi and Agudah) who went on Hachshara and became part of the Yishuv's agricultural settlements. These include my sister and brother-in-law (Mali and Gershon Loebenberg), who went on Hachshara in the Netherlands in 1936 and ended as highly productive members of Kibbutz Chofetz Chaim.

18. See Abraham J. Edelheit, *The Yishuv in the Shadow of the Holocaust: Zionist Politics and Rescue Aliya, 1933–1939* [Edelheit, *Shadow*] (Westview Press, 1996). For details on the Certificates, see "Certificates" in the index.

19. Cf. *Hearings. House Resolutions 350 and 352.* 78th Congress. 1st Session [Hearings]. Reprinted in *Problems of World War II and Its Aftermath, Vol. II* (Washington, D.C., 1976), pp. 187, 243–45.

20. In addition to Edelheit, *Shadow, op. cit.*, see also William R. Perl, *The Four-Front War* (Crown, 1979); Yitshaq Ben-Ami, *Years of Wrath, Days of Glory* (Robert Speller & Sons, 1982). See also n. 21. See my *The Man Who Stopped the Trains to Auschwitz* (Syracuse University Press, 2000), p. 78.

21. See *Four-Front War, op. cit.*, pp. 306–07, 309, 315, 325, 338; *Years of Wrath*, p. 260. One of the boats emanating from Budapest in August 1939 included a group called the "Schonfeld People," although the author had no longer recalled who Schonfeld was. *Years of Wrath, op. cit.*, p. 306. See also Gideon Shimoni, *The Zionist Ideology* (Brandeis University Press, 1995).

22. Hadassah Schonfeld, *Rabbi Dr. Solomon Schonfeld's Rescue Work 1935–1945* [Hadassah Schonfeld] (unpublished Honors paper, University of Westminster, 1997), pp. 23–24 (courtesy of the author).

CRREC'S FIRST MISSION BRINGING GERMAN CLERGY TO ENGLAND

23. Zeirei Agudath Israel. *1938 Report*, p. 1.
24. See my interviews of Rabbi Schonfeld; Retter; Shatzkes, *op. cit.*, *Anglo-Jewry*, pp. 38–39; *CRREC Interim Report* [ca. early 1939]; see also letter by Meir Raphael Springer below.
25. See the term "assimilationists" in the index of my book *Thy Brother's Blood*.
26. Retter interview. See also Norman Bentwich. *They Found Refuge*, pp. 136–37; Fermi, *op. cit.*, *Illustrious Immigrants*.
27. See correspondence of the Emigration Advisory Council in the SP.
28. When I began my research for the book *They Called Him "Mike*," I was unaware that the inspiration for the refugee division of the Zeirei Agudath Israel had originated with Rosenheim. My brother, Dr. Gershon Kranzler, was in charge of the Zeirei's division of Refugees and Immigration from 1938 to 1942.
29. See Shatzkes, *op. cit.*, *Anglo-Jewry*, p. 38.
30. See for example, Yehuda Bauer, *American Jewry and the Holocaust* [Bauer, *American Jewry*], (Wayne State University Press, 1981), pp. 126–28; Shatzkes, *Anglo-Jewry*, *op. cit.*, p. 38. Cf. also my *Thy Brother's Blood*, *op. cit.*, p. 68.
31. Retter interview.
32. On January 28, 1938, Conservative rabbis in Germany sent requests to come to Britain. See also December 16, 1938. SP 183/676. Sa-Saz.
33. Hertz to Viscount Samuel, November 21, 1938. SP 183/676. Sa-Saz. Schonfeld to Schiff, March 1, 1938.
34. *CRREC Report '38–'48*, in *Message*, *op. cit.*, p. 127.
35. Schonfeld to M. Stephany of the Council for German Jewry, December 5, 1938. SP 183/384. See also further correspondence between the CRREC and the Council in January 1939. SP 183/384.
36. Rabbi Alexander J. Burnstein to Hertz, January 5, 1939. SP 183/730/2.

37. Interview with Ernie Mayer. See also his article entitled, "My Teacher, My Savior." *Jerusalem Post*, June 4, 1988.
38. See, for example, Hertz to Lord Reading, November 2, 1939. SP. Bre-Bz.
39. See below, "An Appreciation," by the late Chief Rabbi, Lord Jakobovits.
40. Retter interview.
41. See below, "The Children's Rescue," by Leo Schick. See also *Interim Report*, p. 1.
42. Interview with Meir Eiseman, who lived next to the Hasmonean School.
43. See below, vignette by Felicia Druckman.

CHAPTER 3
CHILDREN IN NON-JEWISH HOMES

1. See Schonfeld, *Memo on Jewish Children*, *op. cit.*, esp., p. 4. SP 183/617/2. See also "Interim Report on Jewish Children Placed in Non-Jewish Homes by Woburn House," [Rabinowitz, "Memo"] by Rabbi Louis Rabinowitz to Rabbi Hertz, March 8, 1939. Copy in my possession. See also Shatzkes, *op. cit.*, *Anglo-Jewry*, pp. 97–100.
2. December 19, 1938. SP. Mo-Mz.
3. See Schonfeld, *Memo*, *op. cit.*, p. 3.
4. December 19, 1938. SP. Mo-Mz.
5. Schonfeld, *Memo*, *op. cit.*, p. 3.
6. Movement to Hertz, March 15, 1939. SP 183/617/2; Schonfeld, *Memo*, *op. cit.*, p.3.
7. Schonfeld, *Memo*, *op. cit.*, p.3
8. Schonfeld, *Memo*, *op. cit.*, p. 3.
9. Schonfeld, *Memo*, *op. cit.*, p. 3.
10. Schonfeld, *Memo*, pp. 3–4. See below, regarding the last kinder-transport from Czechoslovakia. For the risk to Jewish identity, see, for example, Rabinowitz, "Memo," *op. cit.*, p. 2.
11. Rabinowitz, "Memo," *op. cit.*, pp. 1–5.

12. *Child-Estrangement Movement: An Expose of the Alienation of Jewish Refugee Children in Great Britain from Judaism*, [*Child Estrangement*] January 1944, esp. pp. 3–4. SP
13. *Ibid.*, pp. 4–5.
14. *Ibid.* SP.

CHAPTER 4
WARTIME (DOMESTIC)

INTRODUCTION

1. *CRREC Report August 1945.* p. 7. SP 183/617/2.
2. Retter interview.
3. Interview with Yaakov Wiederman, who, with his older brothers, went to Shefford, but whose younger sister remained in London with their parents.
4. *CRREC Report '38–'48. Message, op. cit.*, pp. 133–34.
5. Interview with Dr. Judith Grunfeld. She, who was in charge of running the daily Shefford activities, admitted that he was the soul and heart of this operation. For the vignette, see her book, entitled *Shefford* (Soncino Press, 1980).
6. *Ibid.*, with permission of the author.
7. Pels interview. The money would be sent to them instead of making them come to the office to pick up the money, as practiced by the secular Jewish relief organizations. See also *CRREC Report December 1942*, pp. 2–3. See also *CRREC Report August 1945*, p. 9. SP 183/137/3.
8. *Agudah Report 1941*; *CRREC Report December 1941*, p.3. This focus on the East End, the Jewish neighborhood, was similar to the Nazi bombardment of Jewish neighborhoods in Warsaw at the beginning of the war.

CHAPTER 5
INTERNMENT

1. See Wasserstein, *Britain, op. cit.*, pp. 90–92.

2. For a good unit on the internment episode, see Wasserstein, *op. cit., Britain*, pp. 81–110. See also Ronald Stent, *A Spattered Page: The Internment of His Majesty's Most Loyal Enemy Aliens* (London, 1980). For those sent to Australia and Canada, see "Australia, Jewish Refugees," by Suzanne D. Rutland. *Encyclopedia of the Holocaust*, Vol. 1, pp. 125–26. Also "Canada," by Harold Troper, *op. cit.*, pp. 275–77.

3. See book on Japanese internment by Roger Daniels, *Concentration Camps U.S.A.* (1971). See also my *Japanese, Nazis and Jews, op. cit.*, pp. 57–58.

4. For a good book on the Oswego experience, see Ruth Gruber, *Haven: The Unknown Story of 1,000 World War II Refugees* (Coward-McCann, 1983). For the relief role by Agudah in Oswego, see *Orthodox Tribune*, October 1944, pp. 1, 3, 14, and November 1944, p. 2. For the story of the Jews interned in the United States see Harvey Strum, "Jewish Internees in the American South, 1942–1945," in *American Jewish Archives*, Spring/Summer 1990, pp. 27–31.

5. See above, n. 3.

6. *CRREC Report 1938–48. Message*, pp. 134–35. See also Shatzkes, *op. cit., Anglo-Jewry*, pp. 130–133. For the ability of internees in Canada and Australia to enter schools of higher education, see Elias interview.

7. See "Open Letter," to Schonfeld and the Chief Rabbi of July 4, 1940, demanding representation, since the Nazis had declared them to be *not* German. See also *Message, op. cit.*, p. 153; Shatzkes, *op. cit., Anglo-Jewry*, p. 129.

8. *CRREC Report 1938–45. Message, op. cit.*, p. 135. See also Elias interview.

9. Elias interview.

10. Elias interview.

11. See below, "A Wedding on the Isle of Man," by Meir Eiseman.

12. *Jewish Chronicle*, October 18, 1940, pp. 1, 14.

13. Shatzkes, *Anglo-Jewry, op. cit.*, pp. 128–130.

14. See Solomon Schonfeld, "Great Britain and the Refugees," [Schonfeld, "Britain"] (London) *Times*, July 30, 1940. SP

183/117/3. Also in *Message, op. cit.*, pp. 143–45.

15. *Ibid.*

16. See Shatzkes, *op. cit., Anglo-Jewry*, pp. 118–124, 136.

17. Henry Pels (Secretary of the CRREC) to Rosenheim, March 31, 1940. SP. Ag-Al.

18. *CRREC Report 1941*, pp. 3–4. SP 183/117/8.

19. Schonfeld, "Britain."

20. "Report on Activities of Agudat Israel," p. 8; See also *CRREC Report 1942.* SP 183/287/1; *CRREC Report. 1938–1948. Message, op. cit.*, p. 134.

21. See below, "No Longer A Refugee," by Trude Wiener.

22. Elias interview. See also *CRREC Report 1938–1948. Message, op. cit.*, 135. *CRREC Report 1941*, p. 6–7. SP 183/117/8.

23. See Suzanne D. Rutland, *Edge of the Diaspora: Two Centuries of Jewish Settlement in Australia* p. 344.

24. Shatzkes, *op. cit., Anglo-Jewry*, p. 135.

25. Shatzkes, *op. cit., Anglo-Jewry*, p. 135

26. *CRREC Report 1942*, p. 1. SP 193/132/3. See also *CRREC Report 1938–1948. Message*, pp. 131–32.

27. *CRREC Report 1938–1948. Message*, p. 131

28. *CRREC Report 1938–1948. Message*, p. 131–132.

29. Solomon Schonfeld interview. See also Wasserstein, *Britain, op. cit.*, pp. 172–73. Wasserstein, among other historians, is unaware of Schonfeld's personal role in inspiring Rathbone's efforts on behalf of European Jewry.

30. This factor of immediacy when it came to rescue is a basic element of the Orthodox or better, Torah-based perspective, in sharp contrast to the long-range solutions to the "Jewish Problem" [i.e., anti-Semitism] promoted by the socialist-Zionists. This discussion is highlighted by the speech delivered by Rabbi Abba Hillel Silver during his unscheduled speech at the American Jewish Conference in August 1943.2 For this speech, see Arthur Hertzberg, *The Zionist Idea* (Atheneum, 1970), pp. 592–600, esp., 597.

31. See below. The problem with the socialist Zionists was their absolute, messianic belief that once the state was created, anti-

Semitism would disappear on its own. This was a legacy of the Enlightenment that assumed that anti-Semitism was a relic of the dark, Middle Ages, which would disappear in the face of modernism and the "normalization" of Jews in a state of their own, that is, assimilation on a universal scale.

Rabbi Schonfeld noted to me that the Revisionist Zionists were different in this respect, similar to the role played by the Peter Bergson Group in the United States. For details, see this author's forthcoming work, on "A Comparative Study of the World-Wide Rescue Efforts During the Holocaust by the Orthodox."

His preparation for the postwar era did not in any way mean that he gave up on European Jewry. This is proven by his multifarious rescue and relief activities throughout the final days of the war.

32. Shatzkes, *op. cit.*, *Anglo-Jewry*, 309–310.

33. it is important to remember that when we see Sir Robert Waley-Cohen as an obstructionist vis-à-vis Schonfeld, we are not talking about a "bad" or insensitive person. Rather, one must appreciate the ideological imperative that impelled his action and inactions, and that his sense of priorities differed from Schonfeld's Torah-based priorities. Being accepted as an equal in English society represented for Waley-Cohen and other assimilationists a higher priority than rescue. His insecurity in his status within English society is manifest in his fear that collection of food in middle of the war, or anything else that raised "particularist Jewish" concerns, would make him appear less "English" and therefore endanger his dream of full acceptance by his non-Jewish peers. In this, he was no different from other highly economically, politically and socially successful members of the Jewish "Cousinhood," such as the Rothschilds, the Goldsmids, the Samuels and so on.

This portrait did not fit Schonfeld, no less secure in his status as an Englishman, than as an Orthodox Jew. Nor did it fit Moses Montefiore (1784–1885), a much earlier member of the "Cousinhood," who led numerous causes on behalf of his unfortunate fellow Jews throughout the world. He, too, was secure as an Orthodox Jew and a proud Englishman.

34. Both as individuals as well as in organizations, assimilationist Jews accepted the notion that Jews were citizens of each country, the responsibility of which it was to accept and to rehabilitate its Jewish nationals

35. See Shatzkes, *op. cit.*, *Anglo-Jewry*, pp. 303, 306, 310.

36. See Shatzkes, *op. cit.*, *Anglo-Jewry*, pp. 306–07.

37. However, it did not take long after the war and the revelation of the full horrors of the Holocaust, for even these Jews to realize that Hitler's mass destruction of most of European Jewry did away with any such concept. Therefore, after the war, many formerly assimilationist Jews as well as non-Zionist organizations and changed their perspective. They realized that Jews were no longer welcome in say, Poland, or most could not see themselves returning to Germany, therefore many became Zionists themselves or at least tried to help the Zionist cause by promoting the settlement in Palestine. At the very least, they tried to bring the survivors to the United States.

38. Shatzkes, *op. cit.*, *Anglo-Jewry*, p. 308.

39. Shatzkes, *op. cit.*, *Anglo-Jewry*, p. 309–11.

40. See Schonfeld to Ministry of Food, September 10, 28, 1943. SP. Fi-Foy.

41. Shatzkes, *op. cit.*, *Anglo-Jewry*, p. 311.

42. Schonfeld to G. H. C. Amos, September 12, 1943. Sp. Fi-Foy.

43. Schonfeld to G. H. C. Amos, September 10, 1943. Sp. Fi-Foy.

44. Retter interview. See also correspondence of Schonfeld to Ministry of Food. SP. Fi-Foy.

45. Ministry of Food to Schonfeld, October 19, 1943. SP. Fi-Foy.

46. Schonfeld to Ministry of Food, November 5, 1943. SP. Fi-Foy.

47. *CRREC Report 1938–1948. Message, op. cit.*, p. 136.

48. *CRREC Report 1938–1948. Message, op. cit.*, p. 140.

CHAPTER 6
RESCUE EFFORTS

MAURITIUS

1. The notion of Protective Papers, especially those from Latin America, has not received the attention it deserves, and there are still historians who are totally unaware of these. For the first detailed explanation of the use of "Protective Papers," a rescue tool developed by the Orthodox [Eli Sternbuch, one of the Sternbuch family, representing the Vaad Hatzalah in Switzerland], see my *The Man Who Stopped the Trains to Auschwitz, op. cit.*, esp., chapter 3, 10, 11. This concept was soon emulated by many, but not all, Jewish and even non-Jewish organizations, for example, Dr. Abraham Silberschein, head of RELI-CO, an active rescue organization in Switzerland. On the other hand, Saly Mayer, Swiss representative of the Joint, and Richard Lichtheim, representative of the Jewish Agency, never accepted the use of such bogus papers, although they eventually rescued tens of thousands of Jews.
2. Wasserstein, *op. cit.*, *Britain*, pp. 56–76.
3. Hertz to Cranborne (Colonial Office), August 23, 1942. SP 183/290.
4. Schonfeld to Lord Cranborne, October 30, 1942. SP. Fi-Foy. See also Memo of September 2, 1942 concerning the transfer of rabbis and religious functionaries from all occupied territories to British Colonial Territories. As this same memo points out, Schonfeld intentionally omitted Palestine, but did not hesitate to press for the exchange of German women in Palestine and Jewish women in Nazi-occupied territories.
5. J. Linton (of the JA) to H. Pels (of the CRREC), November 29, 1943. SP. Fi-Foy.
6. J. Linton to Schonfeld, December 1, 1943. SP. Fi-Foy. Closely related to the concept of Protective Papers as rescue tools was the notion of visas to an Allied Colonial possession, such as

Mauritius, which would enable the holder to obtain transit visas through neutral countries. Such visas were valuable because they enabled the Jews to leave Nazi satellites, such as Hungary or Bulgaria. They didn't have to go to Mauritius and they never did. For example, one contemporary historian, Meir Sompolinsky, disparaged Schonfeld's accomplishment in this arena by stating, "Unfortunately, due to conditions on the Continent, not a single rabbi ever utilized a Mauritius visa" (Ph.D dissertation, Bar Ilan University, 1977, pp. IV, 171–187.)

Sampolinsky did not understand this concept of visas to British (or American) possessions as a rescue tool, whether in the case of Mauritius in the unsuccessful case involving "Stranger's Key." The latter was an island in the British West Indies, which Schonfeld "purchased" (with the help of a donor) in order to distribute visas to "his home" or island. Sadly, as Dr. Schonfeld told me, one of the Ministries had approved the plan, but another nixed it. See Shatzkes, *Anglo-Jewry, op. cit.*, p. 270, n. 94.

The truth is that several other Schonfeld rescue efforts involved related ideas, including the "Parliamentary Resolution," discussed below.
7. For a critical view of conditions on Mauritius see Shatzkes, *Anglo-Jewry, op. cit.*, pp. 269–71.
8. Shatzkes, *Anglo-Jewry, op. cit.*, pp. 261–62.
9. *CRREC Report 1938–1948. Message, op. cit.*, p. 128.

CHAPTER 7
RESCUE FAILURES

1. See Rudolf Vrba and Alan Bestic. *I Cannot Forgive* (Grove Press, 1964), p. 250. For the first copy to Kastner, see Randolph L. Braham, *Politics of Genocide* (Columbia University Press, 1981), p. 728, n. 73.
2. Copies of both reports, dated May 17, 1944, given to me by Natan Schwalb, during a taped interview.
3. See Weissmandl's version, *op. cit.*, p. 4.
4. See my *Thy Brother's Blood*, pp. 134–39. He gave me copies of

many of his documents from Weissmandl.

5. Taped interview with Boruch Meshulem Lebovitz.
6. *CRREC Report 1938–1948. Message, op. cit.*, p. 128. See also taped interviews with Mrs. Paszkes and Rabbi Menachem Rubin, two inmates of Auschwitz who witnessed the bombing of Auschwitz.
7. See my *The Man Who Stopped the Trains to Auschwitz, op. cit.*, esp., chapters 8–9.
8. Wasserstein, *op. cit., Britain*, pp. 311–13, 319–20. He seems unaware of the fact that this plea originated with Weissmandl.
9. *CRREC Report 1938–1948. Message, op. cit.*, p. 129.
10. McClelland to WRB, September 16, 1944; Secretary of State Cordell Hull to McClelland, January 15, 1945. WRB.
11. Taped interview with Eli Sternbuch. Copy of the first such papers (Paraguayan) from October 1941, in my possession, courtesy of Guta [Eisenzweig] Sternbuch.
12. For Silberschein's use of such papers, see Yad Vashem. Bronia Kilbanski, comp. Archives of Dr. Adolph Abraham] Silberschein. RG M-20. For a good brief description of the Vittel experience, see my *Thy Brother's Blood, op. cit.*, pp. 102–04.
13. *Thy Brother's Blood, op. cit.*, pp. 102–04, and pp. 7–13.
14. *Thy Brothers' Blood, op. cit.*, pp. 7–13.
15. See my *The Man Who Stopped the Trains to Auschwitz, op. cit.*, esp., chapters 3, 10, 11.
16. For these and many more details about Vittel, see my forthcoming biography of Guta Sternbuch.
17. *Thy Brother's Blood, op. cit.*, p. 173.
18. Interview with Guta Sternbuch, one of the three survivors.

PARLIAMENTARY RESOLUTION

19. *Thy Brother's Blood, op. cit.*, p. 93.
20. From the *Agenda of Parliamentary Rescue Committee, 27th of January 1943*. Cited in *Message, op. cit.*, p. 161.
21. See above regarding Mauritius.
22. Taped interview with Rabbi Schonfeld. Though Shatzkes claims

that the Resolution would never have passed anyhow, as evidenced by remarks by Anthony Eden, the Zionist opposition was not based on the success or failure of the Resolution, but rather on ideological grounds. See Shatzkes, *op. cit.*, *Anglo-Jewry*, p. 172.

23. Schonfeld interview; Also interview with Marcus Retter. He not only recalled the incident, working closely with Schonfeld, he even recalled the approval by the Colonial Office, and the name of the donor, who contributed the necessary £10,000. He also recalled the negative response to him by the representative of the Foreign Office, who told him that although it's true that you can invite anyone to your house (or island) say, in London, you still require permission by HMG to enter Britain. Similarly, anyone with a visa to Stranger's Key, would still need permission to enter the British Empire. Therefore, it was rejected.

CHAPTER 8
POSTWAR CREATIVITY

1. Retter interview.
2. Retter interview.
3. Air Ministry to CRREC, November 14, 1945. SP. Ag-Al.
4. Schonfeld to Ernest Bevin, September 2, 1945. SP. Fi-Foy.
5. Schonfeld to Ernest Bevin, September 2, 1945. SP. Fi-Foy.
6. Shatzkes, *op. cit.*, *Anglo-Jewry*, p. 313.
7. For Reichmann's efforts, see my *Thy Brother's Blood*, *op. cit.*, p. 253. For Tress' [postwar package project], see Yonason Rosenblum, *They Called Him Mike* (Mesorah, 1995), p. 321–27.
8. *CRREC Report 1938–1948. Message, op. cit.*, pp. 136–37.
9. *CRREC Report 1938–1948. Message, op. cit.*, pp. 136–37.
10. Shatzkes, *op. cit.*, *Anglo-Jewry*, p. 308.
11. Shatzkes, *op. cit.*, *Anglo-Jewry*, p. 308–09.
12. See Notes on Sir Robert-Waley Cohen and the Chief Rabbi's Appeal for Kosher Food Gifts for Liberated Areas. Date unclear. SP. Fi-Foy.

13. JCRA to Ministry of Food, February 10, 1945. SP. Fi-Foy.
14. Retter interview.
15. *CRREC Report 1938–1948. Message, op. cit.*, p. 136.
16. The first Mobile Synagogue was donated by a congregation in Melbourne, Australia. See illus. *Message, op. cit.*, p. 155; Retter interview.
17. Retter interview.
18. *CRREC Report 1938–1948. Message, op. cit.*, p. 154.
19. Rabbi Reuven Monheit interview
20. Jeanette Friedman interview of Captain Monheit.
21. Retter interview.
22. Bermant, "Cossack."
23. "Belsen Diary," *Jewish Post*, August 14, 1946. See also *CRREC Report 1938–1948. Message, op. cit.*, p. 136–37.
24. Retter interview.

WESTERN EUROPE

25. *CRREC Report 1938–1948. Message, op. cit.*, p. 136.

POSTWAR RECONSTRUCTION OF JEWISH COMMUNITIES

TRIPS TO POLAND

26. *CRREC Report 1938–1948. Message, op. cit.*, p. 135.
27. *CRREC Report 1938–1948. Message, op. cit.*, p. 130.
28. *CRREC Report 1938–1948. Message, op. cit.*, p. 130.
29. Retter interview.
30. *CRREC Report 1938–1948. Message, op. cit.*, p. 130.
31. *CRREC Report 1938–1948. Message, op. cit.*, p. 139.
32. Retter interview.
33. Dr. Grunfeld interview
34. Retter interview.
35. Retter interview.

36. Retter interview.
37. Unless specified otherwise, this unit is based on the research by Barbara Barnett, who graciously provided me with the manuscript of her forthcoming work.
38. See my *The Man Who Stopped the Trains to Auschwitz, op. cit.*, p. 231.

CYPRUS

39. See Yehuda Bauer, *Flight and Rescue: Bricha* (Random House, 1970).
40. See Ruth Gruber, *Destination Palestine: The Story of the Haganah Ship Exodus 1947* (Current Books, 1948).
41. See Joseph Friedenson, *History of the Agudah*, p. 16. Unless indicated otherwise, this unit on Cyprus is based on taped interviews of Dr. Judith Grunfeld.
42. See Judith Grunfeld interview. See also *CRREC Report 1938–1948. Message*, p. 139. See also the article, "Cyprus," by Nahum Bogner, in the *Encyclopedia of the Holocaust*, pp. 332–39. *Jewish Chronicle*, February 1945. Cited in H. Schonfeld, p. 35. See also SP 183/53/2.
43. J. Grunfeld interview.
44. *CRREC Report 1938–1948. Message, op. cit.*, p 139.
45. Hadassah Schonfeld, *Rescue*, p. 35.
46. SP. 183/53/2.

INDEX

Air Ministry, 255

Alderman, Dean Geoffrey, xvi

Aliyah Bet (the illegal immigration to Eretz Yisroel), 34, 49, 114; Zionist reaction to British immigration restrictions, 49; Labor Zionists opposed (until) 1939, 49; Revisionist Zionists primarily involved with (until 1939), 49

American Jewish Archives, 248

American Jewish Conference, 249

American Jewish Joint Distribution Committee (USA), 53, 54; opposition to the Vaad Hatzalah, 54

Amos, G. H. C., 84

Anglo-Jewish Association, 58; guaranteed Jewish refugees, 46

Anglo-Jewish establishment, 118; assimilationists , 52, 53; feared calling attention to Jews, 83; hindered Schonfeld's rescue work, 52; opposed food collection, 82-85

Anschluss (annexation of Austria by Nazi Germany), 3, 8, 9, 45, 46

antisemitism, 45; Anglo-Jewish leadership's fear of fostering, 59, 79

Antwerp (Belgium), postwar, 103

Arens, Bertha (interview), 239, 242; Harry Goodman's daughter, 239, 242

assimilationists, 245, 250, 251

  see also Anglo-Jewish establishment

Auschwitz, 44, 213; witnesses to bombing, 254; Weissmandl's plea to bomb the rail tracks leading to, 35

Auschwitz Report, 35, 241

Austritt (independent secessionist Orthodox community), 13, 24, 25, 27, 28, 223

Auswanderungsamt (emigration office) of the Agudath Israel of Vienna, 8

Auxiliary Military Pioneer Corps, 77

Avigdor Primary School, 226

Avigdor High School, 217,228; Dr. Judith Grunfeld (Headmistress), 217

  see also Hasmoneaan

Babad, Rabbi Yosef; communal rabbi in Sunderland, 7; principal of Yeshiva Ohr Yisroel, 7, 149

Bais Yaakov movement (Poland), xiii, 115

Bais Yaakov Seminary (Cracow), xiii, 115

Bakstansky, Lavey (Zionist leader), 96

Balfour Declaration, 27; repudiated by Passfield White Paper (1930), 49

Bamberger, Rabbi Seligman Ber (Wurzburger Rav), 24

orthodox immigrants, challenges facing, 47-50; issues of *Shabbos* (Sabbath observance), 50
Orthodox Jews; negative attitude towards, 53
Orthodox Tribune, 248
Oswego NY (internment camp); Jews liberated from Italy (1944), interned in the, 76, 248; relief role of Agudah in, 248

Palestine; British Mandate, 4, 27, 82
Palestine Certificates, 87. *See also* Certificates
Pappenheim, Kalman, 8; Agudah member prominent in rescue work, 9
Paris; Ecole Maimonides, 219
Parliamentary Rescue Committee, Agenda of, 254
Parliamentary Rescue Resolution, 118, 253
Parliamentary Resolution; *see* Parliamentary Rescue Resolution
Passfield White Paper (1930), 49; repudiated the Balfour Declaration, 49
Paszkes, Mrs. (taped interview), 254; witness to the bombing of Auschwitz, 254
Paton, Dr. W., 79
Pearson, Drew (USA columnist), 93
Pels, Henry, 54;
Perl, William R., 244
Petrie, Asenath (Schonfeld's sister), 167
Petrie, Dr. Ernest, 167
Pinter, Rabbi Shmelke; founder of the Yesodei Hatorah Hasidic Educational System (Britain), 118
Pioneer Corps, 231
Poalei Agudath Israel, 116
Poland, postwar, 16, 18; boat chartered in Gdansk to bring Jewish orphans to England, 18, 99, 133, 205, 209; Jewish Communists in, 18; pogrom in Kielce, 18
Polish government (postwar), 111
Polish Government-in-Exile (London), 95
Polish Legation, Jewish Division of the, 92
Posen, Raphael, 141
Preath-Heath (British internment camp), 200
Pressburg Yeshiva, 4, 23
prewar rescue efforts, 45
Prague, postwar, 111-112
Preschel, Tovia (Theodor), (vignette contributor; Jerusalem), 150-155